A BLAZE OF
PERMANENT MIDNIGHT!

"Unflinching . . . probing not only L.A.'s conspicuously consumerist culture but Stahl's own childhood and his married life."

—*Time Out*

"The most searing, hilarious portrait of heroin addiction I've ever read . . . a classic."

—Mary Karr, bestselling author of *The Liar's Club*

"An extraordinary accomplishment. . . . A remarkable book that will be of great value to people who feel isolated, alienated, and overwhelmed by the circumstances of their lives."

—Hubert Selby Jr., author of *Last Exit to Brooklyn*

"A howl of laughter from the abyss of horror."

—Nick Tosches, author of *Hellfire* and *Trinities*

"Jerry Stahl's writing illuminates that dark place where wit and outrage coexist . . . he grabs us and tells a story."

—Brett Butler

"Piercing."

—*Harper's Bazaar*

"Unabashedly lurid . . . highly entertaining."

—*Publishers Weekly*

"What a terrifying account. The headlong, hazardous process—against all odds—is healing, beautiful."

—Geoffrey Wolff, author of *Duke of Deception*

"I loved it!"

—Kevin Spacey

"Horrific and hilarious."

—High Times

"Stahl's prose is a kind of perfection. . . . Drives to a sensational finish."

—Buffalo News

"Jerry Stahl is one hell of a writer. A harrowing, brave, sordid, and, dare I say this, corrosively entertaining book."

—Barry Yougrau, author of *The Sadness of Sex*

"A work of twisted genius by a man who's been there and back."

—Mark Mothersbaugh,
composer and founder of DEVO

"The hyperkinetic style and pace keep things moving."

—Library Journal

"Full-blown, toxic funhouse horror. . . . Stahl has easy, loping, hepster story gifts. . . . Upfront, doggedly refreshing."

—Bruce Wagner, *Los Angeles Times*

"Remarkable . . . alternately hilarious and harrowing, but most of all, searingly honest."

—Daphne Merkin, author of *Enchantment*

"A hilarious, crazed chronicle of the nightmarish world of the junky. Indelible, indecent, sparkling with insight, and more fun than a barrel of monkeys on your back."

—Kinky Friedman, author of *Armadillos and Old Lace*

"A cauterizing celebration of heaven and hell from one dope fiend of a writer, giving us an apocalyptic glimpse of laughter with the Devil."

—Ralph Steadman

"Alternately hilarious and terrifying. Unlike many ultrasensitive, self-serving Hollywood memoirs, Stahl is toughest on his own self-indulgence and hypocrisy."

—Robert Ward, author of *The King of Cards*

"Compulsively readable, intense, funny, and, thankfully, free of piety."

—*Guardian* (London)

"A candid window upon the soul of a man who has walked into the shadow of death and survived."

—*The London Observer Review*

"PERMANENT MIDNIGHT achieves literary magic. This is post-shame writing of the highest order."

—Laurie Stone, winner of the 1996 Book Critics Circle citation for excellence in reviewing

PERMANENT MIDNIGHT

A memoir

Jerry Stahl

WARNER BOOKS

A Time Warner Company

Author's Note:
Some names have been changed, some haven't.

WARNER BOOKS EDITION

Cover photo courtesy of Artisan Entertainment

Warner Books, Inc.
1271 Avenue of the Americas
New York, NY 10020

Visit our Web site at
http://warnerbooks.com

A Time Warner Company

Printed in the United States of America

Originally published in hardcover by Warner Books.
First Mass Market Printing: September, 1998

10 9 8 7 6 5 4 3 2 1

For Hubert Selby, Jr.

Acknowledgments

For their unusual faith and dedication, the author would like to thank the following: George Hedges, Pinenience Joshua, Karen Kelly, and Barbara Zitwer. . . . Gratitude, as well, to the late Bob Labrasca, the still-living David Hirshey, Mitchell Froom, Nancy Cina Lord, Diane Stockwell, Kelly Cutrone, L'nor, Marne Carmean, Michael Melvin, Heather McHugh, Steve Hagel, Susan Squire, Special Agent Glenn, Steve Randall, *Cafe Tropical*, Nancye Ferguson, Hilary Beane, Arty Nelson, Eric and Tina Blakeney, Lisa Jane Persky, Eddie Little, Jonathan Craven, Texas Terri, Lynn S., Mel B., Jim D. and all those who choose to remain anonymous.

Normal people have nothing to forget.

E.M. Cioran

Prologue

HERE & NOW

I'm wearing a diaper. Right now. I'm not sure if it's the June Allyson, TV-advertised slip-on brand, an official Depends, or some no-name, buy-'em-by-the-gross institutional variety. All I know is, I just woke up wearing the thing in this hospital recovery room. Snug and bloody. Pinching so much at the waist it's almost enough to make me forget the screaming hell of the thirteen fresh stitches throbbing due south, on my balls. Or what's left of them. But don't get me going. . . .

This whole deal is not, like, something I'm proud of. Not the kind of thing that makes you want to grab the nearest phone and dial fifteen of your closest friends. On the other hand, I think I ought to mention it. I think I have to, because this—meaning Zip-Loc scrotum, blood-soaked diaper, infernal recovery room—is where I now find myself. Where drugs, for better or worse, seem to have taken me. And this, it says so right on the contract, is a book about me and drugs.

But back to those gauze-wrapped testicles. My genital mummy. The point—oh Christ, oh screaming Jesus, they're bleeding right through the gauze. I'm spotting! But never mind. . . . The point is, everything, bad or good, boils back to the decade on the needle, and the years before that imbibing everything from cocaine to Romilar, pot to percs, LSD to liquid meth and a pharmacy in between: a lifetime spent altering the single niggling fact that to be alive means being conscious. More or less.

It's led right up to this "billiard"—I'm quoting the doctor, a slouching, eighty-four-year-old urologist with yellow hair who said to call him "Buddy"—this "billiard"-size cyst whose removal now has me bruised and oozing. That poison all but destroyed my liver. And the liver, they tell me, is the janitor of the body. It cleans up. My little janitor couldn't handle the overflow, and busloads of heinous narco-residue somehow spilled down there, into huevos *territory. Hence my appearance back here in Cedars-Sinai, my home away from home. The place I kicked junk—twice. The place my child was born. The place, if I can trust Doctor Buddy, where I've just given birth to a scrotal eightball.*

This mortifying diaper-wear is taking me back, sending me careening down toxic memory lane. I can't help but think, lying here in post-op nitrous and dilaudid delirium, of the day the other product of my loins, my baby daughter, popped to life at this esteemed institution. I was thirty-five, between pit stops in the Chemical Abuse Ward. The one time I set foot in Cedars when they didn't want to chop off my arms at the shoulder blades—just to keep the needles out. Not that it would have helped. I would, if one-armed and jonesing, doubtless have *found a way to cook up a hearty spoon of Mexican tar and slam it with my toes. (I met a double amputee in San Francisco whose girlfriend slapped a bra strap around his throat and geezed him in the neck. Another triumph of the human spirit. But slap me if I get sentimental. . . .)*

Let's just say it was that trip to Cedars, the one where I walked in a junkie and walked out a junkie dad, that let me know how far I'd sunk. Even now the details—before, during, and after—make me want to pluck my eyes out and pound dirt in the sockets. There are stories you don't want to tell, and there are stories that scald your brainpan right down to the tongue at the mere thought of uttering. But you can't NOT. Even if you wait until your skull is nothing but a charred and smoking husk, the truth will still be in there, squirming. At this point, there's nothing left to do but let it out.

So . . . by way of time and place: March 31, 1989, I found myself in the sterile confines of the Cedars-Sinai OB/GYN toilet, injecting a bomb-size hit of Mexican heroin while, twenty feet away, my baby daughter inched her way south in my screaming wife's uterine canal.

Somehow, cross-eyed and bloody-armed, I managed to scuffle back in time to witness the sweetest thing in life shoot out of the womb and into Los Angeles. Not, however, before I saw the sheer, unfettered loathsomeness of my being reflected in the eyes of the man delivering my daughter. One glimpse of this little girl's father, it was clear, and Dr. Randomangst would just as soon have shoved the poor thing back to oblivion.

And who could blame him? It doesn't take Jonas Salk to surmise the future of a newborn whose daddy slimes into the delivery room oozing from the arms. I was hell's own creepy beast, and he could see it.

You might say that success ruined me. You might say I ruined success. The eighties launched me on a drug-soaked spiral from feature magazines to sex films to the multi-G-a-week world of network TV. On one level I may have qualified as Young Urban Professional. But that status—newly married and monied—occupied the mere surface of a life whose underside embraced a more tormenting reality of drugs and addiction, betrayal, loss and crime.

Father. Husband. Writer. Junkie. On a daily basis I lived this double and triple life. I pingponged back and forth from L.A.'s hard-core 'hoods to those studio digs, from the comfort of my just-bought home to the rougher confines of the dope house. . . . The hard fact: whatever the universe in which I touched down, Hollywood High or Hollywood Low, among family, friends, or fellow hypes, the only constant was the facade. I was a gangster with the gangsters. I was a Yuppie with the Yups. I was a daddy with the dads.

How I slipped into this abyss—and how I made it out—are questions I'll chase down from one end of this volume to the other.

The truth: This book, for me, is less an exercise in recall than exorcism. And a schizophrenic exorcism at that. Opiates are, by their very nature, about forgetting. When you're in that narcotic haze, memory functions like some mutant projector, a hell-tuned Bell & Howell. As the film goes in one end, at the other it's immediately eaten by some kind of acid, dissolving the second the events transpire.

That was my life on drugs. Experience lived, more or less, then the soothing hiss of oblivion as instantly the moments are burned away. . . . Banished.

The soul, I believe, allows you to forget such trauma. It wants you to. . . . The real record of these years exists on the cellular level. The mind buries the horror. And the body is where it's buried. Hence the sideshow liver they tell me could fail in a year, this recent souvenir in my scrotum, the fatigue and ache and fevered, sweating nights that never end. Until they do.

The fact is, I'm not sure the way this journey will go or where it's going. I only know I have to make the descent—to re-crawl into the inferno and pray to God in His Junkie Heaven I crawl back out again.

PART ONE

LOW END HOLLYWOOD

I used to think that there was no way out, that I would just have to kill myself. When I was reeling in some locked bathroom, blood on my shoes, and someone banging on the door . . . When my wife was pregnant, and I was sure to my sick soul that the baby would be born some eyeless mutant, vegetative at best, because of all the chemicals I had pumped into my veins before I slammed the seed that fertilized her blameless egg . . . When I was in the hospital kicking and my eyelids scraped like barbed wire and my skin felt boiled in oil and every breath was a serrated knife drawn slowly up from my intestines through my lungs and out my gagging throat . . . There was no other way.

And yet, here I am, north of one year needle free. Living life no longer like a human pincushion, seeing my beautiful little girl every afternoon, hating myself only because it seems to be my nature and not because, say, I've stolen a handful of crumpled fives from the purse of a woman who made the mistake of thinking I was clean and really cared, or because I spent the money meant for milk and diapers on another fix.

The temptation is to be clever. To make it all wildly amusing. I published a story once, at thirty days off the spike, about doing dope in the studio where they shot *ALF,* banging so much shit in the sound stage toilet I heard the furry little puppet hissing my name and scratching at the door.

I imagined, in my narco-dementia, that this three-foot furry TV star—no more than a puppet with attitude—could see right through the bathroom walls. Alf was out there, eyeballing all the blood I'd splattered on the mirror, on my fingers, into tiny, scarlet puddles at my feet. And he did not approve.

People thought my story was funny, hysterical. And I was glad. Just because I'd kicked junk, after all, did not mean I'd kicked being a junkie. And junkies lie. It's their primary addiction. Not that I never skirted cerebral hemorrhage imagining a prime-time hairball pawing at the men's room knob while I geezed a speedball and tried to dab the bright red puddles off the floor with paper towels. That happened. But I wasn't laughing about it. I was staring in the mirror and squeezing back the worst tears in the world, tears that came out yellow because, by then, my liver was already telling me what my brain could not accept. I was dying. But not fast enough. I would have to live a little longer, to survive more horror. Which of course meant doing more heroin, the thing that made such horror endurable.

See, it wasn't just the dope. It never is. It was the wrongness of the situation. I wasn't Chet Baker fixing behind the bandstand and blowing his heart out. I wasn't Johnny San Quentin, shooting in his jail tattoos and boosting stereos. I was Jerry Stahl, writing bad TV and hating it. Desperately trying to counter his shame at the loathsome squareness of what he did with the secret hipness of what he thought really was. Only he wasn't particularly hip. And he wasn't, it pains me now to realize, even close to being secret.

You have to understand where drugs can take you. How the once unthinkable becomes routine and the routine, once established, is something you can never, ever think about. You never have to, if you have the drugs.

To some extent, this entire memoir is nothing but a history of WRONG SITUATIONS. Behavior so inappropriate it hardly qualifies as behavior anymore. More like some toxic, nonstop twitch. . . . At *Moonlighting*, on the Fox lot, I had a corner office where I routinely arrived every morning an hour early, locked the door, and fixed to make myself chipper before the arrival of my wholesome co-workers. Some people stopped to get croissants and cappuccino on their morning drive. I stopped for dilaudids. But the transaction, however unlikely or illegal, became just as mundane. As did the whole daily ritual of procurement and consumption.

I was married, gainfully employed and a father-to-be. Though I could not say which of the three terrified me most. My marriage was, from the start, a trifle odd. As was my entrée into Mondo Television. The two: connubial lack-of-bliss and prime-time arrival, occurred simultaneously.

The dope, I ought to point out, was always there. It's not like they stuffed narcotics in the envelope with my studio contract. Your top-drawer Hollywood agents can worm in a lot of clauses, but even they can't guarantee a daily stash of needles and the gunk to stuff them with. This wasn't the music business. It was television. You had to do that yourself.

No, drugwise, what happened with TV was just a matter of progression. It's not like I ever wanted to wake up and just *be* a grossly overpaid, self-loathing, can't-look-in-the-mirror-without-gagging TV writer. A junkie, maybe, but not a prisoner in Hawaiian–Shirt-land.

The thing is, all my heroes were junkies. Lenny Bruce, Keith Richards, William Burroughs, Mike Davis, Hubert Selby, Jr. . . . These guys were cool. They were committed. They would not have been caught dead doing an *ALF* episode.

How I ended up in that high-paid, low-prestige position is, in itself, confirmation of a private theory that my entire adult life is one long lapse. I wouldn't even have had the chance to sell out if I hadn't married it, and I probably would not have gotten married if it weren't, you know, for those darn drugs.

It started—and we have to jump in somewhere—innocently enough, with a kooky little short story in *Playboy* magazine. All I wanted out of life was to write fiction and bang out strange-o magazine features to keep the larder loaded. Which, with some degree of success, I managed to do. And for all I know might still be doing. Except—and this, you just have to believe me, sounds infinitely creepier in retrospect than it did at the time—I sort of wed into the industry. Slept my way to the middle.

My bride, if I may be so bold, was wired into the biz. Just starting, admittedly, but wired in nonetheless. She had seen my earlier, accidental show biz triumph, an X-rated art-cult nugget called *Cafe Flesh. Flesh* slimed into the post–*Pink Flamingoes* Friday Midnight slot at L.A.'s trendy Nuart theater, way back in the S&M Decade.

What happened is when my surprise missus saw the thing, dutiful Development Doll that she was, she concluded I might be exploitable in her own venue. Which turned out to be much more than filling America's need for swinging movies of the week.

Strangely enough, I remember thinking, the first time I saw her: What an odd-looking woman. Kind of like a young, tiny Faye Dunaway with silver hair. Beautiful but strange. Which was right up my alley. If they were just beautiful, I couldn't talk to them. If they were strange, I knew I had a chance.

All my life I'd gone for women who were a little off. I thought of myself as that odd lion who preyed on gazelles who, through some extreme of taste or appealing physical peculiarity, ran somewhere south of the pack. So that, much as I loved the cheekbones, it was the sight of that otherworldly head of silver gray, the harpie's coif on the tiny, elegant doll, that set off the alarms. Under her arm she carried a rolled-up *Vogue,* except that it had been hollowed out, shellacked, and made into a purse. Uh-Oh City.

Five minutes into our sushi lunch in Studio City, when it was clear that nothing could be farther from TV movie usefulness than my meager talents, the girl of somebody's dreams mentioned she wanted to get married. I was still new to the meeting thing, so this didn't strike me as odd.

At any rate, her personal life was a far sight more engaging than my MOW ideas. (Was America, really, ready for *Attack of the Killer Co-Dependents*?) Plus I loved her accent. Those British *R*'s, so redolent of Julie Christie movies, made every detail fascinating. Just hearing the phrase *Chelsea School for Girls,* or *green card,* I was in heaven. This was, of course, before our entire lives mutated to a TV movie.

Needless to say, her nuptial longing did not spring from laying eyes on me. In fact, it preceded any knowledge of my existence. It was, and this should surprise no one, a career issue. A green card thing. Her dad back in England was ailing. She was here illegally. If she left, she might not be allowed reentry to our sunny shores, might be barred at the gates of cinema heaven. In her desperation, Ms. Britannia was prepared to release an easy three G's to the man who married her.

Even now, the romance makes me go a tad misty-eyed. Before me a homosexual friend—a shaved-skulled wild man who played with the Screamers, a primeval L.A. punk claque—had signed on for hub duty, then begged off when he couldn't tell his mom. Which left Sandra stuck on the continent, no means of fleeing the city without making the return on her belly across the Mexican border. Which just didn't seem that likely clutching that jumbo faux-*Vogue* purse.

Months after we reached our mercenary agreement—and the honeymoon check cleared—my ersatz intended and I actually started hanging out. Our first evening together, I stole every codeine in her medicine cabinet. I was fairly shameless, I suppose. But remarkably consistent. . . .

We were on our way to a movie. I wore fake leather pants—a real fashion king—which split up the back getting out of the car in front of her house. I entered her West Hollywood pad clutching my exposed buttocks like a fan dancer and explained that I had to use her bathroom.

I don't know what I planned to do in there. It's not like I carried a needle and thread for emergency crack repair. No, I just sort of stood there, staring in the mirror with the usual first-night "What the hell am I doing?", then took action when instinct took over and my fingers found themselves dancing lightly over the jars of Aureomycin, Motrin, Benadryl, and other useless items until they hit paydirt.

My technique was to flush the toilet on opening the mirrored cabinet, clear my throat a lot as I'm rifling, then flush again to hide the sound of the thing slamming shut. Nothing's louder, in my experience, than a sticky medicine cabinet. Especially when the owner's out there, waiting, and you're already late for something. Inevitably you step out to sideways stares and a studied attempt by your companion of the evening to look like she's been fussing with the plants. My MO, and a prime example of deluded track-covering if there ever was one, was to always leave a few of the stolen items in the bottom of the prescription bottle. Or, failing that, if I'd gone completely mad, to transfer aspirin, Anacin or some similar, useless palliative into the prescription bottle. (Brown ones are best, since the fact that Percodans are yellow, Dristan white, goes undiscovered until yours truly is long gone and out of the suspect pool.)

By the time we left, I'd crunched a handful and rinsed the sludge off with tap water. It didn't take long for the buzz. And I was already wearing Norton, her cat, on my head when she strolled out of her bedroom in fishnets, leather skirt, and magazine purse. (Pet games, in my experience, are always a great way to disguise sudden loss of equilibrium.)

Sandra was a reader for what she called a "millionaire sleaze" from the Valley. Or maybe *I* called him that. His name was Jack Marty, Marty Jackson, Jack Martini. *Something* like that. . . . He suffered perpetual auto angst. For weeks his Jaguar had been sputtering to an inappropriate halt at stoplights all over the Valley. No one could figure it. Jag experts, dealer reps, the whole big-buck prestige car support network scratched their collective head. Until one balmy morning, strolling up the well-tended walk from driveway to door, Sandra heard these . . . squeaks and skittering.

These little squeaks, this *skittering*. . . . Mister Marty, it seemed, had rats in his Jag. That's all! In an act of unwitting charity, the producer'd been playing host to a family of rodents. While on board, the slime-tails had snacked on ten grand worth of British auto wiring. Which really is kind of nice. This being Hollywood and all, there's room for everybody.

Thank goodness my future ex's employer could afford the rat's nest. His one Movie of the Week, however obscure, had made him busloads. It revolved, if I'm not mistaken, around a group of cheerleaders crashed and stranded on a desert island. Something like that. They had to eat each other to survive. Lots of angst and pom-poms. The man had no office per se, and Sandra worked in a North Hollywood ranch house famed for once being the late John Candy residence.

Which bears mention for the sole, sorry fact that, at this stage of the game, I was really impressed. "Hey," I remember thinking, the couple of times I visited, potted up and killing a minute until Sandra was ready to split, "John Candy sat on this couch . . . ! John Candy walked through this door . . . ! *John Candy touched this toilet seat . . . !*"

Greatness really was everywhere, if you could just get invited in.

What I really loved about Sandra—however ironic, in retrospect, considering her Yuppie tomorrow—was that she came from good Bohemian stock. Her mother and father were every bit as arty as my own were the human equivalent of Formica. Her parents, she told me, threw wild parties. Dad was a London book illustrator. An artist. Mom had been married before, to a guy in Stalin's Russia who got disappeared. *Her* father, Sandra's grandfather, founded the U.K. Communist Party. She'd barely escaped back to England with a two-year-old son, Sandra's half brother, now a world-famous neurologist, and never found out, officially, what happened to the love of her life. It was Twiggy by way of *Dr. Zhivago*. . . . And I was completely intrigued.

Unable to do much but get high, write, or worry about not writing, get a little higher, and sleep with women who admired how much I got high and wrote, I wasn't exactly gripped by what you'd call *joie de vivre*. Sandra knew how to live. A skill as arcane to me as glassblowing or conversational Erdu. I'd listen, enthralled, to tales of how she and her parents took trips to Portugal every summer, shacking up with other painters and writers and international happy-artist types.

I'd lie there, in vicarious heaven, as she told lovely stories of dancing on the tables, the only little girl in a summer full of beauty-loving artists, spinning under the colored lanterns while Daddy laughed and Spaniards painted her portrait and everybody drank and sang themselves into some unimaginable Bohemian nirvana. (My own family, every summer, packed off on miserable all-day drives to army bases, where my father spent two weeks in the Army reserves.)

We were, by and large, still more or less in this casual acquaintance category when we tied the knot. So casual was the whole arrangement, the night of the big event I forgot there *was* a big event. Crouched in my back room sleeping off a buzz at six in the evening, I heard the knock on the door and leapt out of my socks.

No one in a drug-fueled stupor likes to hear a knock on the door. It can mean anything. In this case it meant I was about to waltz through a trap door and down a chute that wouldn't break my fall for years and years. All I saw out my back door window, though, was that vulpine little beauty with the silver hair.

I ducked back in the bedroom for narcotic reinforcement—my last high as a single man—and stumbled forth to meet my wedded destiny.

Next thing I know, Sandra and I are speeding off to Burbank with Janine, her sarcastic best friend sidekick, as witness. Janine herself was a stunning Italian woman forever irascible about the size of her hips. A goddess in any other era, she felt like a fat-ass in this one. And nothing or no one could dissuade her of this status. As with any good neurotic, the contempt she felt toward herself was doled out generously to all those in her path.

"Real nice, Jerry, getting married for a fee. What do you think, maybe you can make a career out of it. . . . It's not like you have one now. . . ."

On it went, all the way over the hill in Sandra's plucky, just-bought Toyota Tercel. My thinking, if you can call it that, boiled down to *What the hell?* I can get married, then get divorced, and not have to feel creepy as the years rolled on and I continued to live my solitary, 24-seven loaded life.

Well, yeah! It just made sense. *Divorced. . . . I'm divorced. . . . A divorced guy.* This was a cool deal, beyond the three G's for service rendered. It's not like I had enough respect for myself or the world at large to see much import in the decision. I was, after all, already living like a junkie. I wasn't shooting up smack every day, but still . . . So what would one more bit of surrealism—in this case a gig as green card beard—matter in the grand scheme of things? It's not like I'd been accused of integrity lately. I had no problem with integrity. I didn't have any. To have worried for half a second about what I was doing would have meant taking myself seriously. *"He's divorced,"* I imagined future sweethearts sighing to themselves, *"that's why he's so moody. . . .* " It was like breaking your own leg so people would understand why you limped.

Love really does make the world go round. The question is, go round what?

My last big affair, pre-matrimony, was with Fraulein Dagmar, a married German woman over here to peddle her Performance Art. She was also, I later learned, here to take a vacation from hubby and *der kinder.*

This black-haired, black-eyed mother of two, for reasons still obscure to me, had taken up quarters in the snake room of my porn partner's white picket Hollywood Flats home.

Dagmar and I first laid eyes on each other at a screening of *Night Dreams,* the watershed stretch of sex celluloid that marked said partner and my first, full-length foray into X-land. Hokily enough, the original title was *Day Dreams,* which accounts for the noms-de-porn adapted by my friend the director and myself.

I gave my partner the name "Rinse Dream"—which sounds like a pretentious hair conditioner—and dubbed myself "Herbert W. Day," a moniker that came complete with phony back story. H.W.D., I told the curious, was actually my high school principal's name. He used to pull my pants down and swat me. Now, by way of revenge, I'd see that his sadistic, puritanical ass lived on as a porno legend, the first name in avant garde whack 'n' wiggle movies. (*Night Dreams,* see, snagged major notoriety by breaking the all-important Hot Cereal Barrier, marking the first time in smut-fest history a life-size Cream of Wheat box was used in on-screen coitus.)

The curious thing about pornography, for those in the grim biz of cranking it out, is its singular lack of stimulating ambience. So that the experience of sitting in that tiny screening room—or on the set—watching miscellaneous humping humans earn their daily rate aping orgasm, ranks, on the Arousal Meter, somewhere between folding laundry and *Meet the Press.*

There's no real way to describe that sensation of standing around, chomping day-old doughnuts and slurping bad java, chatting about the merits of retreads versus new tires, while ten feet away some slinky lovely is on hands and knees getting rear-ended by a physical specimen whose defining attribute is a penis robust enough to double as Billy Barty's prosthetic limb, should he ever need one. "Okay, ready for Mayo!" barks the director, and by the time Mister Footlong works up a squirt, the whole crew's so bored they're staging cockroach races behind the set.

All of which is to say, I don't think it was erotic fallout from watching *Night Dreams* that moved Dagmar to sidle on up to me before the credits went up and pose the ever-curious accusation: "Why do you act like you don't notice me?"

To which, of course, there is no answer. If you say "I did notice you," you have to explain why you didn't show it. . . . If you admit their existence escaped you completely, you're in even worse shape. . . . The truth is, the only way I've ever found to make an impression on a beautiful woman is to ignore her completely. (And, considering my track record, you *do* want to take romance tips from me. . . .)

It's a no-lose proposition. If you strike out, you don't feel too bad, since you never really stepped up to bat anyway. If, on the other hand, said beauty, out of resentment or offended pride, approaches you to see what kind of man has the gall to not acknowledge her, not bestow the hosannas to which she's entitled, you end up starting off on a toehold of respect you could not otherwise have accrued.

While the director and entourage remained to discuss the undiluted genius of what they'd wrought, I suggested to Dagmar that we make our escape.

So this lanky, ruby-lipped Teutonic artiste and I ended up slouching arm-in-arm down Hollywood Boulevard at the ungodly hour of ten in the morning. Even at that time of day, the sunlight is so harsh that it drives any sane citizen to take shelter. Only in Los Angeles does the light have that dread-soaked, accusing quality. As if the sun itself were screaming at you, *What the fuck are you doing out in the street, what's wrong with your life?* The city fathers, in some kind of twisted homage, made the sidewalks actually sparkle along Hollywood Boulevard. You can get a headache from the twinkling masonry in between the pathetic stars embedded in the concrete. Making of the great what the not-so-great and the never-will-be secretly want all along to make: a dead and unresisting doormat.

The life-forms were just starting to stir to life on the boulevard. Runaways, mostly, midwest Tims and Tammies, skanked out in Tomy's Coffee Shop, at the corner of Wilcox, plotting their blow-you-for-a-twenty-and-some-crank way through the eye-achingly bright maze of the day before them. Dagmar and I ducked into the Frolic Room, one of the countless morning-friendly bars along this stretch of the boulevard. The kind of place the tourists don't even see and the locals like to hide in.

The only time I like barrooms is early in the morning. Places that open at six, to take care of that wake-up boiler-maker crowd, reassure the likes of me. The warm and fuzzy knowledge that, scattered abroad this noxious landscape, there are legions of others who just can't make it through the day without some form of blessed, soul-killing refreshment.

One difference between dope and alcohol is the booze makes you look worse. The sauce turns you red and the needle turns you green. One turns you into a nightmare and one turns into a nightmarish joke. Dope, at least, preserves you.

You can, if I may propagate the popular myth, shoot it for years and end up a strapping septuagenarian like Bill Burroughs. You'd have to look into his eyes to see the degeneration. His son, Bill junior—author of his own dope classic, *Speed*—drank like the proverbial fish and bellied up in his twenties from liver disease. I knew Billy up in Santa Cruz, used to visit him in the garage he lived in, and it wasn't pretty. He used to whip up a batch of *mah joun,* a honeyed marijuana recipe Dad brought back from Tangier, and spend these strange, timeless evenings reading Faulkner at the top of his lungs. Another victim of the toxic muse. . . .

Anyway, a little ten-fifteen brandy wasn't going to hurt much. And Dagmar and I indulged ourselves on a stool in this murky hideaway, alongside a row of regulars already deep into their disease. Here I learned a bit of her background. It's the details that make human beings creatures of such irresistible freakishness. With her black bowl haircut, armor-piercing black eyes, and cherry juice lips, the bony Dagmar came on like a high-IQ Kewpie doll. In throaty, Dietrich-esque English, she announced: "I haf been owned too long."

I wouldn't have guessed that a single sentence could bring on love—however temporary. But if one could, that was the one. "Who owns you?" I asked.

She knocked back another swig of old Mister Boston and stared at the smoky mirror until the answer came. "My huss-band."

"Your husband." There seemed nothing more to say. So I let it ride.

"He . . . His family . . . They were very important in . . . how you say . . . Arms? During the War. He has the money from the Krupps. You know the Krupps?"

Yes, I knew the Krupps. I had, in my morbid youth, indulged a full-blown fascination for Holocaust porn. I couldn't get enough details of Nazi atrocity. Brand names of oven makers, gas and munitions moguls, details of Henry Ford complicity and Mercedes-Benz's slave labor practices being my absolute fave turf. That I would some day stumble on the flesh-and-blood manifestation of my fetish, slavering over the spouse of an actual gold-teeth rich burghermeister's boy, was more than I'd have possibly imagined.

At the risk of sounding like Wayne Newton's valet, life does occasionally toss off its little rewards.

"Zo . . . I don't know. It's all shit. Shit, shit, shit. You know?" She sighed, a long, slow, eloquent release. Then dropped her hand on mine on the greasy bar. "Zo my husband . . . He is filthy."

Her eyes drilled into my own in the mirror. The cartoons on the wall, caricatures of stars dead and undusted for years, leered down at us like greasy angels. Somewhere down the bar a man coughed wetly.

"Filthy?" I said.

"Is that not how you say? He is filthy rich. It is unbelievable. Every little bitch is in heat around him. He fucks them all. All of them."

"I understand."

I understand. It's what I always said when I had no idea what to say. An old journalism trick, to keep them talking. Although, as I looked in those black-pool eyes, I began to think maybe I really did have a clue. Pain is pain, after all.

Her armaments daddy had banged every maiden on the Rhine. Now she was here, in America, far out of range of his big guns. Ready to fuck him back.

Her long fingers linked into mine. She squeezed. "You do, don't you, Mister Shtahl . . . Mister Shtahlverks. . . . You know," she whispered, suddenly little girlish. "Stahl means steel. You know what is steel, *ja*?"

I said yes, I knew what is steel. I would, at that point, have said anything she wanted. I'd never heard a woman say *"ja"* before. It was all I ever wanted to hear again.

I shortly found myself in a luxury suite, at Château Marmont, site of John Belushi's legendary exit, high over Sunset Boulevard, standing on my head beside my Deutschland doll-baby.

Standing on my head because of the Turkish opium this mother of two had smuggled in her panties through customs.

"I can look like a 'hausfrau,' you know?" she explained when I asked how she happened to sneak the fist-size black ball past the ever-vigilant War on Drugsters.

Once up in the room, we were already abundantly loose from the breakfast brandy. A few riffles through her giant backpack revealed she'd neglected to lay in her much-beloved opium pipe. Bequeathed her, she exclaimed tearily, by Gypsies with whom she'd lived in Afghanistan. It was the Gypsies, in fact, who'd given her the initial ideas for the feather-and-wax masks that now played such a large part in her "performance pieces."

Sans pipe, Dagmar had a novel way of ingesting opium. Hence the headstands. "Ve take off our clothes," she said like the Nazi nurse of every Bar Mitzvah boy's dreams. "Then ve *oom-pah!*"

The "oom-pah" was accompanied by a two-fingered up-yours gesture that left little to the imagination. So, before anything more than a few lugubrious barroom kisses, we had stripped each other in a bedroom of the Château Marmont, broken off black, testicular chunks of evil-smelling drug, and, like partners in a double suicide determined to fire simultaneously, shoved them up each other's hotel-soaped sphincters.

"This is hot, *ja*?"

"Oh, JA!" I gulped, somewhere between a groan and a thank-you.

No time to linger in anal gratification, though. Upon firing, we had to hop off the floral bedspread, kneel side-by-side before the yellow walls, and, head on the carpet, hoist our legs up until our heels touched the swirling paint and our eyes took in the upside-down hotel room. Outside, a reverse palm tree swayed hypnotically. Dagmar's rasping Berlin-decadent-fantasy voice droned on in explanation of our practice.

"You can eat it, but the stomach, accchh, it's horrible. You swallow it and, umm, what's the word, you get this pain and zen you, um . . . *kotzen.* Vomit like a dog. Just like that."

The blood was starting to flow to my face. The brandy swirling in my gut might have been on its way toward *kotzen* territory. Except the proximity to Dagmar's warm flesh—she seemed to exude heat—the sight of her erect nipples defying gravity, wakened my own dangling genitals to defiance of their own.

"You haf to, you now, put ze opium up ze, um, *arschloch,* as far as you can. Otherwise it drips down, you feel it between your legs, *acch,* and it's a total waste. . . ."

In fact, I could feel the stuff gushing north, melting like chocolate left on a hot car seat, sliding ever deeper into my willing bloodstream. In no time we'd stopped speaking. Four floors below us, traffic whooshed down Sunset like the sighs of earthbound angels.

It was time to peel ourselves off the wall. But before we could, in kind of delayed synchronicity, we noticed the knock on the door. Our eyes simply met, acknowledging the thud-thud-thud. Sound, in that state, has reverberation but no fixed locale. It might have been knocking; it might have been a wrecking ball eight blocks away. Before we could decide, the door just swung open. In our haste and passion—for the drug and for each other—we'd apparently left the door unlocked.

In reeled a paunchy middle-aged man in Bermudas and Ray-Bans. A seventies sitcom regular, famed for a face that resembled a Schnauzer, he seemed completely nonplussed as he took us in. Two naked people standing on their heads at two in the afternoon. He paused for a thoughtful moment, took a draw on his fat cigar, and asked, in a thick Bronx accent, "Is that, like, an earthquake thing?"

When we didn't reply, he simply shrugged and tossed the hotel key on the dresser. "Shouldn't leave these in the door," he said as he let himself out, "people get arrested. Even in L.A."

Dagmar and I uncoiled ourselves and crawled to the bed in opiated silence. We were both too gone on that intestinal lowball to do much more than grunt and sigh. In a frenzied slow motion, lips and fingers, tongues and limbs, a single dripping blur—I ended up on top of her, between her parted, unshaven legs.

Our eyes kissed as my hands worked the small and sagging breasts, product of suckling twin boys till they were five, which she seemed to be ashamed of but which I loved precisely because of the life they had seen.

She guided me inside her with her callused palms, writhing wide-eyed beneath me until, in a patois she adapted again and again at the giant moment, she rolled her eyes and wailed at the faraway Fatherland, "*Nein, nein, nein!*" And then, even louder, "*Oi gott!* **I'm being fucked by a Jew!**"

Then she collapsed, whispering her *neins* in my burning ears until we both passed out, entwined and prone in our private, opiated eternities. This was our MO—procto-opium parties and pan-fried Nazi-banter. Whatever the Third Reich equivalent of White Trash, Teutonic Earth Mom, Dagmar would pretend she was it. "*Scuse me, liebschaun-puss, wanna hit me with a couple of them sauerbraten? Howza 'bout you 'n' me turn in early tonight and log some quality Bunker time?*"

Anyway, I started having these Erich von Stroheim in Calvin Klein dreams, and pretty soon it was all over. Duty called, and stout-hearted Dagmar flew back to Himmler's little patch o' heaven to tend to her own Aryan youth.

This was my last real love affair before lurching down the path to matrimony.

• • •

The first problem was just finding the damn chapel. Sandra had combed the Yellow Pages for a suitable venue and settled on the Chapel of Love in Burbank. You'd think they'd really trick the place out, but Bliss Central turned out to be harder to track down than a custom taxidermist.

I sat on the backseat, hunched up and staring at my knees. The sheer horror of the situation produced its own weird rush. "Sandra," Janine carped, "didn't you get directions? I mean, *God!*"

"It's supposed to be here!" my future ex snapped back. In the clinch, her London diction slipped into clipped and vicious.

"Why don't we ask in a gas station?" I chimed in. "Why don't we just have the guy in the gas station do it? Find one that says 'Full Serve.' "

The same holes-in-the-wall: 7-Elevens, notary publics, muffler repair shops, came round and round as we circled the block.

"I can't believe you guys," Janine sneered, never happier than when perched in a posish of high moral authority. She turned with her arms crossed. "Jerry, are you high?"

"It's my wedding day, for Christ's sake. I'm a two-legged endorphin factory."

Finally a sort of Byzantine marquee materialized between two buildings. Faux stained glass. "CHAPEL OF LOVE."

Inside, a tiny birdlike woman in butterfly glasses and sequined dress waited to greet us. The gown went right down to her teacup-size red pumps.

"I am Pia Piarina. You are Mister Cochran?" She had the kind of accent you only hear in dubbed Italian movies.

"Not yet," I said.

"Es-, escuse me?"

"I'm Miss Cochran. He's Mister Stahl."

Sandra was already taking charge, setting the pattern that was to last the duration of our time together: me too fucked-up to function, her handling the details. The walls of the chapel were painted with "couples" frescoes: couples in woods, couples on the beach, couples under an umbrella . . . What made them special was, the people looked like health book illustrations. The men wore windbreakers, the women pleated skirts. Even the floor had been graced with scenes of hygienic romance. Through it all wafted the scent of Lysol, hovering in little aerosol clouds over strategically placed yellow candles.

While handling formalities—checking our license, birth certificate, other documents necessary for legal romance—Pia explained that she'd been an opera singer, but her career had not "bloomed" here in America.

"My husband, too, he is opera," she said. And, as if on cue, an organ began to wheeze somewhere in the back. You had to squint to see beyond the chapel proper—it was a large room lit up only in the middle—but, there in the rear, bobbing over his Hammond, was a thatch-haired, sorry-looking fellow who had better things to do than look our way. He never really broke into song so much as shifted from one lugubrious note to another, switching just at the point when another second of the same wavering tone became unbearable.

"Jerry Cochran," la bella Pia began. "Do you—"

"That's Stahl," I said.

"Excuse?"

"I'm Jerry Stahl," I explained again.

"I see."

Our nuptial hostess had steered us in front of a pastel fresco of two health book types arm-in-arm before a smiling sun. Then, methodical as a mortician, she arranged our bodies in the appropriate manner. Taking my faux betrothed's left hand, she placed it atop my right. This done, she produced a patent-leather riding crop—she must have had it all along, but I didn't notice—and whacked it off her hip when our two paws started to drop.

Sandra and I by then had had sex, but we hadn't held hands before. I've never been much of a hand-holder. The awkwardness did something to me. I just wasn't down for any form of PDA (Public Display of Affection). This may account for what happened next. I got the giggles.

Actually, I began to laugh, hysterically. Not good-natured chuckling. Hoarse, hacking gasps and howls just tore out of me, left me gasping for breath, struggling not to pee in my wedding jeans. "Sorry," I gulped, wiping away the tears, "I'm –aaaggh, huacchh, Jesus . . . I'm really sorry."

Behind me in her role as witness, big Janine must have bruised her tongue from clicking it. Her disgust was palpable. All Sandra could do was shake her head–British reserve didn't cover such contingencies. Pia was beyond furious.

"This is . . . not right! This is the most important moment in your life. For a man and a woman, this is . . . everything. What is wrong with you?"

Twice she tried to lumber past the "Do you, Jerry, take this woman to be your lawful . . ." etc. And twice I burst into gut-wrenching, barking sobs of laughter. By now even her husband stopped tickling the ivories.

"Mister Cochran," Pia screamed at last, swinging her little crop like a jockey off my buttocks. "Mister Cochran!"

"Ouch! Yes . . . I'm sorry," I pleaded. "I'm sorry . . . I'm so emotional."

"You are de-mented!"

WHACK! went the leather riding crop.

"That's right! That's right! When I get emotional, I get . . . demented."

WHACK!

Somehow we made it to the end of the service. Just to round out the evening, Miss Piarina announced she did not take Master Card. She was not about to take checks, either. So it was that I had to stay behind, a connubial hostage, while my new bride and her indignant girlfriend tore around Burbank looking for a cash machine. Pia, Mister Pia, and I stood in awkward silence until the dough was produced. Only when we were leaving, as she was seeing us out, did the feisty prima donna clutch my arm and stand on her red-soled toes to hiss in my ears.

"I know what you do!" she whispered fiercely, spitting the words directly in my brain. "You never come back here, you! I know! *I know!*"

It didn't matter what she thought of me, though. I had the Pia Piarina–signed papers. I had legal documents. I was now a citizen of the nation of the wed and the legitimate, with notarized scribble to prove it.

Marriage didn't exactly fuel our every waking thought, but my legal mate and I did continue to see each other post-Pia. My level of drugdom underwent a sudden shift as well. And not because I'd caught a sudden itch for opiates.

In the autumn of the eighties, L.A.'s drug culture was in a period of transition. The powers that were, whoever and wherever, were changing the menu. Loads—a lethal combination of Codeine 4's and Doriden, a potent sleep aid—had been the drug of choice for the Hollywood Punk crowd since the early eighties. And now, for mysterious reasons of their own, the government was phasing them out. Those much loved loads, source of so much compact inspiration for the Hollywood skank scene, were being phased out. The government vacuumed Doriden off the street, made the things ungettable, and thereby drove countless denizens of peripheral punkdom from the joys of pill popping into more hard-edged, needle-driven activities. Loads—or Dors 'n' fours, as some still called them—were basically a white drug for a certain strata of black leather postpunk alienated types. Down on Crenshaw and Adams, hard by now legendary South Central, the brothers used to stand on the corners and hawk their wares. At the sight of two white boys in a car, they'd step off the curb, wave their hands, and shout you down. It was, in those heady days, a buyer's market.

Think Quaalude: how one day they were falling out of your pockets, the next some farsighted dealer was slinging them for twenty bucks a pop.

It had been years since I'd written a word without the things. I'd turned the process of consumption into some bogus health ritual. Load days, I'd set the alarm for six, make sure I had a steaming vat of java, and plunk the requisite pills down the hatch with a twitch of anticipation and a prayer of gratitude. Within minutes, I knew, I'd be a chattering Gandhi.

One morning I'd no sooner hunkered down to paper and pen when a tap on the door signaled humanity at hand. Normally a hider—one knock on the door and my response, cowering in the bedroom, was complete stillness, active don't-let-them-know-you're-there dread, no matter who they may be—I responded on loads with welling gladness and a dash to the door.

"Come in, come in!" I chirped to the forlorn stranger whose hangdog, Okie visage loomed in the window. The glass was still dewy. I swung open the door to a John Carradine type: six and a half feet of cheap black suit, Adam's apple, and ankles.

"Good morning," I sang, as if I'd been waiting for him. "I bet you'd like some hot coffee!"

The man was a Jehovah's witness. He wasn't used to hospitality. He was used to being shunned. He must have been. You didn't knock on strangers' doors at seven-seventeen in the morning unless you wanted some kind of abuse. My response clearly shook him.

"Have you been saved?" he asked me, suspicion dripping in his voice. "Do you know why human beings suffer? Have you thought about it?"

"Let me get that coffee," I buzzed. "We'll talk about it. This is great!"

I remember he had trouble balancing the mug on his bony knee. And that he sniffed the stuff before sipping it, which he did only once or twice before setting it down on the end table—right, I noticed, on top of a tattered *Pillow Biter,* some fifties' men's mag I'd seen in a garage sale and snapped up for the prose. He didn't seem too pleased to see the Mamie van Doren look-alike on the cover.

"To me, Jimmy"—by then I'd unearthed his name, that he had a wife and three kids in Reseda and that he really couldn't stay too long because he had "an appointment"—"to me, God is like this happy bus driver. . . . He's, like, driving a tour bus, okay? The tour bus of our life, only he doesn't tell us the sights. . . . He lets us pick them ourselves, see, and later we sort of find out where we've been and what it all means. . . ."

"I don't know about that," he croaked. "I mean, Jesus . . . our Lord . . . well, he's the Savior. . . . He's not, well, he's not a tour guide.

"This"—he swept his gangly arm to indicate my living room, its cheesy furniture, the crumbling city beyond and the sky above it all—"this is not a bus."

He seemed so unhappy, I wanted to help him. But after I'd given him six dollars, all the money I had on me, for his stack of *Watchtowers,* he still seemed . . . *edgy.* I did my best to show my interest, which was fairly sincere: "Can *I* write for *Watchtower*? I mean, I'm a writer. That's what I was doing, just now, when you knocked. I was *writing* . . . Uh-huh! Can anyone write for them? I'd really like to do that!" But he still insisted he had to leave.

I don't imagine Brother Jimmy came back to Hollywood much. It was probably safer saving souls in the Valley.

It was a curious confluence of events: this shift from pills and smoke to hard-, or harder-core dope use; from wholesale singledom to no-nonsense domestic union.

When the decision for Sandra and me to "move in together" reared its gnarly head, I had to balk. "We can't live together," I remember screeching. "We're married. It's too corny!"

Foreshadowing what fun "living together" would be for Sandra and me, I got a call during my last, lost days living on my own. It was from one of my aunts in Pittsburgh. Seems my mother, troubled soul, had taken her own life. Or so they thought.

Heroin, at this point, was still a sometime tool. As opposed to a daily necessity. Which meant that it still worked.

And the shot I took before flying east to see my mother off kept me subdued enough to handle whatever I'd have to handle when I got there. And when it ran out, the Valiums would see me through.

What I had to handle, it turns out, had less to do with tragic death than a continuing, difficult life. What happened, see, is that when I got the call, they actually believed Mom was deceased. She had tried to do herself in and in the process suffered a heart attack and gone comatose. Her coma proved not the prelude to her demise, but a respite before her renewed, unhappy existence. Only I didn't know it at the time. I boarded the plane believing I was flying east for a funeral.

I met my washed-out Uncle Cedric at the airport and learned that Mom didn't die after all. No hello, no how-are-yous, but straight to "She's not dead. She's in the hospital. She's in a coma, but she'll be coming out."

There was no reason to visit the hospital, but I stopped in anyway. St. Lucy was mere feet from her current home, a condo, extra handy for the odd session of electroshock. The Edison Medicine, on occasion, being Mom's drug of choice.

Now I don't begrudge my mother her torment. It's the one thing we have in common. I love her. She'd been depressed all her life. And life, along the way, had given her plenty of reasons. My father's own untimely exit left her alone and hopeless to cope with her newfound status. Our house, after his death, became a museum of Dad-dom. His gavel, the flag they wrapped his coffin in, folded up neat and triangular in the army style, pictures of him at various milestones of his career. City solicitor, attorney general, federal judge. All these, and more, mounted, displayed, posted around the living room in black frames. The only thing missing were docents, catalogs, and buttons you could push to hear the story of his life.

Having glimpsed her in her self-induced coma, I returned to her condo. Site of her failed attempt. There to encounter another level of parental horror. This time it wasn't the detritus of memory that greeted me. It was the evidence of unsuccessful death. It was blood.

Blood everywhere. Before I saw it, I heard it: the squish of it in the carpet underfoot. Like stepping in muck from the instant I entered, there was no sense that was not assaulted. I followed the skull-size spots from the doorway, to the kitchen, the kitchen back down her little hallway to her bedroom, where blotches stained her white knit bedspread like a scarlet Rorschach.

The stench drew me to the bathroom, where what I saw burned into the very fibers of memory. Blood on the mirror, appearing, to my reeling senses, to form a single, crippling word: NO. Beneath it, droplets ran and solidified. Like red and frozen tears.

I felt no horror. Only dread. In a kind of mindless spasm, I groped for her tubside Comet, twisted the tap, and, in completely uncharacteristic fashion, set about to scrub, remove, and sponge away every single spot of blood in the otherwise neat apartment.

I labored, on my knees, tears in my eyes and vomit choked back in my mouth. But it wasn't my mother's agony that I mourned. I was neither that advanced nor that enlightened. It was my own stained and stinking death, the unconscious, sunken-heart knowledge of what I myself would someday have to survive.

By the time I finished, the terror that had seized me had mounted to some kind of horrific, prescient vision. I knew, in some unutterable way, that what I'd witnessed, in my mother's madness, was but a preview, a God-given glimpse of the blood tide and savagery that awaited me just around the corner.

Fast forward four months or four years, it didn't matter, and you'd see me, once again, on hands and knees, wiping frantically at blood I'd spilled or leaked or squirted from a syringe. In retrospect, I seem to have spent aeons dabbing panic-stricken at puddles on a million floors. But blood, of course, never really washes away. It filters deep down in the psyche and settles there, in subterranean pools. I knew, without knowing. Like my mother, I would soon create that private hell for and by myself.

I flew back to L.A. and moved in with Sandra. I needed a fix.

Part Two

MONDO PORNO

All right, then. How I even got to L.A. in the first place. How I got to town to take the drugs that sealed the gig that lured the girl that goosed the career that fanned the habit that got me where I am right now.

Nobody grows up in Los Angeles. People just get here. In my case it started in roundabout fashion that took me from New York to Columbus, of all places Ohio, and thence to L.A.

Why Columbus? Because that's where *Hustler* magazine is. That's where I signed on after the career that started off with *Village Voice* gigs and a prestige-y *Pushcart* prize veered mysteriously south, straight to the world of hard-core-in-print pornography.

Dying, in my early twenties, to do anything rather than work for a living, I consolidated the need to make money with the ache to see my name in print by entering the heady world of magazine porn, or "poundcake," as it's known among the pros.

At the time I was living a solo, pot- and speed-laced life in a fifth-floor walk up on 108th Street. A one-room, bathroom-down-the-hall-you-share-with-the-Puerto-Rican-queens-type arrangement.

Gigs came here and there, but I was scraping, until one fine day I spotted an ad in the rear end of the *Village Voice*. "Make money writing Erotica," it said. "Classes forming now."

Well, it's not like that sheepskin from Columbia was doing me any good. So I hooked up with this long-haired older guy named Adams. (By older I mean he was probably five years younger than I am now; he was thirty-four.) And settled in for a few highbrow nights a week nailing down the finer points of "Genital Depictions," "Knowing Your Reader" (though who'd want to?), "Building to a Climax," and the all-important "Come Scene."

The other studes were a creepy mélange of two housewives, whose motives seemed other than purely scholastic, a retired plumber, and an Asian exchange student named Honey who never said much and dropped out mysteriously. In the beginning we'd meet two nights a week and go over our stories. For an hour and a half we'd kick around, say, the best words for vagina. Was "pussy" right? Or did "cunt," "snatch," "lovelips," or, my own fave, "labes" fill the bill a little better?

Adams's apartment provided an odd backdrop for our hot and bothered prosody sessions. Assorted crucifixion scenes graced the walls, taking up space between shelves stacked with a collection of World Bibles. His background, unlikely for a man who made his living penning SPANK TIME, WET'N'WILLING, and MAN-HUNGRY, was in the spiritual realm. He was a graduate of Harvard Divinity School and a nonstop never-see-him-drunk Bud drinker. Function, he explained, of a taxi accident that left him permanently hurting in the sacroiliac.

Blond locks tossed back over his shoulder, he dressed only in suit pants, pressed white shirt, and dress shoes—though I never saw him leave his apartment. He seemed to exist in his own closed little universe. His wife, Jan, a large-boned woman with waist-length ponytail and prominent white teeth, worked full-time for a large church organization.

They were a curiously earnest couple. When Jan would stop in with a tray of pecan sandies and Constant Comment tea for her husband's students, she showed no reaction whatsoever to whatever Socratic poser her husband had lobbed onto the floor. "Wet labia—do they turn us on because of the way they feel, or because the way they feel tells us that our partner's turned on?"

Herb, our plumber, always had the same two cents to throw in in any discussion. "I think odor is important. Scent is the key to your erotic desire. It's a pheromone thing. . . ." It was Herb, as well, who penned what remains my all-time favorite in the eroto-scribbler sweepstakes. "Her breath," the crusty union man intoned, "came in short pants. . . ."

What fruits the eroto-prosing sessions bore had less to do with acquired skills than with the connections gentleman Adams made for me in the wondrous world of glossy mag pornography. I was willing to do anything, as long as it was write for a living. That's all I wanted. I never stopped to consider the morality, personal or otherwise, of what I was up to. Which was perfect preparation for a career in Hollywood.

Thanks to Squire Adams, I secured a chance to sell a story to a truly esteemed outfit: *Beaver Magazine.*

Beaver's editor summoned me to his office to talk about my virgin endeavor. He was a sullen fellow whose proximity to wall-size posters of agitated nudes did little to lift his spirits.

"So," he said, after negotiating a fee for my masterpiece, "what name do you want to use?"

With all the insane fervor of a wannabe convinced that what he's gotten is what he wants, I replied: "My own. What else?"

The guy couldn't just come out and say, "Look, what I'm running is complete crud, you don't want your real name involved." Instead he treated me like a mildly retarded cousin and asked if I was sure about what I was saying. The sick part is, I was.

This was the life! My success with *Beaver* led me to the hallowed ranks of such classic glossies as *Club, Club International, Gallery,* and, gig of gigs, the fake letter desk at *Penthouse.* There bloomed at the time a genre devoted to letters from endlessly perplexed readers, each stressing some arcane practice the writer's girlfriend, sister, stewardess, or mother-in-law happened to clue him into.

Up in the morning, plied with coffee, pot, whatever pills I could get my mitts on, I'd stare at the blank paper until the inspiration for the day's kink quotient popped to mind. *"Dear Penthouse, I know it sounds crazy, but my girlfriend has a thing for doilies . . . Last night, we happened to be staying at her grandmother's house, and the rest of the family had already gone to bed . . ."*

At one point a mag put out by denizens of *The New Yorker,* a little thing called *Real World,* asked me to write a piece describing my odd avocation, under the title "Confessions of the World's Greatest Dirty Letter Writer."

It wasn't much, but it was something. At twenty-one anything seems heavy. For some reason I mailed a copy off to my mom. She not only tossed the thing in the nearest trash bin, she burned it for good measure. No doubt so none of her Hadassah friends might catch a peek.

"You don't really do that?" she asked, segueing into the refrain that would recur with damning regularity on those rare occasions when we attempted conversation. "Your father would die. . . ."

Would, I thought but never uttered, if he hadn't already killed himself. . . .

By this time I was hanging with Zoe, a ballet dancer. I met her at a yoga retreat a previous girlfriend dragged me to in a vain attempt to find some way to curb my king-hell depression.

The retreat was in Newport, Rhode Island. A ten-day,

silent jaunt by the seaside. My third day there, we'd engaged in a group-purging practice called *cria.*

What this involved, in lay terms, was getting up before dawn, traipsing behind some saffron-clad swami to a ditch carved in a cliff over the ocean, and guzzling quart after quart of warm salted water. Once the budding yogi swilled as much as he or she could swill, they swilled a bit more. At which point, predictably, the group tilted en masse into nausea country.

Once pumped to the teeth full of brine, the whole row of us, some twenty or thirty amateur swamis, began jumping up and down, clutching our stomachs, shoving our fingers down our throats. Anything to bring on the warm jets. Bulimia heaven! Twelve minutes of this, and the hills were alive.

Doubtless the first thing a dizzy reader thinks on hearing this fluid scenario is, "How very spiritual!" The kind of thing Job might have picked for a first date. Our communal bile trough bordered the patch of woods that surrounded the Enlightenment Campus. Once my own skull stopped spinning, and I could raise my head without fear of careening into the soup, I caught a strange and curious vision. There, wraithlike in the mist, I saw a small, sloe-eyed female standing with her back pressed to a maple tree. Her compact figure draped in some kind of white gown, she raised one graceful arm and crooked her finger. Beckoning. She spun around, gave a little backward oomph my way with her rounded behind, and flitted off into the woods.

The night after the transcendental barf-fest, I again spotted the Girl in White across the table. She'd selected the slot opposite for maximum eye contact. There was, despite the mounting warp in my own brainwaves, no mistaking the thrust of her glare. Even if I did mistake it, that bare toe nuzzling north from ankle to calf on up to Uh-Oh Territory, would have set me straight.

She managed to slide a scribbled scrap of napkin under

my purified water glass. The single figure: 9, in swirling pink, then a glowing crescent moon, a rough sketch of a gate, a road, and a tree. So much for the spiritual quest. The look in her eye, when I met it, was so crazed, I was not sure if she were proposing a sexual liaison or an evening biting the heads off chickens. Fasting, it was clear from the spun-out devotees plunked in the water-only corner, did things to a person. What it did to her was shocking: I'd seen the same cracked glare in mug shots of Sirhan Sirhan.

Come 8:55, I was already out of the enlightenment dorm, sea breeze whistling up the pant legs of my cotton yogi-wear. It didn't take long to sneak to the front gate, then up the path that led, metaphorically and otherwise, into the woods. Here I was, not just straight, but silent and purified, about to meet some leering wood sprite. But, thank Krishna, I had little time to obsess on my drug-free inadequacies. No sooner did I look up from my stumbling feet than there she was. The girl I'd seen in the mist of the outdoor vomitorium, now completely naked, loomed mere steps ahead of me, propped as usual against a tree.

Well, what to do? We didn't want to break any rules. Or not, at any rate, any more than we had already. So, without so much as an "are you contagious?" we began to get into it. Before long we had our tongues round each other's tonsils and, not long after that, were mashed into the bark of the tree like twin lichens. This being evening, mere feet from the sea, there was a chill in the air and salty mist on every blade of grass. *Tres* invigorating. . . . After the minutiae of our physical introductions, Zoe simply struck her original position, swinging her yard-long hair like a luscious slap across my face, and bent down facing what, by now, had become our favorite maple. Our axis mundi here in Yoga Central.

I entered her slowly, savoring the meticulous muscles in her back, holding on to hips so firm they felt like the flanks of a healthy Doberman. It wasn't long before we were both, you know, almost there.

Which may account for the fact that neither of us noticed the quartet of saffron-clad Yogi pros ambling up the path, out taking a moonlight constitutional.

Before I could do anything to stop her, Zoe let out with a wrenching, from-the-toes-up groan, collapsing with her arms around that tormented maple. Our discoverers, two Yogis and two Yogettes, looked on with expressions of Hindu horror.

I didn't know what to do and heard myself speaking before knowing I was going to. "It's okay," I blurted, "she's not talking, she's groaning!"

Of course, I'd broken the vow of speechlessness myself, but in my native chivalry I wanted to protect the female. At which point, Zoe turned around and smiled—the same sultry half-smirk she'd aimed my way earlier—and I saw the two holy ladies give a tug to the sleeves of their two holy men. Unless I'm crazy, I think they wanted to stay. Maybe it was a Kama Sutra thing: they wanted to critique my technique. Or maybe they were just starved for entertainment. . . . Whatever the truth, off they went, and not another word was spoken.

Once back in the wilds of Manhattan, Yogi Jer hooked up again with Zoe. This was way back in the misty mid-70s, when SoHo still had that soul-nourishing, warehouse-and-zipper-factory vibe. Zoe ran her own studio out of a loft at 92 Wooster Street and kept a tiny apartment on Greenwich. Out of my own apartment, but not yet into hers—she still had some kind of mysterious, three-way thing with a married antique dealer, so I was still a side dish—I ended up spending many a night beneath the wooden seats in the back of her dance class.

Passed out on God knows what, I'd wake up to the pitter-patter of slippered feet doing caffeine-fueled jetés up and down the floor. From my hidden lair under the bleachers, I could remain prone and study the calves of the various ballet addicts in attendance. The only sound, other than the tinkly piano and thump of feet on the wooden slats, was the constant unwrapping of candy bars. Judging from the cast-off wrappers, your budding Gelseys and Mikhails favored Mars bars and Reeses Peanut Butter cups. Yummo! Depending on what I'd imbibed the night before, the crunching sounded like the invasion of Normandy or a pack of meat-eating brain lice that had somehow crawled in my ear and chewed through my cerebral cortex.

It was a hellish way to wake, compounded by the fact that my beneath-the-seat hideaway was right next to the studio toilet, which meant every other chomp and crumple was complemented by the lovely, wholesome sound of self-induced vomiting. The first week or two, I just thought dancers were somehow extra prone to upset stomachs. In fact, the next little *Beaver* check I got, I coughed up the scratch for a jug of Pepto-Bismol. Slipped it discreetly on the bathroom shelf, beside the portrait of Diaghilev, thinking—naively—that it might help ease the upset stomachs that seemed to plague these little Nijinski-ites.

When I finally made the leap, from studio vermin to—what's the word?—bunkmate, I got a better handle on the whole puke situation. I asked Zoe what the deal was with the mountain of candy, nuts, and ice cream her students seemed to consume. By the end of a day the place looked like Shea Stadium after a double-header. I knew, because I swept up. (It was the least I could do, and, as I've been so often reminded, I always do the least.)

Zoe protested ignorance of the situation. "They burn up a lot of energy," she said. "Dancing is hard work."

It wasn't until we'd actually shared living space for a while that I understood what she was not saying. Zoe herself, I noticed, never seemed to eat at all. If a stray loaf of rye bread did happen to end up in the cupboard, it would be gone immediately. In classic fashion, I found out the truth one day when I slipped into the apartment unnoticed and caught her. Other guys might walk in on the little woman riding sidesaddle with the gas man—I caught Zoe with something else down her throat. Her finger.

The sounds emanating from the toilet were so hellish, I thought she was being stabbed. Clearly she wasn't expecting me. I had a meeting at *Club International*, yet another "men's mag," but got the days mixed up and slimed back home on the IRT.

I heard lamp-rattling gasps and dashed to the bathroom. There was Zoe, naked, on her knees before the porcelain throne, jamming her forefinger in and out of her mouth. Her long hair hung over her face. Her breasts rested against the bowl. I couldn't tell if she was actually expelling, because her back was to me. Besides which, I couldn't really take my eyes off her ass. Zoe had olive skin, incredibly soft, despite the phenomenal tone derived from entire days of stretching, working out, swimming, and, of course, pas de deux–ing until she dropped. Her bottom kind of humped up and down as she pumped her own stomach. Her retches tore out of her.

It was like watching a car accident: I couldn't look and I couldn't look away. I don't know how long I'd been staring before I noticed that her left hand, while her right poked down her throat, had a task of its own. Her humping grew even more furious. And I realized that as she was heaving, her fingers worked like drunken maggots between her legs. She began to rock on her haunches. Her head whipped back and forth, the sounds coming out of her more animal than human.

It was such a private moment. Ferociously intimate. I had no doubt no human had ever seen this woman's secret ritual. I didn't know I had dropped my pants—didn't even know I was standing there nursing a throbbing hard-on—until a groan of my own must have tipped her off. She swung around, hand still planted in her thicket of pubic hair, and screamed through a mouth that looked half melted.

"Zoe," I cried when her shrieking ceased. "Zoe!"

But she was beyond hearing. Her eyes flashed like a trapped animal's. The smear of vomit around her lips gave off a primal sheen. She might have been feasting on living entrails. In fact, she was—but they were her own.

Without thinking, I took a step toward her. She leaped up from her crouch by the toilet. Sopping fingers tore at my chest. Strange, wild snarls escaped her lips. I grabbed her shoulders. She took a swipe at my face. I tasted her bile, like salt and mud. Then she dropped back to her knees. She jammed her right hand back between her glistening labia, grabbed my cock with her left, and guided it between those puke-moistened lips.

Her clutch was so violent that I fell backward, hit the wall, and ended up on my back as she gulped and sucked, feeding off my hard-on like a starving jackal.

It was over in minutes, but she remained over me, mouth cupped around my sucked-dry penis. Eyes squeezed shut, she continued working those bruised, shiny lips in a kind of hypnotic rhythm, trying to draw whatever last, remaining drop of sperm might be left. It got too painful and I had to move her head. Finally she collapsed between my legs, rolled her face onto my thigh, and opened her glassy eyes. "Protein," she mumbled, and we both fell asleep on the bathroom floor.

Despite our fevered coupling, the first weeks I spent at Zoe's I was completely sick. Physically sick. That yoga stint, ten days off anything stronger than chamomile, had done weird things to my system. It cleaned me out all right, but the cleanliness nearly killed me. Twenty-two at the time, I'd been high every day for half a dozen years, and the shock flushed my system like Drano. For a while I thought it was just the flu. Except that the flu didn't smell that way. Like I'd been buried and dug up, like my pores were pumping out something to repel vultures. I managed to drag myself to a doctor.

I ended up at Dr. Ronzoni's. Actually Dr. Ronzoni, Jr., since his father, whose original plaque still graced the Bleecker Street apartment building, had died that very week on the table during a kidney operation. I didn't ask the tiny MD why he was back at work so soon—I didn't have to. He explained, while repeatedly ruffling the wads of Vitalis-soused curls piled on his head, that "Dad would have wanted it that way." Dad, see, had worked the very week *his* father died. And, no doubt, in the happiest of all words, Ronzoni junior would show up at the office when his dad, the man standing before me, died. Such a comfort.

One look at me, and the good Ronzoni did everything but recoil in horror. "My God," he muttered, "what have you been doing?"

The plump Lilliputian MD's prognosis was "dehydration." I was dehydrated, like the instant potatoes my mother used to buy to go with her overcooked brisket. Add water, and you could serve me to workaholic cannibals. The kind who just didn't have time to wait for that pot to boil.

Since I'd already been hurled out of my apartment, it made sense on all kinds of levels to just skulk over to St. Vincent's and move in, as per Ronzoni junior's instructions. Doc Ronzoni, he of the chiseled skull and miniature marshmallow body, had prebooked me.

They were wheeling the latest occupant out of the Alky Ward as they wheeled me in. The major difference between us, aside from fifty years, is that he wore his sheet over his head.

Next morning I opened my eyes to a duo of young interns hovering over my bed.

When I came to I saw that they were holding my right hand aloft, examining the fingers. They didn't acknowledge me. They just continued scrutinizing my digits, visibly excited by some feature they'd discovered.

"See," the more fresh-faced of the pair sputtered to his

companion. "Right here, they're clubbed." He was pinching the top knuckle of my middle finger, raising it to his friend's face like the specimen it was.

"You're right, you're right," clucked the second young MD, a thick-necked, frizzy fellow who looked remarkably like Larry Fine, of Three Stooges fame, and reeked of Aqua Velva. The cheap cologne was a welcome relief from the *eau de piss* that permeated the place. "My God," continued the fragrant Larry lookalike, "you don't think . . ."

"Exactly!"

At this point the first little doctor—do they always travel in pairs, or did these St. Vincent flesh slicers just want to share the thrill of treating me?—dropped my paw like a chunk of rancid beef and wiped his own hands on his pants. This was, oldsters will recall, pre-AIDS, before the days when doctors wouldn't even take your check without squeezing into protective gloves.

"Well, what the fuck is it?" I cried, unable to stand the suspense of my own prognosis, as extreme and fascinating as it seemed to be to these two beaming youths.

They could not have looked more shocked if the pillow had yawned and spit nickels. You mean, their urgent features announced, *it* speaks?

There was a pause, then the ambrosial Stooge clone spoke up. "Should we tell him, Donny?"

Just knowing, for some reason, that my doctor's name was "Donny" was vaguely alarming. But I had a hunch Dr. Donny's little Eureka would pack even more emotional appeal.

They exchanged glances—knowing, professional looks such as gods must often share in the presence of mortals—and then Donny-boy shrugged. It wasn't going to be pleasant, that shrug said, but he had compassion. He wasn't completely jaded yet; he'd take the time to talk to this charity ward loser. Patients were human, after all. It always helped to stop and remember that once in a while.

"Take a look at your fingers," he said with studied patience. I saw him roll his eyes at Larry but didn't say anything. What was there to say? "See the nails?" he went on. He spoke slowly, and I could tell he was doing his best to speak in words of one syllable or less. "See the way they're shaped? We call that 'clubbed.' "

"That's right," the son of Larry piped up. "Clubbed."

Clearly he wanted to get in some practice, too, talking to the Little People. "When they're shaped like that," Donny explained, "that's what we call a symptom—"

"A very definite symptom," Larry added.

Here they both stopped. Maybe they were having second thoughts about telling me. It was hard, this doctor-patient thing. The silence dragged on, seconds to minutes, and I had to ask a second time. "So what does it mean? Come on!"

Another meaningful coup d'oeil between junior physicians—what if this guy's unbalanced? what if he bites?—then Larry braved the storm and spit it out. "What it means," he said, his own fingers twiddling with excitement, "is syphilis. You have syphilis."

"And," his more level-headed compadre added, "you've had it for a while. Syphilis comes in three stages. You don't actually get clubbed fingers until the tertiary stage."

"Tertiary, that means third," Larry sputtered. He really was torqued. "The last stage. But," he hastened to add, perhaps sensing my rising panic, "but it's okay. I mean, it can be . . . I mean, there is a possibility it can be treated."

"A possibility? A fucking possibility?"

I was not, admittedly, handling the news with any degree of grace. All I knew about syphilis is that it killed Al Capone and Nietzsche. Not, however, before they both went stark raving insane. Even if they were two of my personal role models, that didn't mean I wanted to expire like them. If these candy-ass bastards were going to hand me a death sentence, the least they could do was give me drugs. Right now.

Right out of their pockets. But I knew without checking that all they were packing was Binaca and aspirin. Useless. . . .

But, it's okay. There's a happy ending after all. Turns out, after I got my blood test and the results came back my last day in the souse ward, I didn't have syph after all. What I did have was a set of not-quite, but-almost-clublike and none-too-clean fingernails.

Apparently, like many a hypochondriac, your budding young medico suddenly imagines he encounters every juicy new symptom he hears about. The difference is, he doesn't spot it on himself. That would be troubling. He finds the evidence on life-forms like me.

Still, even after my successful rehydration, my body remained a sickly thing. From the hospital I endeared my way into Zoe's airy one-bedroom on Greenwich. I don't know if she wanted me there, or if, having gotten involved with me, she was too freaked out to turn me away.

Happily, for her, I wasn't going to be in there for long. By virtue of my niggling success in the prestige world of in-print arousal, I was invited to Columbus, Ohio, to audition for the post of editor at the then king of the hill sex glossy, *Hustler* magazine.

Once actually aground in Columbus, the Auto Parts Capital of America—what Rome is to loafers, Columbus is to brake shoes—the absurdity of my doffing a "professional-looking" suit and tie hit home with hideous vengeance. Not only did the editor who picked me up not have a suit on, he looked, in head-to-toe denim, steel-toe shit-kicker boots and wraparound reflector shades, like he might be leader of the local Hells Angels, Under 5'2" chapter. Had he stood taller than my Windsor, he might have actually been intimidating. As it was, he came across like a swollen but stunted cigar store Indian. With a face full of acne that looked ready to harvest.

One peek at me and it was clear my *Hustler* delegate had

decided I was beneath speaking to. "Sparky," he said by way of introduction, and that was it. No handshake. No friendly hail-fellow, welcome-fellow-pornographer pat on the shoulder. *De nada. . . .*

It may have been the suit. Or it may have been that patchy, last-minute, kitchen-sink haircut Zoe gave me before I'd fled for the airport. But deep down I had a feeling it was something else. As my grandfather Moishe once explained, if you ever forget you're a Jew, a Gentile will remind you. And, at that moment, to put it mildly, I felt reminded. I don't know if the Virgin Mary really does appear on tortillas, but I do know, right there in the airport, the map of Israel mysteriously materialized on my forehead. I didn't see it, but I know it was there. It had to be; there was no other explanation for the look of disgusted wonder on the stunted Sparky's mug.

But, talent will out. After my initial on-site testing—handed a promo for Acu-Jac, an "electronic male masturbation unit," I was shunted to an empty office and asked to crank out a wacky-yet-informative five hundred words—I found myself invited on board. Happily, I was not asked to actually demonstrate the Acu-Jac, which had been my initial fear. Like any other fraternity, I figured the I FELTA THIGH bunch at *Hustler* would put the newcomer through some suitably humiliating sexual paces. Even while sitting there, tugging my ear lobe, trying to think up an angle, I had the uncanny sense my creative torment was being viewed through some two-way mirror. But it wasn't so.

Hustler's High Street headquarters, hard by the usual normal-dormal office buildings and retail outlets in cosmopolitan downtown Columbus, proved to be a hotbed of talented, if slightly twisted, fringers. Most twisted of all, for a first-time visitor, was the relentless normalcy of the place. No 44-D cups careened nude down the halls. No wrong doors opened to en flagrante fellatio sessions. No coupling party-pups spilled out of boardrooms to stain the wall-to-wall hall carpet with wine and drool.

There were four of us, tucked away in a back room on the third floor called the Kinky Korner. Besides me, there were two Mikes, a Tim, and the aforementioned Sparky. But the place was filled with all kinds of arcane characters, one of my favorites being the legendary PeeWee, Larry Flynt's valet. PeeWee'd apparently suffered weight problems all his life, so one Christmas, in an act of characteristic largesse, Larry brought him his dream gift: an intestinal by-pass operation. As fascinating as the mere fact of Pee-Wee's waist-slimming surgery was its awesome side effect.

The polite word, I believe, is flatulence. PeeWee's stomach was legendary, once his guts had been rerouted like free-way clover-leaf, for its gas-blasting capacity. Some things in life a man can't forget. These weren't recital epiphanies. They weren't mere odoriferous sound-bytes. They were full-blown, pants-rippling symphonies. One of which, my very first week on the job, I was privileged to hear, on tape, courtesy of a portable Sony one of the boys had the good sense, like some in-house ethnomusicologist, to lug onto an elevator. Where PeeWee, for reasons too felonious to contemplate, seemed to produce his most extended oeuvres. It went on for at least six minutes.

My job, in those heady early days, consisted largely of cranking out what's known in the industry as "girl copy." You have no doubt seen it, if you've ever stumbled on a glossy spread-eagled female in the pages of some high-brow magazine, one you no doubt found somewhere and opened by accident. And you've no doubt never read it. No one does. But they put it in anyway. Apparently to give young self-loathers like myself the chance to step in and get a toe-hold in the industry. You know the stuff I'm talking about: *"Jennifer's a down-home cowgirl"*—insert photo of naked bovine beauty waving Stetson—*"and when she rides a Bronco, brother, she leaves him branded! EE- HAH!"*

Along with this bit of literature, I had the endlessly strange task of reviewing reader mail. Most of which arrived from our nation's finer jails and penitentiaries.

Prison letters were the strangest, because the authors, apparently recently apprised of *Roget's Thesaurus* in the lockdown library, would tend to write in this ur—William Buckley, Jr., fashion. A style made all the stranger by the fact that, often as not, their sixteen-syllable words were jammed in sad, semiliterate hand into sentences of remarkable incoherence. One, I remember, thanked the magazine for "familitaritizing me and my boon compatriots with a trio of luxuriant parvenus. Especially that one cunt Suzie. . . ."

Larry Flynt, the smut legend who'd founded the magazine, was sort of a pasty specter during my stay in Ohio. Occasionally he'd pop his head into the Korner. Every time he did his resemblance to a full-grown, lard-fed fetus was more striking. Something about his skin tone, the washed-out pink of his lips and pale tufts of hair receding around his round, Baby Huey head, lent the man an in vitro quality wholly at odds with his piercing eyes and apparent genius. But then, maybe a guy who made his fortune in pussy *should* look like he lived in a uterus.

His wife, Althea—dubbed, by the ever-creative Mike Toohey, the "Shaved Monkey"—played Hillary to Larry's Bill. From what I could tell, she oversaw much of the day-to-day stuff so Larry could be free to scale even higher and nobler heights of Pink-dom than he already had. *Hustler* was, for better or worse, the fastest-growing, most controversial publication on the block. Even if the block itself was sort of seedy. Larry, God love him, will go down as the first man in history to break the labia barrier; to, in the argot of the industry, "show Pink." For which a grateful, one-handed public continues to thank him.

Understandably, the lads were less than thrilled at having much of their copy dismissed and criticized by a woman they took to be no more than an illiterate ex-stripper—not that anyone in the office had ever seen her strip, let alone hold a newspaper upside down. . . . An amazing thing about the job was that no matter how much contempt any of us had for the lubricious pap we were grinding out, we all hated having it sent back to us to rewrite.

The focus of most wrath, for us scribes, the man who intervened between us Little Clits and the Big Labes in charge, was a tall and swaggering fellow from New York City named Lance Berman. Famed, in some circles, for hosting a Manhattan X-rated cable show, Lance was, in the jargon of the Recovery Era, a "rage-o-holic," much given to fuming, spume-hurling fits of outrage at whatever atrociously unacceptable shred of copy came his way. Dubbed, once again by the inestimable Toohey, as "the Rabbi," Lance had a wonderfully effective method of containing his temper. He would sit in his office, for hours at a stretch, wearing a black plastic Darth Vader mask over his head.

I had occasion to step into the Rabbi's lair, endure his plastic-muffled litany of disgust over whatever piece of drivel I'd handed him, and then had the hugely memorable experience of having this pouting, Darth Vader manqué leap up, rip the paper to shreds, and throw it in my face. I knew I finally belonged.

The high point of the *Hustler* experience was the banner day King Larry invited me and the rest of the staff, along with assorted media types and a mixed breed of camp followers, to his Beckley Heights home for a celebration. Beckley, for those globe-trotters yet to jet into Columbus for the season, stands out as the Beverly Hills, the Sutton Place, the absolute ne plus ultra of this Ohio hot spot.

I'm not sure if it was a birthday party, the magazine's anniversary, or some sort of grand fete honoring consumption of his millionth hoecake. What lingers in the mind, like a polished jewel, is the singular instant Flynt ushered us all down to his gigantic basement, stood before the throng to say a few words about the humble Kentucky roots from whence he sprang, and then stood back to reveal the focus of the day's jubilee: his little log cabin.

That's right! A little log cabin, right there in the basement, a sort of personal diorama, complete with reconstructed porch, rocker, and Granny's corncob pipe still smoking. An amazing sight, made even more meaningful by the tearful Flynt's emotion-packed explanation for this little hunk of heaven.

It seems, wrapped up as he was in the trappings of success, he wanted to do something to, you know, *remember . . .*

"This is where Larry Flynt comes from," he declaimed in the high-pitched, Pa Kettle–on-helium voice the gods bequeathed him, no doubt by way of counterbalancing his enormous virility. "I grew up in Kentucky, in a shack just *lak* this. You've all seen 'at movie about Harlan County, how bad it was for them people there? Well, where we lived we wished we were Harlan County. . . . There was jus' nothin' there. . . ."

It was, in its way, a touching scene. Here was Larry, whose magazine was not exactly famed for its enlightened civil rights philosophy, stealing a page right out of Alex Haley. White Trash *Roots.* There were, among the backwoods cadets he'd brought to the big time with him, more than a few misty eyes. The only things missing were Buddy Ebsen and Max Baer, Jr., doing Pappy and Jethro. Ellie-Mae, of course, was already on the board of directors.

I might have been more touched, myself, except that that shack looked awfully good to me. I was, at the time, living in the Columbus YMCA, in a room the size of a Cheez-It box. Every morning I got to slime into that shower room, joining the other fellows waiting for an iron lung slot to open up at the VA for a group soapdown.

Half the reason I even took the gig was because *Hustler* was moving to Los Angeles. This was my way of staging *Escape from New York.* The Rabbi himself assured me it would be a month or two when I signed on. Three months after I became a Flynt-ite I was still in Columbus, though I'd finally made it out of the Young Men's Christian Association. My new pad, first floor of a house just down the road from OSU, I'd stocked with a used black-and-white tube and some porch furniture bought at a lawn sale next door. That was it. The whole time I was there I slept on a chaise longue.

Every Friday afternoon I left, back to dancing Zoe in New York City, and every Monday morning I flew back to Spread 'em Central.

Ever the right place at the right time kind of guy, I had the privilege of being on board for one of the more savory spiritual moments in recent American history, Larry Flynt's front-page conversion to born-again Christianity at the hands of Jimmy Carter's sister.

That the president's sibling would sing hallelujah with the world's foremost labia gazer was a phenom in itself. What went down in the trenches the morning of Lar's *Today* show parthenogenesis packed even starker fascination. In the Korner, we weirdos were already wrestling with the reality of working for a racist, puss-pushing yokel whose idea of humor was *Chester the Molester,* a comic strip capturing the hero's kooky problems trying to manhandle little girls.

Now we really had something to be ashamed of. When all else failed, a writer could tell himself he was engaged in some sort of subversive activity. If only in his own mind. The born-again thing blew that right out of the water.

It amazed me, all over again, to see the assembled employees of Flynt Publications, to reabsorb the mid-America, beehive-and-poly-blend beyond-squareness of the just plain folks who manned the fort. Didn't those PTA payroll moms know what was going on here? Didn't they care? Forget Robert Mapplethorpe: you'd expect guys like him to crank out whip-up-the-ass shots. But what about these June Cleaver lookalikes? These workadaddies in purchasing who ordered Vaseline and Kim-wipes? Now *that* was some radical shit. I always tried to imagine what they talked about on Thanksgiving.

When we stumbled out at lunchtime to reup and grab a slab of grease, a flock of shiny reporters accosting us with mikes and tape recorders made perfect sense. Or as much sense as anything else. "No comment," replied employee after employee. As if we weren't porn hacks, we were the Joint Chiefs of Staff. Nobody, of course, wanted to risk going high profile and losing their job. Except, God rest his soul, for the late Mike Toohey, Mister I-Could-Give-a-Fuck.

Mike spoke pleasantly, aiming his freckled, all-American Irish guy features at the shoulder-mounted camera. He had the charm of a six-foot leprechaun. "It's just wonderful! We're going to do a big shoot on the Virgin Mary. Praise the Lord! We're calling it *'Jesus' Mom Shows Pink—A Pussy Hot Enough for Yahweh!'*"

The reporters stared for a second. Then they backed away, before breaking into a run.

Finally the time came to make the cross-country trek from Columbus to California. The drive remains a blur. I spent half the trip curled on the passenger seat of Frank Delia's sporty Volvo. Frank was the photo editor and your definitive New York hipster. He looked like one of those cartoon French guys you'd call Lucky Pierre. Small, dark, and so constantly trailing women, fellow *Hustler*-ites dubbed him "the Dog."

Frank came to chez Larry after an early career making cheap movies with the as-yet-unheralded Abel Ferrara. I liked Frank, even though he was older—already over thirty!—and his sports car had no backseat. Which meant I just couldn't crawl back and curl up like a sleepy five-year-old. Delia-Dog wouldn't care. He could carry on three or four sides of a conversation all by himself, then tell you to stop talking and let him get a word in.

By the time the gyno-meisters actually made their move, I was on the brink of some form of physical collapse. Still, I probably would not have had the gall to curl up and snore. I was already the resident weirdo, I didn't want to add narcoleptic to the list of my peculiarities. In fact, I would have liked to help drive. But, macho, A. J. Foyt–like specimen that I was, I couldn't drive a stick.

Somewhere in Missouri I switched cars, joining the managing editor, a sharp-dressing New Jersey dude named Zigmund. The great thing about "Zig," as those on the smut farm liked to call him, was his absolute devotion to the *Hustler* organization. Unlike the rest of us, who looked in the mirror and wondered what went wrong, the Z-man was a *Hustler* ecstatic. He didn't just like his job, he was proud of it. Which made for a series of interesting entrances in bars and coffee shops across the country. A slender, smiling fellow with more than passing resemblance to famed fifties mimic Frank Gorshin, Zig was given to strolling into a joint, looking around at the assembled locals, and announcing in his booming Perth Amboy voice, "Step aside, we're the *Hustler* boys!"

Which, as I recall, went over big in Lovelock, Nevada. Everywhere else I think they felt sorry for us.

We arrived in Los Angeles during a season of unceasing rain. My first drive down Santa Monica Boulevard, to *Hustler*'s Century City headquarters, the overlarge plant life fronting the boulevard actually frightened me. It seemed so glandular, the enormous, fleshy ferns and cacti reaching toward the street as if to lure pedestrians into some fatal, steroid-laden embrace. There were, however, no pedestrians, so perhaps the plants had already eaten. . . .

Here, I thought, with a certitude that startled me, is the city I'm going to die in. A place where everything that can kill you is beautiful and green.

A Hollywood moment! Even now, I can still have them. . . . Amazing. I'm at my computer, dredging up these heinous memories, when the phone rings. And it's an agent. A high-powered one. She told me herself! And, not only that, her company represents Larry Fishburne. A terrific actor. And Larry's seen my stuff. That's right. Larry's seen the article on which this tome you're reading now is based, and he's, like, interested. Majorly interested. "We're talking option," she said. "Do you understand what I'm saying?"

I tell her, "Yes, yes, I understand. It's just that . . ."

"Just what? What? Tell me, this is business here."

"Well, call me a fool, but are we talking about the same Larry Fishburne? The guy who played the dad in Boyz 'n the Hood, *the young soldier in* Apocalypse Now, *Ike Turner in the Tina Turner movie?"*

"That's right," she says, "that's right. He's terrific."

"He is," I agree, "he's incredible. One of my favorites. It's just that, just, you know . . ."

"Just what?"

"Well, I know he's an amazing actor, and I'm not saying he can't do it, but you really think a black dude can pull off a neurotic Jewish guy from Pittsburgh? I mean, I'm not saying he can't pull off the stretch. . . ."

"For God's sake," she says, and now I really feel bad. I don't want her to think I'm some kind of bigot. Or worse, that I have no imagination.

"No, wait," I say. "Wait. . . . You know what?" I pause, as if the idea's just coming to me, the muse just plopping onto my shoulder and getting a grip. "You know what? I think it's a great idea. Really. I mean, it adds an extra dimension, but that's good. That's good. It's like the guy's not just a junkie, not just really alienated behind that. He's, like, black, too—and he doesn't know it. Yes! I think I'm loving this . . . honest to God. I think it can work. . . ."

Not surprisingly, there's a vast silence on the other end. I can hear somebody in the agent's office clicking around with high heels. Either that or she's auditioning tap dancers at the same time. Minimizing that pesky lag time with an in-house talent search while talking to dorks like me.

Finally she comes back on, her manner completely changed now. Her words are no longer clipped and thrilled, but very de-li-ber-ate. Very slow. Like she's talking to a very young or very stupid—sadly, pathetically stupid—possibly brain-damaged child.

"Mister Stahl," she begins, and already I know I'm in trouble, with this switch from "Jerry, bubbelah!" to the IRS auditor–like "Mister." "Mister Stahl, we are not talking about my client playing the role in question. We were talking—at least I was talking—about his purchasing the material for possible development."

"Well, of course," I say, trying to form words through the cringe that has lodged on my face like a sucking barnacle. "That would be wonderful, too. I mean, that's probably the best idea. I mean, you know what I mean. . . ."

There's another pause. The clicking has stopped. It's been replaced by a slurping noise. Like a little kid sucking up the last of his chocolate milk with a straw. I don't even want to speculate what that is. . . .

"Mister Stahl," the agent says briskly, as if, after a pause,

she's decided not to just slam down the receiver, to at least be civil enough to close the conversation as if everything—most notably yours truly—were normal. "Mister Stahl, we'll get back to you on this."

"That's fine," I say. "Whatever." And then, in a complete fit of lameness as sudden as a sneeze, I add, "And tell Larry I'm glad he's interested. I loved him in Deep Cover."

Another pause. I'm cracking a sweat now. I feel like somebody handed me a bag of money and I dropped it down a sewer grate. Even though I know the likelihood of anything anybody says in this town ever happening is roughly equal to the chance of weasels raining down from the heavens with little yarmulkes on.

"Mister Stahl, one thing," the agent adds, taking a breath as if she hates to say what she's about to say, but she really, you have to understand, she really has to. "Mister Stahl, please, if you two happen to speak, don't call him 'Larry.' And, whatever you've heard, don't call him 'Fish,' either."

I have to admit, I hadn't heard the "Fish" thing. I hadn't heard anything. I like the guy's acting, but I haven't spent a lot of time sitting around dreaming up nicknames for him. That this woman, a complete stranger to me, apparently thinks I have merely confirms something I've always thought about the movie business. Everybody in it is convinced they are the absolute center of the planet. A one-man axis mundi. And everybody else, losers that we are, exists with their noses pressed against the glass of their blessed and personal inner sanctum.

"Okay," I say, too tired at this point to make a fuss. This is how it happens. They call you up and say you've won the lottery, then when you start to think you've actually got the cash, they let you know they're not completely sure about it; in fact, there's a good chance the lottery's been discontinued, and anyway, most likely your number is invalid anyway. . . . But they'll be in touch. Build you up when you

didn't ask for it; knock you down when you start to believe. That's always the deal.

"Okay, what do I call him?" I ask, like I'm ever actually going to talk to him. Like this wasn't just one of those calls you occasionally get as punishment for ever having stuck your nose in the rhinestone trough that is Hollywood.

"Call him Laurence," she says, "with a 'u.' Like Olivier."

"Laurence with a 'u,'" I say. "Like Olivier. Got it. And you're his agent?"

A pause. What's this? "I work with his people," she says, and hangs up before I can inquire further. Even this lovely, apparently, was just working her little angle. For all I know, she's the agency masseuse. But what the hell. Why do I feel so . . . unfulfilled? Like I've been taken on a slow ride on the up escalator, then hurled headfirst down the stairs.

That's the trouble with this business. People are always offering you things. And as soon as they're mentioned—even if the idea never occurred to you before——you feel like you really want them. By the end of the conversation, whatever they're dangling before you—which you didn't know existed three minutes ago—has now become an absolute necessity. At which point whoever called you in the first place can feel comfortable taking it away. They've done their job. . . .

This is Hollywood's dirty little secret. It's not about making movies. Are you kidding? Forget that shit about "the Dream Factory." It's about manufacturing frustration. Preening movie stars making people out there in Dirtville feel like shit. People in offices making people who don't have offices bark like dogs. All of them generating their daily quota of hopelessness. That's the quantity in question. And the factories are always going full blast.

So ends my Hollywood minute. For no more than the sixty-thousandth time I remind myself, if my child didn't live here, I think I'd move to Peru.

PART THREE

TELEVISION VIRGIN

Fast forward half a dozen freelance feature magazine gig-packed years of subsistence living—I'd gone from the medium depths of *Hustler* to the medium heights of *California, Playboy, Los Angeles,* and assorted in-flight mags—and here I am ready to alter destiny.

My blushing green card bride had established some kind of professional cahoots with a man named Tom Patchett, future *ALF* mogul and, at the time, producer of an English transplant by the name of *You Again?* This short-lived saga, featuring the raw charisma of Jack *Quincy* Klugman and young John Stamos, marked this writer's first strange foray into TV-land.

Thanks to the missus—who used her access to slip a nutty little story I'd published in *Playboy* right under the man's nose—Patchett decided I was a writer with a good deal of latent yuck-huckster potential. He thought the story showed "real funny." Meaning, in the argot of the industry, I just might be one of those humans born with that extra "sitcom" gland, a random bit of anatomy righteously esteemed in TV-ville.

So, thanks to his generosity and vision, I was herewith invited to join the hallowed ranks of network scribes.

Did I think twice? Did I balk? Did I consider, for a single self-respecting minute, that I might be heading down a road whose destination loomed somewhere in the opposite of

Dreamland? No. I never considered *anything*. To consider meant to plan. To plan meant to hold the self in some kind of esteem; to look in the mirror and know who looked back mattered.

I just didn't give a fuck. An attitude stemming less from arrogance than complete cowardice. Of course, I didn't care. How could I? My father cared. He struggled. He believed in something. He had goals. He crawled his way from the coal mines to the federal judiciary. And what did it do for him?

My father. My father. I never thought of him; I never stopped. Mostly, on the cusp of some decision, at any kind of crossroads, his vaguely sinister, always inscrutable face floats by like a full-risen moon. He gave me no advice. We had no heart-to-hearts. Only once, on the subject of my sister marrying a self-described radical poet in the wilds of free speech Berkeley, her refusal to take parental money, despite dire poverty, did he offer what could even faintly pass for paternal wisdom: "Pride is stupid." Uttered with a scowl, I think, for one who suffers unnecessarily from one who necessarily suffered.

Pride is stupid. Thanks! It may not have been much, but I certainly took it to heart. Actually I typed "hurt." Which may be more truthful.

You could accuse me of a lot of things in those days, but pride was not one of them.

This being Hollywood, the man who hired me was fired, and I ended up being summoned by the legend himself, Big Jack Klugman, to help fix a script whose story Tom and I hashed out in our first, festive meetings. Unlike Patchett, a tall, buttoned-down man who'd started out penning *Newharts* and continued to wear a gentle, semibemused, Newhart-like expression from then on, Klugman was all business. And bad business at that.

All I remember of that first, fraught story meeting is that Big Jack spit pea soup on my shirt. When I walked into the office he was busily slurping from a plastic spoon. Blowing on his Styro takeout container, he actually shot a glob of viscous green onto my collar. Big Jack played it accidental. But I knew better. The word *contempt* does not come close to the man's expression as he reeled off nuggets of TV genius it was my job, as scribe and supplicant, to render feasible on the teeny screen.

"This is not working," he howled, clutching my sorry outline and waving it at me. "Don't you understand?" he repeated like some agitated mantra, his face so close to mine, I could smell his eyeballs. "Don't you see? Are you stupid? Don't you *see*?" Through his entire tirade, I had this irrational feeling I was being screamed at through a TV screen. His leathery features seemed no more real to me than Elmer Fudd's. Such is the curiously diminished impact of celebrity. So saturated with cast-off *Quincy* visions, brain-drek from half-digested *Odd Couples* and old *Twilight Zones,* the mind cannot wrap itself around the notion that the star of all these 2-D memories is suddenly three-dimensional.

It only took that one story conference to realize that here was a process every bit as squirmy and morally uplifting as an in-depth proctologic exam. The idea was not to sound smart, but to make your meal ticket's moronic notions sound entertaining. It was clear a man would have to imbibe something on a regular basis to suffer this kind of success. If you wanted to make it in television, I sensed, you'd just have to roll up your sleeves.

You'd have to do something drastic, it was that grotesque.

Writing, to me, still packed an aura bordering the divine. An attitude that Hollywood renders absurd, to say the least. My first visit to chez Sandra, I saw something that shocked me to my toes. Before me loomed piles of writing. A gaggle of scripts stacked high as a Shetland pony from her Navajo throw rug halfway up to that cottage cheese ceiling your low-end L.A. pads all seemed to have. Casting a panicked gaze round the living room, I saw every corner had its own leaning tower of creativity. The coffee table supported another fifteen or twenty efforts; the couch and rocking chair were cluttered with still more.

Call me naive. I felt like a jeweler who'd landed on some planet where diamonds were shit from dogs. And treated accordingly. "Who writes these?" I murmured, still dumbfounded so many souls were partaking of this holy act.

"Who writes them?" Her expression said she couldn't tell if I was insane or just slightly retarded. "Are you kidding? Everybody writes them."

"But why?"

Until then, for the most part I'd circulated in magazineland, an arcane branch of reality where something called prose was practiced. Sure, I'd helped pen a stretch of celluloid myself. But it was all just treading water while working on the Big Book. The novel. The thing that real writers really write. I just didn't get it. The vision was inescapable: all over Los Angeles there were houses and offices, apartments and car trunks, all full to bursting with some earnest soul's attempt at crashing the entertainment barricades. It was like *Day of the Triffids,* with scripts instead of Triffids. I imagined them one day rising up, growing teeth, and simply eating everyone in sight. First they'd chomp the boneheads who'd put them on the page, then they'd go after the development drones who judged them harshly before attacking en masse the studio smoothies who denied them life. Abortions could pile up for only so long, and L.A. was a city stinking with excess.

Once enlightened, the sheer breadth of screenplayitis revealed itself at every turn. Before hitting Los Angeles, I didn't know many writers. Now it was impossible to find anyone who wasn't. Once tuned in, the signs were everywhere: you couldn't slime into a 7-Eleven without the clerk bouncing a spec *Cheers* off you. Their first language might be Armenian, but that didn't stop them.

I suppose I should have celebrated my good fortune. Without meaning to I'd stumbled into Fat City. Imagine *What Makes Sammy Run* with Sammy so out of it he didn't see his feet move. I once heard Lily Tomlin say she's the only person she knew who came to Hollywood to be a waitress but couldn't get work and ended up acting. Exactly how I felt. Who knows why we betray ourselves? In a world of infinite possibilities, I chose only those that stung.

Or maybe it was just the cash. Mister Put-on-Earth-for-Prose showed remarkably scant difficulty shedding his pretensions. Money has such strange powers. And not only for what it can buy. Or not just. Society has always said: Make money. Artists have said: But there's something else. Cliché City. But in Hollywood there's the Big Lie that you can have both. A lie you want to believe.

Somewhere, in *On Becoming a Novelist,* John Gardner discusses how writers must explain what appears like their rank failure; why they work so hard for so little, why they have to sacrifice for the privilege of failing. It's so much more comfortable making a living. In "show business." Why, you suddenly get respect! From relatives, dental assistants, that whole ilk. . . . It feels so good!

"What do you do?" Me—with studied casualness—"Oh, I write a little thing called *ALF.*" "You do? Why, my little niece in Chatahoochee just loves that little guy. Ooh, this is so cool! What's he like?" Sometimes they even ask you for your autograph. Talk about feeling great about yourself!

Eventually, as mere dabbling on the little screen swelled to something like steady employment, the need for creative—call me old-fashioned—freedom quickly sank to distant second behind the itch to power down the jumbo bucks. Creativity is the opposite of TV. Creativity means sounding like yourself. TV means sounding like whoever wrote the pilot. The pay's swell, but it's tough sledding for the hardcore delusional intent on maintaining the facade of free will.

But what the heck? Let's not rush into things. Self-delusion, as Voltaire reminded us whole centuries before inner-child angst, is the key to happiness. How better to maintain that facade of contentment than coating one's nerve ends in poppy gauze?

By the first few times I stumbled into *ALF*—the lanky Patchett, God love him, held no rancor I'd stayed on board to whore for Klugman after Happy Jack sacked him—I'd already developed the peculiar malady that would plague me throughout my TV comedy career: a chronic inability to find anything the staff found funny funny to me. Indeed, my penchant for IV-mortification management had its trial run in these early *ALF* episodes.

I was not on staff, I was that most loathsome of interlopers, the freelancer. The way the television business is set up, all series are required to farm out two shows a season to outsiders. It's a Writers Guild thing.

Not surprisingly, you're competing with everyone from the producer's brother-in-law to lunkheads phoned in by agents whom someone, by dint of deal or poker debt, owes a favor. Even worse, though, is the sense, sitting in a room full of skilled Professional Writers, that you might as well be working for Allstate insurance. Except that the Allstate guys might be a tad more colorful. Between whacks at "Alf Wakes up on Uranus" plots, the swells on hand were as likely to be kicking around tips on mutual funds or studio shake-ups. On the plantation, you soon learn, everybody's always got an ear for what's happening in the Big House.

These were all ace individuals. The kind of people you probably *want* to spend three hours with in a windowless room. Discussing stories that mean less to you than Inca fertility myths. It's I who couldn't relate. A glitch that could be overcome only by making myself, *avec* chemical additives, somehow relatable. I can't describe that numbing disorientation the first time I heard two otherwise lovely fellows, two writers, penny loafers propped on the table, chatting happily about the real estate market. I mean, I didn't know about real estate. Real estate was for . . . Other People. For, for lack of a better word, squares.

Not that land and mutual funds are somehow heinous in themselves. Or, for that matter, that there's something wrong with four well-scrubbed nonpsychotics in buttoned-down shirts and jeans with creases milking their frontal lobes for family fare. Far from it. To a man, your Bills, Bobs, Jacks, and Toms were amiable. That's what makes it so awful. The relentless niceness.

See, I always thought creativity had to hurt. That talent was another name for torture. Not in this venue. One session round the proverbial table, coffee served by that extra-pleasant honeyed blond "assistant," and the revelation stings like a jellyfish: I have no reason to feel fucked-up. This life could be perfect.

Forget *The Dick Van Dyke Show*. Here were no lovable eccentrics lobbing bald jokes at Mel Cooley. (On the other hand, Morey Amsterdam didn't shoot dope.)

The pros involved were swell, though they did have a little fun at my expense. My virgin stab at a first draft—after my thin-soup idea (Alf sees a giant cockroach in the bathroom and ends up in therapy) got boiled down to something resembling coherence—rang in at something close to a hundred pages.

The good news is, thanks to a cache of cocaine, I wrote it in a night and a half. The bad is, half-hour shows are supposed to run about twenty-two minutes—which shakes down to forty-four pages, two pages a minute—and I turned in enough for a mini-series. When I'd asked about length, see, the prepped-out fellow on board as story editor informed me that ninety, ninety-five pages was perfect. Little did I know he was making carnival with my ignorance.

People didn't walk in there not knowing *anything* about writing for television. At least not until I got there. L.A. boasts two grand universities, USC and UCLA, with entire programs devoted to mastering the niceties of plot points, commercial breaks, and "dramatic arcs"—not to mention how long a sitcom should be.

I just didn't know. And the clammy shame of my ignorance served as one more reason why I had to medicate my mind. Another man might have bought a how-to book, but not me. I chose to stay dumb and suffer all the way to the bank.

"Wake up and smell the coffee," snapped the human tassel loafer when he handed back my outsize script. The fluorescents gleamed off his Armani wire-rims with real malevolence.

My smack use, which had wavered from lax to steady, edged ever closer to full-time status with my toe-in-the-water entry into Mondo Tube-o. Sandra and I now occupied a lovely two-bedroom apartment in a stretch of untrendy Hollywood Flats down in the Fairfax district. My wife had landed a slot as D-girl—or "development person"—for yet another cheesehead producer. I never paid much attention to her work, but I do know all of his projects seemed to involve stewardesses. Their boyfriends were always TROUBLE.

I'm not sure what happens, but it doesn't matter. Even an outsider like me could see making movies was the least important thing anybody did in Hollywood. Sandra seemed to work for a succession of Armani'd mooks who pulled down all kinds of money for not producing at all. The whole idea was getting the budgets. Everything after that was busywork—and Sandra was very busy. This left me the whole day to get high and scribble while she went off to Land of a Million Scripts.

The real novelty of living with Sandra was how civilized it was. She had, in her repertoire, things I'd never thought about: silverware, matching plates . . . friends in the Industry . . . and, of course, *Dinner Parties.*

The only way *I* could handle a dinner party was to time my opiate intake to coincide exactly with the arrival of the first guest. Like so much of drugdom, I had it down to a science. If, say, the soiree was at our house, I'd time my consumption to coincide with the doorbell. That was my cue.

Ding-dong. Then, "Can you get it? I've got to pop in the bathroom for a minute. . . ." At other people's parties I'd have dark-cornered tête-à-têtes with the opposite sex. These centered around my confessed unhappiness at my present situation. Nothing, it seemed, proved more alluring than the admission of misery. One constant recipient of my not-so-secret discontent was Karen Powers, a screenwriter and intimate of Patti Smith, Robert Mapplethorpe, and that whole crowd back in her Manhattan days.

Karen was older, a diminutive package of soulful angst replete with red hair, haunted eyes, arcane literary taste—not to mention martial arts training and a serious, private devotion to the underground deities of Santeria. She had probably bathed in goat blood—how could I not be smitten? Here was someone as outré and alienated as me. A bona fide Hollywood outsider. Nothing ever turns me on so much in a woman as unhappiness.

"I don't know, Karen, I can't fucking stand the life I'm living. You know what I mean?"

"I know. It's horrible here. These people! Sandra used to be different. She was so full of life before."

"Exactly! Do you ever just want to get out of here? I mean, fuck the screenwriting? Fuck everything?"

"Are you kidding? Do I ever not?"

Of course, Karen didn't do drugs. She didn't have to. She needed a fix, she could steal a hit from a lifetime of Catholic guilt. She had a stash of it, and it was horrifying. I dug her immensely for it. All I did was spill my miserably vivid little beans. There were no secret liaisons, only secret pain. It was not about exchanging bodily fluids. I was, after all, enjoying myself. Pretending the dope rush was fueled by love for something besides the dope itself. Later on I'd learn to turn the smack buzz to a six-hour fuck. Just than I was still learning. That this carried its own built-in betrayal—of myself, my wife, and, most important, the women who shared their own scarred souls with me—was more of an insight than my own shallow psyche could fathom. It wasn't just that I never called; I never remembered even speaking to them.

Sandra's absence—for that matter, her ten-hour-a-day work schedule—left time for my real love affair. Which was consummated most days by a morning visit down to the wilds bordering South Central, to see the hefty Guatemalan lass who'd become my first full-time connection for *chiba.* Dita, short for Gordita, because of her ample, stunted girth, lived in a sprawling, ten-to-a-room complex down around South Central, near USC.

Dita epitomized a breed unseen in the TV/big-screen evocations of hell-hustling dope peddler. She was not a "street dealer." She was, in the argot of the needle scene, a "house connect." Despite the bullet-pocked stucco exterior, her apartment had an alarming neatness. In the breakfast nook, where business was conducted, a festive bouquet of plastic flowers graced the table. Four place settings depicting a smiling gaucho were laid out around the basket. And on the wall above her stereo console, the customer faced a collection of photographs: her three sons by an absent father, framed and mounted so each glowing lad shone as the center of a white tin rose.

Miguel, her hulking eldest, was an avid *ALF* fan. We'd run into each other on days he cut school. He never failed to ply me with some new bit of alien arcana. Did Alf think in English? Did he ever sneak back to Melmac, his planet of origin? Did he have a dick? All this while, belt looped around my arm and through my teeth on his mom's plastic-encased love seat, I'd be fixing a shot and getting off, listening to the ten or twenty little kids perpetually running around the courtyard outside. Every time I stopped to visit Dita, I'd have to run the gauntlet of knowing moms and babies who sat along the wall of the dried-up megagraffiti'd fountain and watched my entrance. They never said anything. But the kids could not help laughing and pointing at the sallow gringo in the Cadillac. My answers to the *ALF* test varied in detail according to the potency of his mom's product and the amount I shot.

Sometimes I helped Miguel with his homework. Plucking the needle from my arm, I'd swab off and lean across the kitchen table to tackle a tricky multiplication problem or help compose a book report. Miguel was seventeen, an acne-racked high school junior who on a good day was able to read Dr. Seuss. I was never much a nodder; and the dope high perked me up, made me want to do some kind of good. But it wasn't just that. I liked the kid. Miguel had no attitude whatsoever about the fact of my coming by to bang smack at ten in the morning. That was his mother's business, and he respected his mother.

The only thing that bothered him was Dita's involvement with Rosa, the prim, bespectacled ER nurse who shared her bed and did most of the cooking. It wasn't the lesbian thing. It was a complaint any teenage lug in the world could have understood. "She's okay, you know. . . . It's just that, when Mom's not around, she yells at me like she's my mom. . . . Mom never makes me pick up my sweats and shit. . . . Rosa's on my ass like a pimple, man. . . ."

It's hard to describe the feeling of belonging these little visits gave me. The twisted sense of family. I could have no more informed Sandra of my east of USC jaunts than told her of my niggling habit. Deranged as it sounds, it was these contacts, slight as they may seem, that kept me human. I'd spend most of the days by myself, seeing Sandra off in the A.M. and greeting her arrival home in the evening. The time in between, I needed something. And Dita was kind enough to provide it. For a price.

Sandra and I more or less realized we had problems but maintained the polite facade that all our difficulties were the sort that could be worked through, *managed,* made better with the benefit of time and simple decency.

On the career front, I'd simultaneously nailed yet another *ALF* gig and been hired by the ever-friendly swells at *Playboy* to do an interview with Mickey Rourke. This meant winging down to New Orleans, where the Mick was midway through shooting the oddly regarded *Angel Heart.* He and his entourage were ensconced in a high-priced luxury hotel off the French Quarter, the Windsor Court. And *Playboy* was flush enough to spring for the $250 per day it took to slide me in there, too. My plan was to loll around in Hef-financed splendor, banging out that alien furball rewrite between sessions grilling the James Dean of His Generation.

Mickey Rourke and Alf. The two would seem to represent polar-opposite entrées on the contempo show biz menu. But if I'd come to learn nothing else in this kooky industry. I'd learned this: When the assignee is fucked-up enough, it really doesn't matter what the assignment is. It's all hellishly grotesque and inappropriate.

Right out of the gate, dope facilitated a gig so hopelessly twisted, a saner scribe would have tossed his Eberhard Faber over his shoulder and walked away fast after the first ten minutes. Another *Playboy* writer had already been lobbed onto Planet Mickey, found wanting by the inhabitants, and summarily tossed back into the galactic wastes. So it was up to me to try to meet the hard guy thespian's rigorous personal standards, whatever they turned out to be. My shot at acceptance was to begin at the Cafe Roma, Mickey's surrogate office, catty-corner to the swanky Bev Hills hair salon in which he's part owner.

Thank goodness, one of the less remarked-upon benefits of narcotic functioning is the enhanced ability to remain absolutely deadpan in the face of any and all breed of bad news. With enough Hamburger Helper coursing through the veins, "Your puppy's been napalmed" elicits the same measure of animation as, say, "How 'bout those Dodgers?" Which comes in handy. My first meeting was with Lenny Termo, the hangdog fifty-plus trusted buddy M.R. kept glued to his side. At this point in his life, Mickey and Lenny lived, worked, and traveled together. And Mickey, powerful H-wood legend that he was, had written into his contract that any movie he was in, Lenny T—who looks like a Sicilian Zero Mostel—got a spot in, too.

If Lenny liked you, you were in. And Lenny was nothing if not likable. It's just, some of the things he said were a tad . . . peculiar. Which made the wonder of narco-stoneface that much more compelling. Indeed. My first exchange with Termo, the ex-Manhattan *schmatte* dog uttered a curious thing. After an introductory spiel about the primacy of loyalty in a cutthroat scene like Hollywood, he rattled the following. "Let me tell you how I feel about Mickey Rourke. If Rourke got bit by a rattlesnake on the head of his dick, I'd get down on my hands and knees and suck out the poison!"

Well, hey! What can you say to that? Anyone under less medication might, at the very least, flinch at such a two-fisted sentiment. Hard not to. Happily, loaded as I was, my mug was wholly incapable of registering any reaction at all. Except, perhaps, for a ho-hum nod of agreement before smiling, "Me too!"

Of course, it wasn't the phony compliance that was so difficult. It was wrapping your mind around the sort of psyche that conceived of such a squirmy proposition in the first place. Still, this was the verbal hurdle the aspiring Mickey acolyte had to scale. It fell somewhere between twist-o loyalty oath and double dare.

So, count me in! With scant ado, I was greenlighted to meet with Mickey once or twice in his humble local digs. (He kept a manly two-room walk-up in what passes for an outré section of Beverly Hills, plastered with the sort of old-timey, back-of-the-barber-shop boxing posters you'd expect from a guy who inspired toxic cockhead loyalty.) Once I'd winged down to old New Orleans, there was another henchman to try to impress, this one a Jersey-born bodyguard type named Burb Berbelstein. Or something like that.

Burb, if initially more of a tough customer, proved every bit the sweetheart Lenny did. His MO, up front, was more the "Where you come from? Why the fuck you think my man should talk to you?" variety. He had a small bullet-skull plunked impassively on bouncer's shoulders. But, being a Jewish thug, he was warm *and* scary. Once the subject of d-r-u-g-s came up, however, I confided a bit of my illicit substance history, and Burb confided his own ex-Manhattan-junkie roots.

The truth, in fairness, is that I was less a big-time ex- than big-time future-junker. But why get technical? Hell is hell. Whether you'd already been there or were just on your way, you still shared the same stretch of psychic real estate. On such common ground trust could be established. "He's good people," Burb made a show of telling Mickey over the hotel phone before I'd met the Man. "He's been there, babe."

Once ensconced down south in my luxury Windsor Court suite, the sheer surrealism of the whole endeavor reached instant, epidemic proportions. Somehow I'd managed to scarf up half-a-dozen scarce-as-worms'-teeth loads. This I complemented with a film canister of fluffy coke, for staying relaxed and awake when it came time for those post-interview *ALF* installments. This combo, happily, helped the stressed-out stranger blend perfectly into the alcoholic splendor of the quarter itself. Right out of the airport, it was impossible to find more than five souls who did not seem to have "go cups" grafted surgically into their hands.

Beyond regional grotesqueries, there was the darkly weird, sheltered-from-the-public, hothouse atmosphere of Mister Rourke's neighborhood. The crypto-macho vibe first wafted from Lenny's Cafe Roma pronouncement was further amplified among Mickey's other cohorts. He had on his "staff" another fellow, a slinking, skinny little Miami blond named either "Zeke" or "Billy"—I can't remember. Billy/Zeke's job, it seemed, was to hang around as human lightning rod for Mickey's spontaneous, seemingly unprovoked and horrendous wrath. In other words, he was paid to eat shit. And the man in charge gave him plenty of helpings.

My first night chez Mick, the simple Q&A deteriorated to a monstro five-hour session listening to Mickey as he set up and played with his toy soldiers. Here was the new Marlon Brando, hunched over an end table, fiddling with little men, the hunky bad boy out walking his inner child. In person Mick's face hung a little lumpen, a little pasty and pockmarked. But the star himself came off friendly enough—once he saw you weren't going to look at him funny. If you could handle his world, rang the unspoken rule, and not say anything about it, then you were more or less welcome to hang out.

Each tiny figurine—cowboys and knights, drummer boys and Indian chiefs—had been lovingly hand-painted, right down to their bloodshot eyes. For what seemed like decades, star-boy rambled about each fave figurine, in turn. How he'd like to, y'know, "be" the bare-chested Indian straddling his palomino. "This guy, see, can ride sidesaddle, so when some motherfucker's coming up behind him, he can swing around and shoot an arrow—KEEWANGEEE—straight through his scum-sucking heart. . . ."

And so on. Between soldierly fantasies the amiable and soundly sheltered Mickey would suddenly whip around and snap at little blond Billy/Zeke. In person his much vaunted edge did not come from that cultivated biker vibe or the residue of his "life on the street." It sprang from the sense that like any spoiled second-grader, he was just as likely to give you a dollar as pick up a stick and poke your eye out.

"Hey, man," he barked at me, nodding toward his sullen lackey, "see this sorry pussy? Total fucking loser. Right, Billy? Jerry's a writer. He's a smart guy. He'll want to know this. Come on, Billy, tell Jerry what a fucking loser you are.

I mean"—he grinned, lowering his voice to a sinister croak—"if I asked him to crawl on his soft white belly, right now, just crawl over here and beg me to keep from firing him, he'd do it. Right, Billy? You'd crawl, wouldn't you, you fucking faggot. Sure you would."

Now the whisper exploded to a deranged scream. "Come on, Billy! What's the matter with you?" At which point, in some hideous mutation of Burt Lancaster shaming Tony Curtis out of his argyles in *Sweet Smell of Success,* poor Billy would put down his *TV Guide* crossword, or whatever the hell he was doing, and cast his sorry, played-out basset visage his master's way.

"Hey, Mickey. . . . Come on, man. Why are you doing this? Stop messing around. . . ."

"Don't fucking talk back to me! Don't you fucking talk back to me!" Rourke had a way of shouting and smiling at the same time. Then, looking at me as though I were part of the gag, he shook his well-moussed head. (His hotel medicine cabinet, in fact, contained nothing but mousse—twenty-four identical plastic bottles.) "Jerry, man, do you hear him, do you believe the way this little faggot talks to me?"

What becomes clear, in time, is that Billy's not the only one being singled out for humiliation. I'm the one who chooses to sit and witness this performance—without saying a word, without lifting a finger—if I want to get an interview. By simply hanging out, watching in strained silence with the rest of the crew, I'm going along. That's the deal: I want to get next to Hermann Göring I have to let him gas a Jew or two to unwind. My very acquiescence is a shameful thing.

The horror. . . . Rourke could blow from zero to a hundred in the space of a cringe. And even if you knew it was acting, and Billy/Zeke knew it was acting, that just made it worse. Because you knew there was no reason for the torment. No reason other than the rank desire to mind-rape another human by way of distraction. And invite, as in "incriminate," a third party—namely yours truly—to sit still, in admiring silence, while the drama unfolds. Ugly is not the word.

It went on and on. The kind of night where every moment seems to stretch into hours, and the hours expand until your head bursts. Rourke maintained that sleep deprivation was his drug of choice. I never saw him take a whiff of anything, never saw him imbibe any substance more potent than a Bud. . . . And who knows. Maybe it was that sheer venom that kept him running. Not the kind Lenny'd volunteered to suck, but some deeper, more toxic variety.

After a stint of this kind of fun, there was no way I could just slime back upstairs to my suite and tackle that pesky *ALF* job. The night of that toy soldier marathon, something in Billy/Zeke's trampled-below-dirt display wrenched a few rogue emotions loose in me, too. Perhaps the mere sight of such abasement drew out buried pockets of my own self-abasement. Feelings engendered up north in Sandra-land.

Whatever the case, I gulped another load and stumbled out into the steamy French Quarter dawn. By then the moon was already setting. And I found myself holding on to a mailbox, rushing mightily by this Voodoo shop tucked away on a side street I'd strolled past earlier. Regaining my sea legs, I stood before the window and, in classic B-movie-style, looked up from the display of monkey paws, incense, Marie Laveau dolls, and candles and spotted a figure looming behind me. A figure in a red dress whom I hadn't heard approach, yet saw reflected over my right shoulder.

"You look kind of sad," she said. Her hand on my shoulder all but melted me. I didn't know how starved I was for human touch. The woman I saw when I turned around was not going to show up on the cover of *Seventeen.* She was a full-faced blonde, and her lipstick was a little askew. I don't know if her dress was a size too small or her breasts and hips a size too big.

"You're looking at my stockings," she said with a hoarse laugh when I turned around. "I'm not wearing any!"

Which of course made me check out her legs. Her calves tapered au naturel into two scuffed-up, black spiked heels. "Down here, it's too damn hot for stockings. Leastwise it is for me. I can't see why a girl even needs the things, 'less she's gonna strangle somebody!"

There came that throaty laugh again. "Man, you are a gloomy Gus! You up late or up early?"

Whatever I said, it wasn't clever. Something like "Are you working, or just being friendly?"

"I'm talking to you," she said. "That's what I am. I'm only wearing this party dress 'cause the motel I'm staying at lost all my jeans. Damn manager there got hands like helicopters, if you get my meaning. Wife just sits there in a wheelchair by the screen door. Don't say a damn thing."

I didn't know if it was residual self-loathing over sitting through the Rourke spectacle or some new batch of angst at my entire existence. Distance, as was now becoming clear, had the singular virtue of both removing you from hell and giving you a detailed overview. I just wanted to spray my brain with Lysol, kill all the germs.

Sally told me all about her journey up from Mississippi, the little boy she left behind, the money she'd be sending back there to her grandma once she got a good job. Until she made enough to bring him here to live with her. "Although," she confided as we turned the corner up the red carpet to the hotel lobby, past the mildly amused glance of the uniformed night man, "New Orleans is not the kind of town you want to raise a child in."

It wasn't like I thought, Now I'm cheating on my wife, when we stepped into that lavish suite the magazine provided. I was too tired for that: wiped out from the psycho-endurance contest and the dawning awareness of the narcotically maintained lie I'd been living long before.

All I know is that the touch of Sally's soft, ample flesh,

after so long when sex was just another deal I'd stayed high to forget about, set me right on fire. We rolled onto the paper-strewn bed and, kissing like a couple of drowning asthmatics, tore off each other's clothes. Sally grabbed my hand and slammed it between her moistened thighs. "I don't know why I'm turned on by a xylophone boy, but I am!" I'd never thought about the term *lusty wench* before. "Sweetheart," she cried, "I could play 'Dixie' on your ribs!"

We'd dialed room service before tumbling onto the Sealy, and by the time our surf 'n' turf tray arrived we'd already landed in a heap. Sally was a hungry girl. And I found, for the first time since hitting New Orleans, I was starving myself. I couldn't even remember the last time I'd had an appetite—didn't even notice how Dachau-like my own once buff physique had become until I saw myself in the mirror. "Boy, you thinking of moving to Biafra or what? Get over here and stuff your face!"

I obliged. And, Sally naked beside me in the sheets, we sat and tore at the victuals spilling off the platter. I bit the heads off the jumbo shrimp and spit them in the wastebasket. Sally wiped lobster juice on my belly. We ended up rolling back onto the thoroughly ravaged tray, landing on the gardenia-print carpet. I just wanted to bury myself inside her. And never come out again.

Sally plunked her face in a dish of blueberries, blueing her lips, while I hung on to the other end of her and slammed until my neck snapped. I wasn't very good, but I was thorough. When it was over she turned her fruit-stained face to mine and said, "That's what they call an Italian tune-up. Just head out to the desert and drive a hundred miles an hour to see if everything still works."

"Does it?" I gasped, so out of shape from pot, pills, and angst that I could barely breathe.

"*Comme ci, comme ça,*" she said, "but you shouldn't go so long between drives."

The rest of my stay she just hung there, lounging around the room so I could pounce on her when I got back in. I don't know if she was homeless, a hooker, or just the sweet southern high school dropout she claimed to be. Down on her luck and in a friendly mood. Whatever the truth, I slipped her a few hundred without making a big deal out of it. And she didn't make a big deal of putting it in her purse. Before we split, she took a ragged wallet out of her jeans—by then I'd bought her some tops and Levi's—and held it open before me. There was a picture of a towheaded five-year-old, plopped on a pony and waving a tattered cowboy hat over his head Wild West style.

"That's Jamie," she said softly without looking at me. Her eyes stayed glued to the curling Polaroid. "It's been two and a half years. But I know he remembers me. I mean, I talk to him on Sundays. Well, some Sundays. . . . You know, when I can."

I didn't know what else to do but hold her. She pressed her face into my chest but kept the picture in front of her, touching it lightly with her finger, running it gently down over her long-lost baby's face. It seemed so strange to me, the idea of a child. I couldn't imagine having that kind of presence in my life: some little creature with the power to haunt your every thought if you weren't with it. It was painful to see. Three minutes after she'd been rolling on crunched lobster shells, squealing loud enough to shake the chandelier, the lost little girl beside me was racked with a sadness so profound it brought on silent tears.

She rocked against me, arms wrapped around her dimpled knees, fingers still clutching the snapshot of her Jamie, and I felt a chill I couldn't even name. No way I could have known what was coming. Maybe I did. Because the truth was looming, just beyond the curtain that separates us from our certain tomorrow. *Just wait until I'm a father.*

I had an inkling, just from the sweet Mississippi girl collapsed beside me, that I didn't even know what pain was. That, like it or not, I was about to find out.

The flight back, I was too weak to do much more than concentrate on not sliding into the aisle. The booze and drugs had taken their toll. Beyond cleaning my syringes, I didn't have much use for alcohol. But Miss Mississippi had a taste for Jack Daniel's. I must have matched her one drink for five, but it was enough, in tandem with everything else, to keep me walking sideways. By the last week I'd simply kept Sally tucked away in the suite. She wheeled the TV into the bathroom and spent most of her time watching soaps from a bubble bath. I wouldn't have minded being alone, but her proposition was beyond reproach. "You can do your work, baby. Just come over here and stick it in me between pages."

Well, writing is such grueling work. Especially polishing up that *ALF* dialogue! After a day of that—not to mention those nightly sessions in sado–movie star–land—a boy needed something to unwind. My coke had run out, but my temporary roomy, she of the pink blush baby fat, reeled in some more, along with what she called Beaucoup Cajun Bush. Grass so strong, I actually noticed being high. Which, for a constant puffer like myself, marked no small claim.

Whether it was the accumulated horror of watching Mickey toy with Billy/Zeke like a child plucking the wings off a fly, or the unspoken awareness, with this much distance, of what I'd be returning to in L.A., I pushed my hotel slap-and-tickle as far as it would go. Somewhere between Mickey Rourke and *ALF,* I needed a transition. And what better than tying a pink-skinned teenaged mom from Tupelo to the bedpost and feeding her crawfish?

My life, in the abstract, sounded so perfect: here was me, a newly high-paid writer; here was Sandra, a budding young execette. Why, we were saving money! We were house hunting! We went away for weekends! We ate in restaurants nine nights a week!

Marriage, like my habit, felt like a temporary arrangement. Even if I knew the longer I went with it, the harder it would be to kick. Life can be lived as a temporary arrangement. Life *is* a temporary arrangement! But the longer you go without changing, the more obscure the likelihood you ever will. After enough time passes, the idea of any other way of life grows ever more misty.

I believe, and I'd rather drink dog water than say this, that what I got strung out on, more powerfully than mere Mexican heroin, was comfort. Conformity. The okay-ness of it. The stylish roof over my head. Maybe I made the money, but Sandra took care of the paperwork. All I had to do was exist. More or less. It's a grim truth: some souls feel more at home in prison. They commit crimes to stay there. Because, bad as it is, at least they have a known source for the agony. They know who and what to blame. It was no different when, at the flaming height of adolescence, I'd been shipped off to this hideous Episcopalian boarding school, there to rage against the assholes who ran the place, who kept me so constrained. Why not blame *them* for my misery?

Then again, even if I wasn't entirely cognizant of my swirling inner turmoil, others were. In particular, in one of life's stranger episodes, a pack of telepathic trance channelers I'd signed on to infiltrate in my last, pre-full-time tube *Playboy* gig. Amazing, the places revelation rears its nasty little mug. . . .

Channels knew how to turn themselves into human telephones by entering a trance and stepping out of their bodies to let the spirits in. This enabled the rest of us to pay money and gather round, not just to hear the Other Worlders speak through them, but to bask in the wondrous energy their formless entities just seemed to emit, like benevolent swamp gas, while they told us what's what.

The reigning spirit, at the time, was a blow-dried shaman

from Marin County by the name of Lazaris. To look at him, you'd think he was just as likely to sell you a Winnebago as insight into your eternal beyond. In the year or two previous, he'd become the darling of the Hollywood New Age set, duking it out with Mafu, a perky ex-policeman's wife named Penny on this plane, for the souls of everyone from Michael York to Suzanne Somers. Laz had, in fact, made quite a splash on the late, lamented *Merv Griffin Show,* where he appeared with York and his missus and gave the portly host messages of Hallmark-like intensity from the Great Beyond.

("We have earthly things to do, called commercials," blurted a respectful Merv at one point. "We know of such things," quipped Lazaris, wrinkling his nose, cuddly-puppy style. I mean, he's never been incarnated. The guy dwells in some timeless ether. But, by God, he knew about commercial breaks!)

Unfortunately, the day I hooked up with Lazaris, I was having a little opiate crisis. My three-days-on, one-day-off arrangement had progressed, because of my usual Gordon Liddy–like willpower, to more like one week on, five minutes off. Which would have been fine, or at least endurable, on any other day. But not when you're scheduled to meet a spiritual giant. You can't hide from a mind-reader.

No sooner had I sailed into his room at the Airport Marriott, where the spirit's corporeal self, one Jach Pursel, was staying while in Los Angeles, then bad things began to happen. Instantly this teddy-bear, RV-salesman-of-the-month type bursts to life. The *contorto* stuff was part of the excitement of channel watching. Call it the "easy listening" equivalent of carnival geek. It's not easy letting some strange spirit sublet your body. It's hard enough keeping your own in there! As soon as Jach had packed his own psyche off to the metaphysical holding tank, Lazaris swooped in and piped up with his trademark opener. "All right," pronounced, due to accent or transmission problems, "Oo rate!"

"Oo rate, we're picking up a strong signal." Then another nose-wrinkle, a little craning of the neck, while the subject of his scrutiny shifts on his seat to keep from sticking to the Naugahyde. That darn kick-sweat!

And for the first two, two and a half minutes or so, it's okay. Not pleasant, but all right. Like being trapped in a room with an acid-tweaked Norman Vincent Peale. Until, sudden as a summer storm, the jovial entity bolts forward and grips the arms of his chair. I think, Heart attack! I think, Stroke! Then, off his love seat like a human cannonball, he hunkers over me, meaty paws on my shoulder, and lowers his apple-cheeked, shining visage inches from my own.

"We didn't know," he cries. "We didn't know!"

And there are, I can see them, tiny tears in his eyes. "We feel so much pain! We cannot continue! So much pain, we are sorry, but we do not feel . . . We cannot . . . The spirit does not choose to experience this at the present time."

With this he backs up, plunks his poly-blend bottom back on the hotel chair, and smiles sadly. "We see dark colors. We see grave, grave negativity! We see . . . shall we say this? We see you have a hole in your aura!"

Dark colors I could have handled. Negativity was my bread and butter. But a hole in my aura? What in life prepares you for that kind of news? I stood up, watched in horror as the suit-and-tied sensitive twitched back to Jach, who now reassumed his Regular Guy demeanor. I had, I realized, been rejected by an all-knowing entity. What does that tell you?

"Strange," was all Jach said in a mild voice when he'd fully returned. He looked at me for some kind of explanation about what had just happened. He, apparently, hadn't been there when the heavenly messenger was cracking a sweat. "Very strange."

"I'm . . . delighted!" was all I could sputter. Why stay around to explain? What if he called *Playboy*? What if he told them they had a potential bell tower guy out there interviewing psychics? A member of FMA—Future Mansons of America? The rest of the gig, I was careful to stay amply loaded when interviewing brain invaders. To a one, up to and including the lovely Mafu, they remarked on my happy nature.

Of course, it took a while to recover from my Marriott jaunt, but I'd learned a lesson. My days among the weirdos were done. The cosmos had my number. It was time to come in from the cold. Mere moments, in the cosmic sense, after I slimed on back to my Fairfax drug den, the chance presented itself to worm into the opposite reality. To the very heart of convention. The world of Normal White People. The world of Yuppie angst. The world—slap on those L.L. Bean hairshirts, everybody—soon to be known and loved as *thirtysomething.*

Thanks to yet another woman, I managed to parlay my initial, sneak-thief break into TV paydirt to that most legit of entrées: Creative Artists Agency. That's right, CAA. Maybe Mike Ovitz didn't leap out of bed each morning and say to himself, Hey, I think I'd like to finance Jerry Stahl's smack habit today! but Herr Mike, or at least the troops he commanded, had that general effect all the same.

Steve Sticket, as it happens, was a twinkly, cherubic little fellow who represented, among others, Gina Wendkos. Gina and I went way back. My first *Playboy* gig, in the year one, I'd zipped back to Manhattan to cover some schlocky new comics. I was staying, ever the earnest hepster, at the Chelsea Hotel. And one fine day, minding my own business as I crossed Twenty-sixth and Sixth, I happened to raise my eyes to meet the incredibly blue pupils of this tiny, androgynous beauty behind the wheel of a mammoth brown station wagon. Ten minutes later we were bouncing off the walls of her loft. This was, let's all join in a deep sigh, back in the late 70s, when you could go from eye contact to major wall-bouncing in the flick of an eyelash.

G.W. had progressed to playwright, come west, and, in

classic fashion, transformed herself from the belle of Manhattan performance art to the queen of mainstream TV here in Hollywood, where real artists come to fatten up and die. In no time she was living in a house the size of the Taj Mahal and complaining about "that damn Jacuzzi!" But all this is beside the point.

Gina, to make a long, sordid story short and simple, was grand enough to toss the enormous weight of her cachet around the agency to get them to sign a mook like me.

That's how I landed on that couch, staring at this cherubic suit named Steve Sticket, answering questions about my "vision of myself in the industry." Of course, I didn't *have* a vision of myself in the industry. But drugs and apathy helped me fake it.

They were used to people pledging their firstborn to get a shot at a sitcom gig. Souls who spent their lives cranking out spec *Jake and the Fatman* scripts. I was a whole other ball game. I was that wacky magazine guy, the kook who did the off-the-wall porn, the one who always wears black, says all kinds of peculiar things, used to zoom Gina, and now lives with a TV exec. All this and those coveted *ALF* credits to boot! I stood out, in short, as that most beloved of eighties entertainment commodities: safe edge, the "dark" guy who took a little explaining but got the job done.

There is, as any sane man can imagine, no real advantage to succeeding at something you loathe. But by now the pattern I'd started in that Burbank chapel had been established. I signed with CAA's crack TV squad the way a beer-drunk seventeen-year-old enlists in the navy. Blind high when he X's on the dotted line, he wakes up from a blackout in Fort Benning. In my case, instead of boot camp, I'd set sail for TV-land, a journey deep into the heart of small-screen darkness.

So it was, what started as a mutant career move swelled to full-time horror. By the time I'd stumbled out of *ALF* the necessity of IV mortification management outweighed any fear about its inherent danger.

Worse still, my Latina connection, Dita, had by then developed a hellacious taste for crack. Which made her once reliable presence a hit-or-miss proposition. One day I knock on the door, find it's already open, and push my way in to find her flat on her belly, half jammed under her bed and swinging what at first I think is a broom handle and turns out to be the barrel of a shotgun.

"It's Rosa," she cries when she sees me. "The whore! She's under the bed with Carlos, the landlord. That *maracon!* I know they fuck at night, when they think I'm asleep I hear them. I feel the heat off their skin. . . . Ha! They see me, they go out the window."

I start to reply: the window is on the other side of the room, it's locked shut, and the bed could not possibly fit anyone larger than a child underneath.

I start to say this when she grunts her way out and climbs back on the bed, and I see her eyes. The flat-out insanity. While I stand there, helpless, she sits on the bed and nods. "Uh-huh . . . uh-huh. . . ." Running the bizarre scenario again and again behind her eyeballs.

Despite her rage, her smiling fury, there's unearthly steadiness in her hands as she squeezes two fingers in the front pocket of her old jeans—I never saw her in anything but these same man's Levi's—and plucks out a wad of tinfoil. She's still muttering as she unwraps it. Peels back the shiny crinkles to get at the chalk-white nugget of rock underneath.

I once did a piece on funeral homes, looked in a box full of cremated human, and was shocked to see, not dust, but tiny, chalklike white chunks, each no bigger than a knuckle. . . . No different, I now think, than the twenty-dollar rock Dita's got in her plump brown hand.

So I say nothing. Just sit down as she pulls the straight pipe from her jeans pocket. Shoves the chunk into the blackened copper Chore Boy wadded in the end. (The Chore Boy people must be absolutely thrilled at the crack epidemic. There's not a crackhead in the world who doesn't suck his rocks through the crunched copper coils. It's a million-dollar industry, and the giants on top cashing the checks must know it's not all coming from clean kitchen counters. The only oven that's getting cleaned is the ghetto. . . .)

By now, pipe in hand, her smile's gone twisted. "Bastard!" she hisses. "Whore!"

She stops muttering just long enough to fire a six-inch flame from her pearly green, three-for-a-dollar Bic lighter. I start when the torch singes her hair. "Careful . . . Jesus!" But she doesn't hear. She's beyond hearing.

Dita wears her black locks in the fly-catcher style, a slanting fan arching out over her forehead in the fashion favored by oldtime Mexican ladies, "authentic" restaurant hostesses, and the just-off-the-boat Latinas you see squeezing mangoes in Pico-Union. I smell the burning follicles. See a single, feathery tuft singe and curl. Dita takes a hit, oblivious. Closes her eyes. Opens them, horribly, to reveal nothing but whites, a faint crescent of brown iris still showing on top. She waves the pipe in my direction before exploding in a torrent of coughs and cursing. This is not what I want. This is the last thing I want. But she's so insane. I take it just to make sure the shotgun stays where it landed, plopped across the pillow of her neatly made single bed. I don't know if it's real: I've never even seen a deer rifle. I just want to get the fucking heroin. But now I've walked into this private party from hell, and I can't get out.

"Bastard," she cries again, eyeing me with that same deranged gaze when her eyes roll back down in their sockets. But they're still not right. The veins in her throat bloat and squirm like birthing worms. "You too, huh? You too? Right! You fucked her, too! Under the bed? Right!"

"Hey, Dita. It's me, Jerry. Slow down," I say. The pleading cracks my voice. "Come on! You're tweaking, that's all. Smoking too much of that fucking *rock*."

"Too much!" she shrieks. *"Too much!"*

She throws back her head, howls at the ceiling. It's the funniest thing a *tecato's* ever said. She's still cackling as she reaches under her brocade pillow. Goes for the tin box with the skull and bones taped on top, above the words LA CALAVERA scrawled in red, curling pen. I can hardly stay in my skin till she pulls out some stuff. This is months before I'd sat down and slammed cocaine—the only high more hellish, and unstoppable, than smoking the rock. I can't say I enjoy the sensation of my heart slamming up against my ribs like a rabid rat in a cage. In fact, I want the feeling to stop. It has to, I half think, half scream, through my sweating eyeballs. Or I'll fucking die. . . .

So here I am: the jones that got me here amplified to this blood-soaked, over-amped stare by smoking crack. Twenty minutes ago I might have been sick without smack. Now sick's the least of it. Sick's the best part. No, now I'm going to implode, splatter the room with my seized-up nerve ends if I don't get down. The things you do to be sociable. . . .

In the midst of this picnic, Miguel, Dita's son, lumbers in from the back room. There's still sleep in his eyes—and the haunted look you get from passing out in your clothes, not knowing when or by what you're going to be wakened next. He looks homeless in his own home, ten years older than the first time we met, less than a year ago. He'd gone from eager boy to sad old man. Clearly Mom's crack habit hasn't exactly enhanced life in the household. Miguel lights up a little when he sees me, then spots the pipe in my hands. He scowls and continues in silence toward the door.

I want to talk to him. I want to say something, but I can't. I watch him darken and turn inward. I sense his hurt—one more betrayal—but say nothing. The hand clenched around my heart has shut my voice off, too. I can't talk. Can barely handle just sitting there without tearing at my own throat or snatching her nicked and disappointed old gun, jamming the barrel in my mouth and sucking lead. Just to stop the clanging bells in the back of my head. Two puffs and I hear insects whispering in apartments five doors over. I can only imagine what must be echoing in Dita's brain right now. What kind of e-mail from the Planet Doom. . . .

I feel horrible about Miguel. We had a kind of friendship. I was someone he could talk to. But now I've crossed over, just like his mother, into crackland. I want to explain: I'm not like this, but . . . How do lips work again? What do you have to do to form words and project them into the air in front of your face?

I give up, stare fixedly at nothing. Before my scalded eyes, the paint on the walls starts to shimmer and bubble up. Like boiled vanilla pudding. The whole world's on fire, but the flames are invisible. Their presence apparent only through sheets of heat that waft over the skin. I can't see the flames, only feel them. What time is it? I look for a clock. Accidentally glance at the mirror over her dresser, see my face: the image chokes my heart. My skin shines strawberry red. My eyes looked dipped in nail polish. Fucking Christ, I need a fix, but my hands are shaking so massively, it's all I can do to hold them still in front of me. If I let go, I might flap right up to the ceiling.

Dita catches my eyes, and I see she's been laughing. "You went out, hombre."

"Just a whiteout." I shrug, like it's the most natural thing in the world. Like I have ministrokes all day long. No big deal. "I'm okay, I'm okay," I go on, though my tongue swishes in and out of my mouth like a lizard's tail. I feel like I'm speaking through helium.

Dita is still cackling. But she's just insane, not heartless. In an act for which I'll always bless her, a blast of compassion that somehow transcends her soon-to-be-fatal crack madness, she's fired up a spoon on the house. Drawn a needle from her shining tin *CALAVERA* box and sucked up a pinkie's length of chocolate-brown *chiva* through the cotton.

I take it gratefully, with quaking hands. Utterly naked in my need. And without even tying off, make a fist, jam the needle in Highway 101—the bulging, crook-of-the-elbow vein I've mined since the beginning—and sigh with rank gratitude as the blood boils red up the register like a cartoon thermometer.

"Yes-s-s-s," I sigh, and fall back against the wall behind the single bed, upsetting a tiny shelf with a six-inch crucifix.

Dita doesn't bother to right it. Just pinches a squidge of china off the gram for herself and smears it on a small square of tinfoil she's flattened against an end table. No bigger than a pack of Camels. Dita never shoots up; only smokes. After rolling a straw of Reynolds Wrap with practiced hands, she puts it between her lips, aims the tube over the smudge of heroin. She holds the foil steady with her left hand while she flicks the Bic and holds the flame beneath the dope with her right. A single, practiced puff draws the stuff in a straight chocolate drip from the top of the foil to the bottom, with no waste. Chasing the dragon.

"Uh-huh," she says, as if the answer to some question has just come to her. "Uh-huh," she says again, and flashes her crazed but more relaxed glare in my direction. "So, Jerry, how's your wife?" she asks, and laughs so hard she bangs that little shelf again, knocking another crucifix to the floor.

"Oh, right," I say. And, getting up, I realize I've forgotten all about Sandra. Forgotten all about the day ahead. We have a house to look for. Of course, I could not talk to Dita about buying a house, any more than I could talk to Sandra about smoking rocks and shooting up with Dita. These are two separate worlds: I just happen to be in both. And neither.

Without even knowing if I've been there fifteen minutes or an hour and a half, I stumble to my feet. Lurch out of Dita and Rosa's bedroom, past the table with the plastic bouquet, the beaded framed photos of her sons. Only stopping at the door when I realize I've forgotten what I came for.

I turn around to pick up the gram of dope before I leave. My head feels full of boiling seawater. I'll have to stop for a quart of milk before I head home. To make it look like I've been somewhere. . . .

It is, when I make it to my car and check the clock, 7:45. The ladies have already gathered on the lip of the dry fountain. They sit with their legs apart, their long embroidered skirts tucked in between and babies on their knees. Brown impassive faces in a splash of colored cloth. They look my way when I go by and look away when I look back.

Maybe Sandra will still be sleeping. . . . The dope, at least, has taken hold. I'm awash with precarious benevolence when I start the car. A new day!

I cut over to Rampart, north. When I see a boy peddling flowers in front of an out-of-business tire shop, I stop. Mexican roses, sprayed with God knows what. Perfect! While I'm opening the car door, the handle jams and I half fall out to the sidewalk. Not yet eight. My money's wadded in my pocket, and the bills spill out when I reach in to get it. "Here," I sing, "here, take it."

The boy, who can't be any more than ten, does not look happy about the transaction. In fact, he looks scared. But why? I slap a couple of bills in his hand and lurch back to my Caddy.

"Señor, Señor!"

"Yes?" I holler back. Maybe he does like me. . . . Only I wish he wouldn't call me "señor." "Yes?"

"You forgot chor flowers."

"Right, right. . . ."

I grab them, the mood all but gone, and throw the diseased buds on the backseat. What is wrong with me? The fucking cocaine has bit into my high like a jackal. I'll have to reshoot when I get home. Christ! Now I see the blood on my fingers. Must have gouged my arm somehow. Gotten bloody when I pulled down the sleeve. I don't remember. But the scarlet stains my fingers like a butcher's. God knows what the kid thought. Good thing I saw him, in case I got pulled over later. Nothing like reaching for that license, polite as Ozzie and Harriet, and handing the thing over with fingers dipped in human spillage. "Oh, it's nothing, Officer. Just doing a little slaughtering back at the smokehouse. . . . It's sheep season, you know. . . . So how's the nightstick business?"

Jesus! I'm going to be parading through strangers' houses in an hour and a half, and I feel parboiled. I pat the lump in my shirt pocket. By now I've already adapted the year-round, long-sleeved fashion favored by hard-core needleoids. You can shoot forever without a trace if you have fresh needles. But I never do.

Scoring heroin I can do. But this *house* thing! Not the least of the horror is the mortifying parallel to the show my wife's now deeply linked with. The one I'm fated to write in the soon-to-be future. I imagine the feature headline and want to vomit: BACKSTAGE WITH THIRTYSOMETHING!

Aren't we the eighties couple? Oh my oh my. . . .

• • •

As usual, Sandra does all the work: the bank, the loan, the realtor. Passive lump that I am, I just hear about it. It's a given in our relationship that these real-world things—finding a house, a dentist, or the right light fixture—are her bailiwick.

In my own accursed way, I loved Sandra for her competence. Loved her the way the man without hands loves the nurse who spoons in his gruel: with a mixture of shame at his own handicap and gratitude that he's found someone patient or deranged enough to help him overcome it.

But then, my mother did not even let my father drive. And God forbid we should sit too near an open window! Mom had a friend whose son had his elbow whacked off by a passing moving van. All because his mother let him lean out the window. She had a legion of mysterious friends, all of whose children suffered extreme, unimaginable calamity because their mothers weren't as caring as she was. One boy, son of yet another errant mom, had to have his feet surgically removed because he wore tennis shoes with no socks and a cut in his foot got "sweat-infected." My sister and I may not have known how lucky we were to have such a careful mom; but our intact feet and elbows are living proof how such caution paid off.

Whenever the two of them hopped in the family Valiant, it was Mom who manned the wheel. And, more important, Dad let her. Other kids' daddies drove their families, but not mine. In our house, Mommy drove. It was, like my lovely's fiscal dominance, a simple given. The picture's indelible: here's Mom, fingers clenched on the steering wheel, eyes drilled forward, tooling along at her patented twenty miles below any given speed limit. I'm crouched behind her—you never rode in our car, you crouched—eyeing a fleck of lint in the frizzy flip she wore every day of her life. Dad's slumped over in the not-good-enough corner, there on the passenger seat.

He used to sit in a kind of half twist, his back against the car door. I once believed this was so he could look at my mother while they chatted, but now I don't know; maybe it was so people in the cars alongside couldn't see him.

As a child I did not just witness this abdication of paternal power, I absorbed it. Decades later when it came time to select my own mate, I found one to whom I could hand over the wheel.

The first house we looked in, a dirty-white stucco number in the shadow of the ABC broadcast tower in Los Feliz, I found myself drifting into the bathroom while my competent half chatted with the lady of the house about foundation-crumbling and earthquake sturdiness. Sadly, I found nothing more exciting than Motrin in the medicine cabinet. Though the cap had been left off and a handful of the little buggers scattered wantonly around the bottom shelf amid Q-tips and Desenex, this peek into the matron's state of mind supplied little more than a shiver of guilty excitement. Nothing grander than what a career Peeping Tom might garnish on a slow news day.

It wasn't the medicine chest strikeout that threw me, though, it was that jumbo TV tower looming over the backyard. The specter of constant, low-frequency vibration: hidden cancer causers, beaming waves of tumor food right through our bedroom window. No, thank you!

See, I may have been a junkie, but I knew about health. I knew what was bad for you. I didn't eat meat, either. No chicken or fish, either. Vegetarian for years, and proud of it. You think I'm going to put a piece of steak in my mouth, what with all those Frankenstein hormones they pump in?

Heck no, I was a California junkie. Rarely a day went by when I did not stop into the Beverly Hills Juice Bar, to douse my internal organs with a double shot of wheatgrass and a carrot juice chaser.

So okay, in a pinch, maybe I *did* have to draw up a syringe full of toilet water to cook up my tar. That was different! I mean, hey, you boiled that. That's what the lighter and spoon were for. Even if, all these years later, I've washed ashore with a permanent case of hepatitis C, I'm sure it can't be that questionable spoon fluid. Not a chance. I probably kissed some girl who forgot to brush her teeth. . . . There are so many nasty things going around these days, you can't be too careful. . . .

You have to be vigilant.

We must have looked at a dozen houses. After a while the domestic invasions melt down to a single, intimate sensation. Usually smell. There is, always, a peculiar odor. But sometimes—in the case of a man who sat alone in the dark and greeted us with a highball in one hand and a toy stuffed bunny in the other—there was, quite distinctly, a waft of old socks, the sharp, popcorny scent of sweat-through Ban-Lon gone crisp undersole. "Sock-sniff," is what you'd call it. But loneliness is its name.

The bunny-man was the only one home. His house up on Bronson Canyon squatted halfway up a small hill, set back from the street by an overhead trellis where morning glory and bougainvillea battled it out. Outside, thanks to these tangling vines, the air positively massaged the nostrils. Inside was that toxic cloud.

I was surprised, when those two olfactory fronts collided, that it didn't just rain right there at the front door. But somehow, we stayed dry.

We never got any deeper than the verandah. There, beneath a chandelier that looked like a bronze rat's nest, complete with dabs of green copper guano, Sandra met my eye with one of those let's-get-out-of-here signals that married couples develop. I shook the bunny-man's hand, surprised by his iron grip, and we ducked back outside.

"That guy was spooky," Sandra said as we strolled once more through that cavern of bougainvillea and morning glory, gulping great lungfuls of fragrant air. "Did you smell that place?"

"Maybe he collects socks," I said. "Maybe all his friends collect vintage wines, and he wanted to do something different. You know? Some people lay in prewar Lafitte, he has socks from 1930."

"That's not even funny," she said, standing aside to let me unlock the passenger door.

"Maybe not." I shrugged. "I'm just trying to give the man the benefit of a doubt. Anyway, the odor thing hasn't held him back any. He had to do something to pay for that place. I bet there were lots of rooms in there."

"Six. Not counting bath and rec room in the basement."

"Rec room! Wow!" My eyes would have glazed over if they hadn't started off that way, pre-glazed. "I've always wanted to be a guy with a rec room."

"Why?" Sandra snapped her seat belt with a snort. "You seem to have no trouble getting wrecked without one."

"Ouch!"

I fired up the car. How could I not love this woman? A mouth just like the sweet thing who bore me.

"Something's definitely wrong there," she declared. "He probably married some woman with money and drove her off with his odor. Now he gets the house."

"You think so? Jesus!"

Two minutes, and she's already indicted the man for moral turpitude. I felt obliged to come to his defense.

"I don't know, I kind of dug him," I said. "Sitting in the dark like that. . . ."

"You would," she sniffed, but not without affection.

I think we both stepped into the Cadillac feeling good we didn't have to live like the sit-in-the-dark, bunny-clutching homeowner. Bad as I was, I wasn't like that.

I didn't own any stuffed bunnies.

Even as we pulled up to the house that eventually became ours, I remember thinking, Do I want this? Not do I want this particular home. But do I want any home at all? And if I don't, what the hell am I doing? Why am I going along?

Not that there wasn't something about the place. First glance, what you noticed was the cacti. A nice little terrace of it. Every bit as forbidding as the mound of spikes Vlad the Impaler was said to have left on the road to his kingdom by way of scaring off potential invaders. Except, of course, that Vlad topped his barbs with human skulls. But there was time for that, too; we'd just have to find the right landscaper.

In the meantime there was the rest of the house to survey. Just a block and a half off Sunset Boulevard—walking distance to primo urban sleaze—the place itself set far enough back on the hill to afford a majestic, Mediterranean-like view of Los Angeles. (L.A. always looks majestic if you're insulated.)

While my all-business better half trotted in to absorb the interior, I found myself skulking up the tiny path that ran alongside the house to the backyard, where what I saw, looming large as an R. Crumb blonde, was the Cartoon Cactus.

The Cartoon Cactus, some twenty feet of rubbery spiked needle-tree, sporting juicy red growths of no known origin and, though I didn't know it then, awe-inspiring pink blossoms that show themselves and open only on moonlit nights when it's in the mood. What I did know, just looking at the thing, was that it symbolized everything I loved and hated about the city I lived in: at once fake-looking and genuinely dangerous, colorful to the eye and fatal to the touch. If a pterodactyl had flapped out of the banana tree bunched behind it, I would not have been surprised.

Beside the surreal plant life stood a sort of glorified shack, a smokehouse in the thirties when the place was built, turned into a studio by the failed writer who inhabited the place before us. I knew he was a failed writer because when I stepped in to have a look at the place, the first thing I saw on the desk was a treatment for a *Beany and Cecil* movie. He was either very late getting off the mark—*Beany and Cecil* had to have been off the air since I was, like, nine and a half—or so out of his mind he thought his ticket to Hollywood heaven would be a revival of some never-that-popular-when-it-actually-existed kids' show.

I imagined, in a blast of astral identification, this fellow sitting out here, the sun beating down on the tin roof and his wife off earning the money to keep him sitting there, banging at the typewriter with this wretched idea. Scene One: *Beany finds buried treasure on sunken Pirate Ship. Cecil contracts shingles.* . . . My kind of guy! Whatever the inside was like, I knew this was the spot for me.

Once inside the vibe was even better. Sandra was plunked in the kitchen with the soon-to-be-former owner and her mother, discussing the divorce that made this particular bit of commerce a necessary move. It was all coming together: that lug nut off in the backyard dreaming up doomed cartoon treatments, hitting the bricks without even cleaning up his desk, and his wife, this stressed-out stringy blonde with a thousand-yard stare, left behind to pick up the pieces, stuck here trying to take care of business while he finds some other cute face to wait tables while he hunkers down and contemplates his next big brainstorm, no doubt a *Heckel and Jeckel* epic.

This wasn't just any old house. It was, as a banner over the front door may as well have proclaimed, HOUSE O'UNHAPPY MARRIAGES. Not that I needed any more signals from the Marriage Gods, but just to hammer home the rightness of this move, I slunk into the bathroom and took a looksee at that all-important medicine cabinet.

After a moment's disappointment—nothing stronger than over-the-counter Empirin—I shifted the outer row to the side and hit paydirt. Plunked right there in front of me was a jar of Dexedrine. *Hey, I haven't done speed in a while!* And squidged in behind that, between the Massengill and some meat tenderizer (people put all kinds of things in medicine cabinets; sometimes it's better not to know why), a jumbo, three-quarts-full jug of Hycodan. That lovely, triple-script, lung-soothing hydrocodeine syrup. Just looking at the stuff's enough to make a guy want to have bronchitis. But why wait? This was a banner day. Why, I was probably going to buy a house. I was probably going to buy *this* house! If that didn't call for a gargantuan gulp of narcotically charged cough syrup, I don't know what does.

I hadn't even seen the rest of the house. But I already loved the bathroom. If I were Carlos Castaneda, I'd tell you

I found my power spot. Tell you I saw myself, months up the road, sitting naked on the toilet, bathed in sweat, both feet planted on a black sweatshirt dropped like a puddle around my feet, one sleeve wrapped tight around my arm and a ragged, chewed-up cuff clamped in my teeth. . . .

In my vision, it's barely daytime. The sun's too sick to come up yet. Blood drip-drips onto my freezing ankles. I'm on my second or third vein, looking for a hit, wishing the fucking bluebirds would stop chirping and just die till I can connect, finally, plunge home the wake-up hit that will make it all right, make the day endurable, make this body, this room, this house, just exactly on the planet where I want to be.

Fuck yes! I left the mirror with a final, knowing smile. *I'll be back. . . .* Then I remembered to flush, ran some water, and strode out of the bathroom all but singing.

"Sandra, we should take it! This is the place. . . . Baby, this is the place for us!"

My last moment in our old apartment was emblematic of the new life for which I was embarking. We'd spent the day before packing. Moving shit into the living room for the movers, two trippy guys named Maurice and Beppo who were both skinnier than me, yet wholly capable of hoisting entire couches, complete with their cushions, onto their backs and down a couple flights of stairs. They didn't want food. They didn't even want water. All they had to have was their forty-ounce Cobras, and they were stoked.

At that time, not yet having sunk into crack-world, I didn't realize forty-ouncers were the grease that kept the rock machine flowing, the low that kept the high intact. But it wouldn't have mattered. At least not to me. Fuel was fuel. And even if the two Hispanic fellows arrived sweating profusely, got soaked through their chinos just turning a doorknob, let alone hauling entire dining room sets, so what? I knew a thing or two about chemical nutrition. I just didn't quite have a handle on theirs.

The whole process, not surprisingly, required an excess of nerve soother. Ever since the day we'd decided on Chez Silverlake, I'd been jumpy as a lab rat. Sandra, of course, took care of everything. God forbid I should get involved with the drab mechanics of loans, interest, mortgage rates, or anything else. No, thank you. The day we were actually ready to vacate, and the apartment almost completely empty, I stopped back at some ungodly hour, two or three in the afternoon, to pick up a remaining box or two and make sure there was nothing left. That we hadn't forgotten anything.

So there I am, sitting on a crate full of abandoned dinnerware, legs crossed, whistling the theme from *The Match Game,* idly holding a lit pack of matches under a spoon I'd had the good luck to dig up from underneath a serving tray at the bottom of the box. It was less a spoon than a ladle, but what the hell. A little crusted gravy mixed in with the heroin wouldn't hurt. It was the same color, anyway. Might even make it go down a little easier.

Nothing more perverse, really, than shooting up on a sunny day, with the light streaming in, right in the middle of a beautiful weekday. Sure, most of your junkies prefer that dark cave thing, and I'm with them, but sometimes, like just then, you want to just do it like it doesn't matter.

What happened, I suppose, is that I anticipated shlepping a box down to the trunk of my car, then skulking back up the stairs for my farewell taste. Instead, being a good dope fiend, I decided not to wait.

Those were the good old days, when I still had veins. I slipped in the needle, felt that delicious prick, got a nice red register, pulled back the plunger, and was just about to thumb it home, when *Hello?*—the door swings open and in walks my landlord, Mister Fishman, a towering old Auschwitz survivor with haunting, acid-burned cheekbones and an eternal sweet, sad smile on his face.

Luckily, I'd just gotten to know Fishman a little better not two months previous. I'd stopped by his apartment to pay the rent and the door was wide open, Fishman at the dining room table with his head in his hands, and all the chairs in the living room on their side. "My vife," he cried when he saw me. "It's Esther . . . my vife, she got out!"

What happened, he managed to explain, is not that the little old lady left him for a good-looking cantor. She'd simply gotten loose. We both had to fly outside to try and catch her.

Mrs. Fishman, see, was deeply senile and given to midmorning escapes. And since Fishman, though still mountainous, was feeble as a kitten, he told me, because of both astronomical blood pressure and bad gout, it was up to me to run down the street and find the poor lady. Which I did, wedged halfway into a crawl space under another apartment building. She still, according to her husband, imagined she had to hide from Nazis. And, during her dashes from their apartment, couldn't pass up an open window, a basement passage, even, occasionally, an open garbage can without stopping in her tracks and squirming in.

That morning, I'd pulled the old woman from the crawl space as gently as I could. (In that neighborhood, the sight of a hapless Alzheimer's victim, half naked or crying on the curb like a child, was common as a cat up a tree, alarming no one.) Carrying her in my arms like a baby, I brought her back up the stairs to my landlord's apartment. Her dress, a faded green polka-dot print that must have been sixty years old, was ripped off her shoulder. Her sagging but voluminous old-lady breasts were fully exposed. And she had, in the course of the morning's excitement, passed water. Fishman, however, treated her with a gentleness that made me want to cry.

If I ever have to wonder what love is, I only have to think of him then, the way be half cooed, half whispered to his wife in Yiddish as he put her back together.

Fishman, however, was not cooing at the sight of me. He

was not saying a word. He stood quietly by the door while I finished my business. The same sad smile played on his face. I finally stood up, doing my best not to weave as I picked up the box of dinnerware and walked across the empty room. He just held the door for me and let me pass. Not until I was halfway down the stairs, taking a breather on the landing, did he step back out of the apartment and call down to me.

"Mrs. Fishman said to say good-bye to you."

I looked up at him, feeling weirdly grateful, feeling, if this makes any sense, forgiven. Our eyes held. And, perhaps sensing from what he'd just witnessed that I would need it, he added softly: "Good luck. . . ."

"You too," I said. "And thanks. . . ."

Then I walked out in that L.A. sunlight and wanted to die. Though I didn't know from what.

Last night I had the dream again. The same one I've been having since I made the decision to write this book and peel off the scab that's formed mercifully over the memory of my drug years. I'm in a dark room, perhaps a closet. A single shaft of light slices through the space between the sliding door and the wall. I've left it open, a crack, so I can see out. Children's voices drift in from somewhere outside. It must be daytime. I don't know. It's always dark where I am. Just enough light to see my syringe. To tie off, with quaking fingers, and fix. Or try to. Because every time I pump a vein, every time I work the needle into my leatherlike flesh—more, at this point, like hide than human skin—my hand shakes so violently, I pull the plunger all the way out of the rig. The dope inside spills in a warm dribble onto my leg, my stomach, my wrist. I try, desperately, to jam the thing back in, to draw a few drops from the puddle that's formed on my grimy clothes. My dead man's clothes. But there's nothing there. This happens over and over. I'm so dopesick, my tears taste like urine. It's as if the air itself were made of broken glass. I try to stop twitching. To stay still, to stop my very breath, let the pain stay inside. The slightest movement grinds tiny shards into my pores. Breathing is like gulping from a bag of claws. I want to die. Want to pass out. Want to stop . . . this . . . fucking . . . feeling. Until, in my desperation, I throw myself on the ground, in the hidden dust, and roll onto what feels like a bag of tiny bones. Fumbling beneath me, to lift myself up, is like trying to roll over a heavy corpse. My own corpse. But I have a sense, in my sweating nerve ends, I have a sense of what this bag is full of. And yes, I can't believe it, but yes, I'd smile if I could still feel my face, the bag is full of rigs. I hold it, with tremendous effort, up to that shaft of light. My God! There must be half a dozen, all loaded, all pulled back, capped, 100 cc's of ready-to-shoot speedball. Except, what's this? I look closer, I can see the filth that streaks the surface of the rig. Some kind of mildew. Narcotic rubigo. Needle after needle, I pull out of the slimy bag. Lift into the light. And they're all the same. The fluid inside, through some process of time and rot, fetid as pond scum. I see little hairs. Tiny, floating pieces of things. Visible bacteria. But I'm so sick. Can't you understand? I don't care. I don't even care what's in them. I just need a shot. Just need to not feel what I am feeling. To silence the screaming in my cells. So, God help me, I don't even bother to tie off. I just make, with the last of my remaining strength, just make a fist, try to rouse a doughy vein and plunge one in. Yes! This time there's no trouble. The point slides through easily. Blood registers. I close my eyes, thanking Jesus, when, just before jamming home, I look down at the needle. Only now, it's not full of fluid at all, not even filthy water. . . . It's—so help me!—it's my father's face, distorted and tubular, squeezed grotesquely into that plastic shaft, dark eyes staring up at me. Like a fetus in a test tube. Mutant, furious, forgiving. . . . "Oh Daddy, Oh Daddy. Oh—"

My own shouting wakes me up. My arms are twined around each other. My heart hurts from beating.

This is the dream I have.

PART FOUR

KIDDIELAND

Lest you think I awoke spontaneously addicted and gainfully employed, it's probably necessary to fast backward. To dip into the hellacious batch of damaged synapses known as the past. . . .

I'd been getting high since I was fourteen or fifteen. It started in earnest when my dog killed himself. Samson, a frisky little black-and-tan, apparently crawled into the garage where they found Dad slumped behind the wheel of his spanking new Oldsmobile with a ball game on and the motor running. They say death by carbon monoxide is like going softly to sleep in a giant gas station. Relentless daily drug use, through high school and beyond—*way* beyond—was my way of not finding out.

I hadn't intended to explore the link between my father's exhaust-pipe passing and my own, more lugubrious stretch of suicide. But I see now, before I can get to the fruits of my toxic hobby, I've got to get down to the roots. This kind of self-exploration stands out as wholly antithetical to the life, or, more accurately, the life of the mind on drugs.

The whole point of drugs is to keep you from thinking. The dead stay buried, along with all their ugly artifacts.

My family—dead father and still alive, terminally tormented mother; my Katmandu-dwelling Buddhist sister—falls into that category. And I can't say I'm thrilled at the prospect of examining them. To the extent heroin addiction was my little Vietnam, starting with my marriage is like starting with My Lai.

Childhood, for some of us, is the prison from which we must escape to enter the world. Where I learned to do drugs, on a daily basis, was Pottstown, Pennsylvania's Hill School, famed for accepting Tobias Wolff's forged grade-point average in *This Boy's Life*. And later expelling him for smoking. . . .

My parents went away a lot when I was little. My father worked at different times in Harrisburg, Philadelphia, and Washington, D.C. He was a lawyer, in the public eye, city solicitor of Pittsburgh, then deputy mayor, onward and upward to attorney general of Pennsylvania, Lyndon Johnson–appointed director of something called the Lawyers Committee for Civil Rights under Law and, eventually, a federal judge on the Third Circuit Court of Appeals.

That is the Cliffs Notes version. You can imagine how proud I am: Dad was an immigrant made good as public servant; son's a drug-taking pornographer. . . . Say no more. (When I was nine, I kept a little diary and wrote: "If my father were a garbage man, instead of mayor, I could do what I wanted to do.")

On those occasions when Mom went to stay with him, they hired various neighborhood ladies to stay with us. Now that I've stumbled into parenthood myself, this seems appalling. These weren't family. They weren't friends. They were friends of friends. Grandmothers, widows, never-marrieds, off-key strangers, a whole herd of postmenopausal lovelies with plenty of free time.

Most prominent of whom was Mrs. Neugabine. I remember Mrs. N. for a lot of reasons. Number one, she smelled like rancid ham. And second, she liked to snuggle with me after school. I don't know where my sister was. Off at high school, I suppose, hanging out at the Debate Club. All I know is, when I came home, Mrs. N. would be waiting for me. Propped on her side on our downstairs couch—not to brag, but I think we were the first to own velour—waiting for me. . . .

By the third or fourth day (she stayed with us about two weeks) the after-school snuggle had become ritual. Other kids came home to cookies and milk. I came home to Mrs. Neugabine.

"Hi, sweetsy boy," she'd call, fingering the wattles that hung down from her chin to her neck, lying there in the yellow tropical flower muu-muu she wore every day. Though there was nothing tropical about her. Her body was immense, freckled, saggy . . . as if the skin had to cover large spaces from bone to bone, and there was nothing underneath. If you've ever seen tent caterpillars, you know what I mean. It was as though if you weren't careful, you'd put your finger through, as you might through old parchment. . . . And God knows what you'd find inside.

Her face, by contrast, didn't look like parchment at all. It looked like a rubber mask. Tight little features jammed atop a mound of soggy flesh, like a cherry plopped on a melting sundae. The sweet motif is no accident. Her hair was bright orange, a color you don't see anymore. A shade not found in nature, only in candy corn, and it clashed horribly with the pasty liver-spotted ball of her head.

Mrs. Neugabine had a thing about candy. She brought a big glass goldfish bowl filled with sourballs. Her favorite, though, were jujubes. Back then they used to come in a little box for a nickel. After three or four chemical-flavored nubs, you could sort of sit back and feel the cavities. What Mrs. N. liked to do was tape a jujube to each of her nipples. I never saw her do the actual taping, so I don't know the details. But when I got home, and she summoned me over for the after-school snugfest, instead of chowing down on Twinkies in front of the Three Stooges, my ritual when Mom was in town, I sat down beside her. I watched her smile that creepy ham-smell smile and lower the half-moon neckline of that lovely muu-muu, inch by fleshy inch, until the peculiar fruits of her afternoon taping were visible.

"So, sweetsy-boy, want some candy? Wanna jujube? Got some right here, doncha know. That's right! Got some right here stuck to my oochies!" At the height of it, her whole manner of speaking would slip into a kind of ur-Charo mode, so that I found myself lumbering around atop this sixty-plus industrial accident head with candy on her tits and a bad Brazilian accent.

Still, I can't sit here and squeal about child abuse. It didn't take Anna Freud to know the whole deal was not PTA sanctioned. I knew there was something not exactly Dick, Jane, and Sally about the setup. But thank goodness, I survived to become absolutely normal.

The first day or two I simply plucked the things off. Fumbling with the tape—I don't know what she used, but it would have made a great commercial, along the lines of the indestructible Timex spots running at the time—I'd have to twist and pinch the incredibly plump old-lady nips. Much larger, in case you were wondering, than the attached jujubes. Once she got me in there, though, Mrs. N let slip that lots of other little "sweetsies" liked to bite off the candies. "You know, like little puppies. I call them puppy bites." So, already laying down the pattern of overobliging behavior when it came to women, I leaned down over her jumbo bosoms, while she tugged at the ever-pliant muu-muu neckline and threw back her head of orangeade hair. For some reason, the tape—could she possibly have ordered it special?—tasted like mint jelly, so that even before I worked my canines around the main course, I already got a tongueful. Then I'd get down to it. After the first couple of nibbles, it wasn't so bad. I'd forget what the fucking things were attached to. Just clasp my mouth around crisscrossed Scotch taped candies, trying to work one of my pointy molars underneath the stick'um and tug upward.

After a few minutes of this, her whole body would give a

shudder. Then I'd sort of half lick, half chew, at the miniature fez-shaped candy, lapping as if my life depended on extracting every last molecule of factory flavor. Mostly she stuck on the cherry ones. Though I noticed at about a week or so into it she'd switched to orange (no doubt to match her bouffant). Whichever tinge, the left nipple always matched the right. Whatever else you could say about her, she was color-coordinated.

The old lady never hurt me. But by the second week she was reaching south to my penis, checking to see if "my l'il pup was happy." "Happy little boys," she told me, "have happy little puppies." And while she checked on young Rover I continued worrying her nipple like a terrier, chomping, nibbling, biting, gumming my way around the by now licked-to-a-sorry-nub candy remnant. I'd work on one, then quickly loll over to the other, prompted by her hand on the back of my neck, petting and squeezing. By the time I got one tiny prize the other would be almost as licked down, and I'd make quick work of that one.

The whole business took no more than ten or fifteen minutes. When I was done, she'd quickly pull up that muu-muu, squinch the tape into a single sticky ball, and become instantly businesslike. Never once did I achieve anything that might be called orgasm. Only once, because of a combination of nerves and after-school Hawaiian Punch, did I actually squirt anything, and that was nothing more mature than pee. Lucky for me, the orange-domed sitter didn't notice and simply proceeded to wrap up as she always did.

"All right, little man, all right, no reason to dawdle. Let's get some supper ready before your sister comes home. What do you say to that? Candy's well and good, but a young boy has got to eat his blood meats if he's going to grow up strong."

With the exception of the ringworm Mrs. Neugabine seemed to have given me, a half-dollar-size splotch of psoriasis rosea right there on my cheek for the world to see, I was none the worse for wear. Penny-candied baby-sitter nipples are supposed to be, well, disturbing. But the jujubes were a onetime event. And nowhere near as disturbing as what passed for routine. What about the crazed green of my mother's eyes or the fact that she lay in bed in the dark for much of my childhood? What about being the only Jew in a grade school of eight hundred or so? What about my sister and me picking the dried food from last night's dinner off the fork we were handed to sit down and eat tonight's with? What about my father being the only guy in the neighborhood who wore a white shirt to work? What about the way he used to bang his fist through the plaster, knock his head through a wall after fights with his wife? Or how, for whatever reason, those holes never got fixed, so that the inside of our house was like a museum of my father's rage: a shattered door here, a ragged, exposed-wire hole there, to remind us of the way we lived should we ever be inclined to forget? . . .

Childhood stands out as a series of minuscule horrors. A pattern of baffling dread. The moment I became aware, what I became aware of was *shame.* There was nothing else. At three and a half I heard my mother utter a threat that even to this day fills me with a terror so penetrating that shame moved into my cells and hung up curtains.

You see, I had a problem. I used to stain my underpants. Used to, no matter how much I wiped—and I rubbed until my preschool sphincter chafed like sanded mahogany—leave a residual smudge of shit that moved my loving mother to paroxysms of rage. The fear of which, on a daily basis, became the dominating fact of my early childhood.

If you leave one more stain, I'm going to hang your underpants on the line where all your friends can see.

Her face scrunched up close to mine, those green eyes glowing like tortured emeralds, clutching my crap-caked underpants by the band and dangling them before my face.

So close I have no choice but to breathe in the evidence of my own shame.

Well, all these years down the road, what can I say? This isn't about *Oh, my mommy made me feel so bad, I shot heroin when I grew up.* Not even close. People endure worse, infinitely worse, and turn out to be upstanding citizens.

It's just that *I* have a three-year-old child now. And she, being a three-year-old child, occasionally has the sorts of messy little problems three-year-old children have. Including the same one I had. Which, as Uncle Sigmund guaranteed it would, centers around the display, retention, fascination, and occasional leakage of poop.

Whether I was playing whiffle ball, throwing rocks at cars, or running around the neighborhood looking for empty bottles to turn in for pennies and cop Popsicles at the corner store, one part of me was there, doing the playing, throwing, or bottle hunting. But another part, the deeper, secret part, was squeezing my ass tight and praying to the Allah of Underpants that there wouldn't be a streak there when I got home. Because I knew, if sweet Mom delivered on her promise, I would have to kill myself. That's all there was to it.

I had the plan, too. I figured—and I don't know where I got this—but I figured, Okay, if she goes ahead and hangs the shame-stained undies out there, as she put it, **FOR ALL MY FRIENDS TO SEE,** then I will simply run down to the basement, turn on the dryer, and hop in. That's it. I'll just hit the spin cycle and whirl myself to death.

That thought, more than any other, gave me peace through the night.

Eventually, I stopped shitting altogether. Sometimes for weeks at a time. The memory of one such stretch, in the unlikely location of Fort Jordan, an army base deep in the heart of Georgia, can twist my viscera to this day. Our family didn't take vacations. My father, who was at the time city solicitor of Pittsburgh, had served in the military reserve his entire life. Which meant, instead of taking two weeks at the beach, like normal people, we hit the road and went for a dreadful stay at an army base. Fort Dix, Camp Drumm, Fort Sheridan, and a whole lot more. . . . We hit them all. Fort Jordan, though, way down in Georgia, stands out for a number of reasons. Not the least of which is the motel turkey baster incident.

Dad stayed at the barracks. He was a major at the time, assigned as a Judge Advocate General. Mom, sis, and Junior, however, stayed at some red clay motel—I believe, in fact, that's what it was called, Red Clay Motel. *"Where we treat everyone like a redneck . . . !"*

Days were spent lolling around the pool or, better still, hanging out at the base, waiting for Dad to finish up doing whatever he did. I certainly never knew.

All I knew is that, instead of his usual so-old-it's-shiny baggy brown suit, he wore a tan uniform and snappy hat. Plus his shoes were suddenly shiny. Sitting around the motel when he came to visit, the old man spent an inordinate amount of time huddled over his Kiwi can, buffing up his black brogans.

While my mother and my sister bonded with other part-time army gals, I would sneak off to a dusty parking lot behind a barracks and watch the guy on guard duty.

There was, for some reason, nobody else around. Just me and this poor soldier marching back and forth, back and forth, on this sun-heavy patch of dirt. For a few minutes, I remember, I watched him. I'd never really gotten so close to a soldier before. Seen one up close. So when I yelled, "Hey!" and he didn't turn around, it was slightly disturbing. Thinking, perhaps, he didn't hear me, I yelled again. "Hey, you! Hey, over here!"

Still nothing. Which was strange, Spooky even. I had, of course, been told to be quiet before. To go away or get lost. But to just be ignored, as if either you didn't exist or the person you were shouting at weren't human—that was something new.

After more unsuccessful shouting, I started marching alongside him. Staring sideways and up at the soldier. Who was, looking back, just a skinny kid with bad acne and a golf ball Adam's apple. No doubt suffering enormously at having to march up and down in full uniform, rifle on his shoulder, helmet on his head, for no reason at all, while this fucking pipsqueak in T-shirt and Keds pestered him like a three-foot mosquito.

At last, unable to take it anymore—my entire worldview, such as it was, shattered by the specter of this automaton in green fatigues, a robot in army boots—I whirled around, picked up a clump of dirt and, in one of those rare decisive moments, those actions so pure we don't know we're going to act until the action's over, hurled it right at his head.

Ka-Chunk. . . . The thing exploded off his helmet in a puff of red dust. And still the soldier boy kept marching. The Adam's apple didn't bob. It was, there's no other word, mind-bending for a three-year-old boy. As if one of the Grade Z monster movies I loved to watch on Chiller Theater, Saturday nights, had come to life, right here in Bumtickle, Georgia, in the form of this trudging army man.

When one chunk didn't do it, I picked up another, hurtled this one at his stomach. *Ka-poomph!* Still nothing. I tried another chunk, then switched to rocks. I was in a fever now. Was this guy human? Were soldiers something besides flesh and blood?

Pretty soon my arm felt leaden. And still nothing! So I switched to gravel. Scooping up great handfuls, I hurled them at him. Showering the poor gawky loser in uniform with rocks the size of peach pits. I *had* to get a reaction. Otherwise, I somehow knew, it meant that one of us *WAS NOT REAL*! And I already suspected, long before I made this trek to Soldier-ville with Mom and Dad, that that someone was me.

By the time my frantic mother showed up to grab me by the hand and drag me away, I was a shrieking mess. . . . And the soldier just kept marching. Or so I thought.

"What is wrong with you?" my mother screamed at me. "That boy is crying! What did you do to that soldier?"

And suddenly, when I looked at the marching youth, I saw that what she said was true. He *was* crying. Sniffing back tears. Clamping his lips tight as he walked what had to be the longest, most horrible walk in the world.

I stole another look, one last glance over my shoulder as my mother pulled me to the car so fast my ankles dragged in the dust. Only then did I see the bright streak of blood on his forehead. The dirt-bomb blotches on his back, his legs, his stomach . . . I had not even seen what I had done. . . . I wanted to obliterate the image as soon as it burned into my eyes. A sensation, oddly enough, that was to define my every waking moment decades down the road.

But I did not have long to think about it. Because once my mother had thrown me in the backseat of our two-tone Plymouth, driven to our lovely Red Clay digs, and dragged me to the room, there was a whole new torment to endure.

"I know what's wrong with you, young man"—reaching deep in her suitcase, fishing through the giant slips and panties as my own brain filled with screams as silent as the muddled soldier's, *please God not that!*—"what's wrong with you is, you need to do a BM."

"Mommy, no!"

But there was no getting out of it. I knew what she was grabbing for. And my guts curled like pan-fried rattlers at the prospect. It was—be still my sphincter!—turkey baster time. I was a constipated child. Mom was going for her enema.

Oh, Christ!

Had I some hard stuff at the time, I would have taken it myself or slipped it in her Maalox. Either way, I might have saved myself the nightmare of hot soapy water inserted through a tube the size of a Roman candle. Almost as scary as the actual act was the sight of the enema. I don't know where she got the thing, but the bulb was not just huge, it was . . . *foul.* A smudged-up orange rubber thing that looked like one of those horns Harpo Marx kept in his belt. Except Mom wasn't honking at Margaret Dumont, she was penetrating my rectum.

Mostly, from the miasma of childhood, it's the sense of difference, of being an outsider, that permeates all memory.

Brookline, the section of Pittsburgh I grew up in, boasted lots of Slavs, Poles, Italians, Irish, and two Jews. To the right of us were the Pazehawskis, to the left the Bombellis, and across the street were the Carrigans. The neighborhood, in fact, contained more parochial schools than public. My friends all went to Resurrection, known colloquially as "Rezzie," and I can't tell you how many times a hate-squeezed Suzie or Timothy stopped me on the way to school to grab my arm and ask me why I killed Jesus. By the age of six, I was convinced I must have done it in my sleep.

The neighborhood lurked somewhere in the lower-middle-, upper-lower-class strata of reality. With the exception of us, who could easily qualify as straight middle or, after a fashion, upper. See, Jimmy and Regie's dad drove a meat truck. Kenny's sorted mail. Ricky's humped in the steel mill and Danny's worked the swing shift down at Duquesne, one of the breweries.

My dad's official title was city solicitor. But he served as deputy mayor when the actual mayor, one Joe Barr—known to City Hallers as "Mush-Mouth," a moniker whose import, in retrospect, might best be left to surmise—was off doing whatever mayors did when they weren't mayoring. I don't have much in the way of Dad memorabilia, but I've hung on to one yellowing photograph from the *Pittsburgh Post Gazette* of my father, in trademark black baggy suit and tie, clutching a sickle next to a gaggle of what were then called little Negro children, for a staged photo of a groundbreaking ceremony for a playground in the Hill District, Pittsburgh's answer to Harlem. Beside that, above a caption "Mayor demonstrates that Pittsburgh can be a swinging city," he's riding on a swing between a pair of little black kids.

You'd have to know the old man to know just how peculiar these pictures were. He was so *quiet.* Never elected, always appointed. A short, strong guy, built like a Welsh coal miner, black hair brushed straight back with a strange silver patch on the left front of his hairline. Black-rimmed glasses.

He once told me that all he had to eat on the boat over from Europe was stewed tomatoes, and just looking at them, even thirty years later, made him queasy. That's it. Where he grew up, how he got here, what it was like when he landed . . . all that stuff I had to pick up after he was gone.

I knew he had it hard. And I had a sense of how my own cushy life must look to him and felt constantly guilty about it. Even though he never said anything—and probably didn't think it. I loved him, but I couldn't be seen with him. Shame again. We never really spoke about his own ordeal, though it now seems fascinating.

From what I can piece together, he was born near Lithuania to a Russian father and Lithuanian mother. His father, I believe, was a schoolteacher. And a Zionist. When my father was two, the three of them were trying to escape civil war–torn Russia, to make their way to Lithuania and thence to Palestine. Problem was, while his mother could get into the country, his father, being Russian, could not. So they had to stop, in some godforsaken border town, and wait for the proper papers. Instead of papers, though, his father got shot, one victim among millions, and died without ever getting out of the country.

My father and grandmother, having already trekked through the ravaged countryside, somehow make it to Lithuania. They live somewhere east of Vilnius. At this point America rears its ugly head in the form of a cousin named Harry. Harry's a grocer in Kittanning, Pennsylvania. He's recently widowed, with two sons. And he's sent word he'd pay the freight for my grandmother's younger sister to come and take his dead wife's place.

Younger sister, though, doesn't want to get on a boat to emigrate to a country she's never seen, let alone marry a man she's never met.

My father's mother, however, wants more than anything else to snag some kind of future for her son. For Jews, for Lithuania, for all of Eastern Europe, the writing is on the wall. At least to her. She tells her sister she'll take her place. *She'll* go to America. And, having decided, she has to make the kind of decision no mother should ever have to make.

Harry, through some cruel whim of his own or the U.S. Immigration Department's, can only send one ticket. Mother can come. Her son cannot. It comes down to this: to save her child, she must doom him. Leave him behind while she goes to America with the sole, sustaining hope in her heart that someday, as soon as she can, she will send for her little David. Someday, though, turns out to be eight years later.

I try to picture my father, at the age of ten, setting sail by himself. I compare his experience to mine at the same age. A comparison that haunts me in all my dealings with him. I seem somehow to have known the story of his childhood my entire life. And awareness of his hardship informs my feelings about him—more accurately, informs the feelings I imagine he has about me. Like the night, at yet another army base, when they take me to my first movie, *Anatomy of a Murder,* and I can't sit still because, at that age, it's the single most boring experience I've ever had, and I end up walking all over soldiers' and their dates' toes, making a nuisance of myself.

At the end of the evening, my father steams at me. "Other boys would feel lucky to get to go to a movie!" And I wonder . . . no, I *know:* "Not other boys, Dad, *you.* You would have liked to go to a movie. And you can't stand me because I can and I don't even like it."

The fact that he had to ride in steerage, by himself, gulping horrible stewed tomatoes all the way across the Atlantic, while I, at the same age, got to sit around slurping Sugar Smacks and watching the Three Stooges after school, pretty much made me guilty for ever breathing a happy breath. Even though, once again, *he never said anything.*

All the old man ever said, and that rarely, was that the reason he was so short is because he got no milk as a child. That was it. Years later, stumbling upon a college short story he wrote about his village, I read about his shame at being the only family in the village who didn't have their own cow. Which explains everything or nothing about my discomfort at the plenty he provided me, and my sense that he resented my comfort. If *we* lived in the village, we'd have had a goddamn cow, you know?

The guy was nothing but good to me. But he never had a father, and I never didn't—until a few years later—and such a setup, I suppose, bred guilt as inherently as love.

I've been reading from a Memorial Session held by the Third Circuit Court of Appeals, on which he served with distinction from October 31, 1968, to February 1970, when he had what they describe as "the accident." Speaker after speaker recalls his brilliance, his kindness, his sensitivity to the rights of others, his unstinting devotion, love of the law, gentlemanly manner as student, official, and finally, judge. It just goes on. And, as I read it, I think: Here I am, son of the legal equivalent of Gandhi, writing this book packed with needle and candy action. Talk about your downward mobility. . . .

I came into the world sensing his accomplishment, his amazing ascension from unloved immigrant stepchild to esteemed and conscientious public servant, a man whose life left others' lives better off. And, though he never lorded it over us, never, in fact, acted anything more than a guy who used to take a bus to work and wear undershirts around the house, I felt *doomed by his goodness.*

There *was* something horribly oppressive to being the son of a man about whom no bad could ever be said. In a way, I could relate to my father—and to what I imagined to be his sense of otherness. The boy who entered kindergarten at ten, speaking no English. Suffering mightily, as one can imagine, from his provincial classmates. This wasn't the Lower East Side. Hub of the old ethno-melting pot. This was Kittanning, PA, where everybody knew everybody else.

Just so you know how old thirty-nine is, I can remember, in kindergarten, having to stand in a circle to hold hands and say the Lord's Prayer before school every morning. I'd be lying if I didn't confide how happy I was not to have to do that the next year. Because, even though it was only words, I felt like I was betraying all manner of rabbinical ancestors I didn't even know I had. I felt the eyes of my fellow kindergartners, who seemed to be constantly looking, at least in my imagination, to see what Jerry the Jew would do.

When that was over we had to listen to the damn Bible readings. Only it was never "our" Bible—and how I knew, at four, which Bible was "mine" is beyond me. It was theirs. Every day was another fucking Peter and Timothy story. "My Bible" sported guys like Hezekiah and Aaron. They had Pete and Tim. (I had Uncle Shlomo, my next-door neighbor had Uncle Buzz.) Sometimes I'd try to cover my ears, without anyone noticing.

Somehow, when I couldn't manage to block it out, they always seemed to be telling the loaves and fishes story. Jesus standing there in his robe, tossing bread on the water. Once again I knew this wasn't a story for "my people." If it were "my people," there'd be some old guy named Moishe with his pant legs rolled up, dumping lox and bagels out of wax paper.

My father was brilliant enough to leap from kindergarten to fourth grade in a single year, and I had enough smarts to excel myself. I was born with brains, but that was just one more thing to feel weird about. My IQ got me sent to a summer school for "the gifted"—which translated, near as I could tell, to girls with pop-bottle glasses and boys who played the violin in French. I may not have fit in in Brookline, among the working-class Catholics, but I didn't fit in at the temple, among the suburban Jews of Mt. Lebanon, either.

Mt. Lebo, see, was where the rich lived. Not mill hunks and brewery drivers. Kids in Mt. Lebanon wore buttoned-down shirts and penny loafers. Kids in Brookline wore Ban-Lon gaucho shirts and Italian fence climbers. Mt. Lebanon was home to "cake eaters." Brookline was greaser and hood country. And I belonged in neither.

Throw in the strange-o Mom factor, the fact that I'd been startled into poop trauma and cried more than a boy my age, or any age, I suppose, ought to, and you're getting a picture of the dope fiend as young whiner. But fishing for the big truth, you can't throw out all the little ones that come up squirming on your hook, either.

One of the more horrific moments of my childhood was the Denny Holmhoffer incident. Denny was my best friend from up the alley. Son of a postal clerk and mom who did church work, both fanatic Methodists. One night, in a rare to the point of unique display of father-son chumminess, my dad took me and Denny to the Ringling Brothers circus. We rode the streetcar from the Civic Arena downtown back to Brookline. Denny and I sat next to each other on the ride. My father took a seat opposite. When we got off—also no big deal—me and Denny walked home together. My father, again, hung back a little.

I'm eight or nine at the time, Denny's a year older, but the same size as me. A slight, bucktoothed kid, brainy in math and uncatchable in a game of tag. When Denny went through our yard and up the alley to his house, and I followed my father into the house, my parents immediately went into a conference inside our kitchen.

I still didn't pick up on the tension, until, reaching in the fridge for a glass of milk to wash down a post-circus Oreo, my mother suddenly turned to me. "Jerry, your father and I want to know if you and Denny were holding hands."

"What?"

"You heard us," she snapped, the phosphorescent charges going off in her eyes under the harsh kitchen light. My father stood behind me and closed the fridge. "Daddy says he saw you."

"Dad?"

Of course I denied everything, when I could tug myself out of shock long enough to respond, but the message was sent and there was no retrieving it. My own parents suspected me. And, though it was not true, though I knew it wasn't even close to being true, that fact somehow made it even worse. Because if I wasn't, to lapse once more into lingua mama, a "little limpy," what the hell was I? At least there was a name and a description of that fate-worse-than-death condition. But the cloud I lived and breathed under had no known description: I was just different. My own parents knew it.

Everything about my mother was a source of prepubescent agony. On the low end of the Mortification Scale there was her name. *Floncey.* Not Ruth or Irma or Sally. Floncey, short for Florence. On a more twisted level, there was the single, hideous fact that, knowing how weird she apparently felt I was, I could not help feeling weird right back.

My sister, five years my senior, who hit Berkeley in the Free Speech years, became a lawyer, dropped out, moved to Nepal in 1975, and never moved back, has a theory. It follows feminist lines. Mom is a smart woman. She had degrees—in child psychology—she worked in New York City during the war. After which, like all good women of the era, she hooked up with a man and sublimated her IQ to the drudge of homemaker-hood and suffered accordingly. I think the Miltowns helped, however. There was always a handy jar of these prehistoric Valiums in the bathroom.

It should be said that I love my mother. I can't be in a room with her for more than three minutes without getting into a screaming fight. Can't bear the sound of her voice. But I love her, even if we can't stand each other, for all kinds of reasons. Not least for some of the very same things that, while growing up, rendered her a source of profound embarrassment. Things I've since come to appreciate, even if they still drive me crazy. Like the way she talked. Ask her how she felt, she'd tell you, "Like a nickel's worth of dogmeat." Ask her where her kids got their brains, she'd say, "They didn't get it licking the wallpaper." Ask her what she thought of her son, she'd sneer, "Misery guts."

"Sarcasm" doesn't quite describe it. I didn't feel like a source of amusement. I felt like a walking punchline. Until I was a little older, then I just felt like a joke. (Then again, I wouldn't have wanted to raise me, either.)

All of which points up an incident in my own early childhood that lingers in between lived event and dream, memory and approximation.

I've come to call it the Invisible Handicap situation. I was born with a defect. Nothing in the missing nose, hole-in-the-heart, thalidomide flipper category, but a defect nonetheless. It all had to do with a malformed hip, some hink in the joint that's left me, to this day, sporting a left knee slightly higher than the right, plus a pair of calves that look as if they were hacked off two different people—both skinny and white—and transplanted to me.

As my mother used to tell it, when I finally got up off my haunches and started paddling along, I "rolled my hips like a drunken sailor." At two, my movements were peculiar enough to lend the impression of already being the inebriate I ended up.

Dr. Tyne, a world-class Pittsburgh pediatrician, specialized in treating children born with bone disorders, correcting them without surgery. Beyond curative powers, however, was the little matter of appearance. Dr. Tyne favored short white wavy hair, brushed straight back and kept wet, and always wore the same attire: black suits with pants, white shirt, black necktie, black dress shoes.

The doctor's eyes seemed to swim behind these steely wire-rims, large as pickled eggs. But one sensation looms: Dr. Tyne, up close, smelled of something secret, something tainted, moist. . . . Dr. Tyne, whose fingers clutched my bare thighs in damp, hot fingers. Who told me, in odd, fluttery tones, to pull this way, to pull that way, to push, child, push. . . . Dr. Tyne, who I didn't even know was a woman.

All I knew was that the burly yet disturbingly rounded figure made me feel a way I didn't understand. The sight of her/him, the blinding white mini-pompadour, the smooth and rounded jowls. Creepy-making. But not half so much as her waiting room. For here was another world altogether. A vast kindergarten-size sprawl of tricycles, slides, games, and crippled children. That's what scared me. The little boys in wheelchairs, girls whose wrists were strapped into shiny steel braces, all manner of metal appliances affixed to the limbs of kids the same age as me. It's as if, clutching my mother's hand, I'd stumbled into a damaged parallel universe to the one I thought I inhabited, a world of limping little boys in cowboy hats, shrieking, broken two-year-olds on their mommy's lap, unable, you soon realized, to ever leave their mommy's lap. . . .

"But Mommy, I'm okay, aren't I? . . . Aren't I?"

"Of course you are."

"But Mommy—" The question I could never ask. *But Mommy, why am I here?*

The difference between me and the screaming towhead whose withered limb dangled like a sagging afterthought out of his short pants was that *what I had was invisible*. Otherwise he was the same as me. We were both crippled. Only he was crippled outside. And I was crippled inside.

That was it. I was there, I was one of them. You couldn't see it. But I knew. I knew. . . . And I would spend the rest of my life simultaneously trying to forget my condition and making sure it never changed. . . .

• • •

Jacobo Timmerman wrote that you become a man the day you see a policeman plant his boot in your father's testicles. My equivalent, this being a civilized country, took place in the chambers of the United States Judiciary Committee when I was fifteen. My father had been nominated by Lyndon Johnson to the Third Circuit Court of Appeals. Part of the process involved a session in front of the Senate Judiciary Committee, whose Big Man was an old-school Mississippi bigot by the name of Jim Eastland.

Whatever excitement or pride I had in my father's ascendance quickly turned to horror once we got to Washington. I still remember the smell of that mahogany-paneled hearing room. Cigar smoke, and furniture polish, and something else. Some kind of stink that flowed under and around the shining tables and old, withered men in suits.

I had never seen my father grilled in public. He looked so small in his chair. He clenched his lips tightly, till they shone almost white. I recognized the gesture. It was the expression of pain. The one he wore when my mother screamed something particularly cutting in front of my sister and me.

Senator Eastland kept this rattail cigar clenched tightly in his sneering lips. Each time he leaned forward he blew smoke in my father's face. He spit out his questions like chunks of rotten meat. *"What makes yew think yew're qualified to be a judge? . . . How long have yew been a lawyer? . . . I understand that yew weren't born in this country, is that true? . . ."*

Of course I was high on something, even then. A handful of Mom's tranqs, if I'm not mistaken. But that just made the moment more absurd. It did not make it any less painful. Absurdity and pain, I was to spend the greater part of my life relearning, are not mutually exclusive. Not even close.

The horror was doubly amplified by the fact that Eastland had scheduled the hearing on Yom Kippur. And my father, the Jewish immigrant, faced the conflict of his life even as he faced the opportunity of a lifetime: whether to make a stand or swallow his pride and accept the bigot's terms. Which he did, and for which he paid.

By way of reconciling the gnawing conflict: attending a lower-class inner-city public school after my father's ascendance to the judicial heights, it was decided that, for my junior and senior year, I'd be sent to a boarding school. I'd never known anybody who went to prep school. But the prospect, from the PR-driven pamphlets that flooded our mailbox once the decision was made, loomed at once tantalizingly thrilling and frightening.

Since my father would be spending much of his time in Philadelphia, it was decided a Pennsylvania school would be best. And the academy decided on, as fate would have it, was a blue-blood haven by the name of the Hill School. The Hill, I was to learn, boasted a tradition as snotty as Exeter's, if not quite as well-known. Scions of the rich and well born, from James Baker to Bunker Hunt, Oliver Stone to Harry Hamlin, attended the Hill.

"Culture shock" does not even begin to capture the awesome social scare thrown into me my first, fatal days in the company of these sons of the ruling class. For starters, I'd never even seen a stereo. Never learned how to tie a tie. Never, needless to say, done drugs the way they did drugs here.

Before heading for Pottstown, PA, site of the sweeping campus—literally up on a hill, above the native peons—I was shipped off to a place called Wolfeboro, in New Hampshire, to attend summer classes to ready myself for the academic rigors to come.

It readied me all right. But not in any way that had to do with algebra. No, it turns out the only other Hillies shipped to summer camp were the fuck-ups. Gifted, underachieving discipline problems. Which, this being the year of Our Stoned Lord 1969, meant the druggies.

You can imagine how badly I wanted to fit in when one of the older guys at the camp popped into my tent and made his friendly intro. His name was Sipes. He wore baggy shorts and Top-Siders—neither of which I had ever seen before—and looked exactly like young Leslie Howard.

"So, Stahl," he asked, flopping down on my absent roommate's cot, "what do you like better, mescaline or acid?"

Well, it's not like I'd done a lot of either. I'd done mescaline once, when I was fourteen and my sister slipped me some, but that was it. So of course I told him the truth. As casually as I could I said, "Acid. As much as I can get. As much as I can do."

And that was that. My fate was sealed. Those were the days, for those of you who never lived through them, or have since forgotten, when people were divided into two groups. Heads and straights. Jocks and hippies. Freaks and squares.

By the time the school year rolled around, and I was actually in Pottstown, wearing a school tie and blazer every day, complaining with the rest of the guys about the mandatory haircut—short hair was bad news—I'd already established my freak credentials. It was at Hill that I really learned how to do drugs: all the time, and like you weren't doing them at all.

My buddy Sipes, and the other grotesquely monied sons of Industry giants, taught this bonehead working-class geek from Pittsburgh how to gulp 800 mics of blotter and maintain at dinner with the headmaster and his ferret-faced wife, or make it through chapel without screaming at the blood dripping off the stained-glass saints.

When I returned to the school after my father's death, my

junior year, it was with the lovely, liberating peace of mind that NOTHING MATTERED ANYMORE. If a man like my father, who never did anyone any harm, who had, in fact, helped mankind immensely, if a man like him could just die like that, what was the point?

After that my already considerable consumption rocketed into the boundless category. Something happens when you do hallucinogenics daily, for weeks at a time. You walk through a door in your brain. It shuts behind you and you just don't care.

It was all about staying deadpan. Where better to learn about taking drugs than in a community of the absolute straightest people in the world? Prep school was like narcotic boot camp.

All the older guys I admired took vast quantities of drugs. Of course I can't name any of them now. They've all gone on to take their true place as Captains of Industry, stalwart and substantial Republicans, whom it would not be cricket to expose as youthful flame-brains. By my last two years of prep school I could not conceive of an earthly existence that was not spent inordinately, inappropriately high. Even if no one knew it but you.

Over the years, of course, the chemicals changed. But never the attitude. In a way, I suppose, drugs helped me sustain my adolescence, this absurd stance of fuck-the-straights rebellion, right up until the time I kicked smack for the last time.

Not until I stopped doing drugs altogether did I feel like a man. Not until I walked out of that fire did I have any idea what the word even meant.

It feels like I went right from pubescent to senior citizen. But what are you going to do? I'm lucky I caught myself. I might have ended up the only man in the rest home who still thought Jack Kerouac was cool.

So I'm talking to the one writer I know, Hubert Selby, Jr., the man who wrote Last Exit to Brooklyn *and a soul who's slogged through his own share of trauma, narcotic and otherwise, in his sixty-five years on the planet. I'm talking about the fact that, up to now, I thought my childhood was okay. Not great, but more or less okay. But now that I'm writing about it, I can only come up with nightmares. The scary interludes that erupt like fissures in the normal reality. Whatever that was. . . . So that the whole thing comes off like some kind of horror show. And Selby says sure, that makes sense.*

"What do you expect?" He laughs when I tell him I'm dying behind the fact I can't write happy when I look back at the kid shit. I can only write grim. "What the fuck do you expect?" he howls, giving me that demented cackle. He's a slight man, almost not there at all, missing most of his ribs and three-quarters of his lungs. He says he's been dying since before he was born. And it shows. All his weight seems to be in his eyeballs. He looks like a demented Donald O'Connor: black Irish, with a crazed laugh and scorched blue eyes that see through the back of your head and into the universe.

"Listen to me, man, you're not going to write about what you had for breakfast every day. You're not going to write about the three squares Mommy and Daddy put on the table.

You're going to write about what hurt you. What fucked you up. . . . Just make sure, when you're writing about it, that you do it with love. That's the secret. Write about the torture. But before you sit down to write about it, pray. . . ."

Which feels exactly right. What gets chronicled are the scary interludes, as opposed to the normal-dormal stuff. I haven't described our house—I've only told you about the holes my father smashed in the doors and walls. That's just how it comes out.

It's as if there's a landscape—we'll call it childhood—which exists in your mind. It's completely familiar. Unspeakably familiar. Until in the middle of the night, when the sky is blackest, lightning cracks through the firmament. And in the crush of sound, amid the madness and the blinding flash, you see your world: home, trees, rooftops, your own hand, in an entirely new way. Illumined by fire. Flashed for half a second and then gone. And it's that image, that savage, rip-through-the-curtain vision, that lingers. Not the reality you see every day. Not the world you walk around in. No, it's that spookhouse glimpse, the scorching peek through the blackness, that stays in the brain.

That's what you remember. Or, if you're a writer, what you write about. . . . That's what's so strange. Sometimes I feel like a writer, sometimes I just feel like a snitch. Although, in the end, the only person I'm ratting out is myself. At this point, I don't even know the difference between truth and shame. If it hurts—if I don't want to say it—then it must be true. That's the only compass I have.

The trick is to lay out the soul but let the brain and body float on and on.

Which is what, with that needle in your arm, you think you're doing. Until you realize, inevitably, that you're not. That you're just generating more pain, more penance for the one sin you couldn't help commit. The sin of being born.

That's what you remember. Or [illegible] [illegible] [illegible] [illegible] [illegible] [illegible] [illegible] [illegible] [illegible] [illegible] Sometimes I [illegible] [illegible] [illegible] [illegible] [illegible] [illegible] Although, in the end, [illegible] [illegible] [illegible] [illegible] [illegible] [illegible] [illegible] [illegible] [illegible] [illegible] [illegible] [illegible]

PART FIVE

TV I.V.

By the time I hit *thirtysomething,* I had this bad habit of spraying a bloody jumbo Z on the tiles of whatever TV show toilet I happened to be shooting up in. Kind of like an intravenous Zorro. It was my way of saying "Just because I happen to be here, writing an episode of *thirtysomething,* that doesn't make me ONE OF YOU REEBOK PEOPLE!"

Maybe I *did* overreact, tweaked by that nasty, subconscious realization I just couldn't shake: *I was perfect for the show.* The horror! Because I *had* the wife, the home, and there was probably a baby on the way. And some part of me wanted all that. I hated admitting the extent to which I could relate to the very things I considered most despicable.

To enter a story session for *thirtysomething* was to enter a chamber of privileged pain. Requiring not just a stash of well-banked anxiety, but the smarts to articulate it in TV-ese. Shoot me up with Einstein's brain fluid, and I still couldn't outline my way from trunk to car seat. The left side of my brain had succumbed to atrophy years ago. During our first story meeting, Ed Zwick, the Harvard-trained half of the duo who came up with the concept of prime-time Yup Opera, literally barked after my recitation of plot: "That doesn't mean anything. . . . That's just sentences!"

TV kings are allowed to bark. That's their right. But, sensitive flower that I was—he only did it once—this had the odd effect of rendering me utterly incapable of finding my simple way from the third-floor elevator door around the corner to the Bedford Falls office. I dreaded the mere chance of a barkfest. I used to sit in Marshall Herskovitz's office, during these endless sessions, and gaze up at the medieval tapestries that graced his walls.

Once inside the office, awaiting my turn at story bat, I'd sit on the low-slung reception couch, pretending to leaf through magazines but actually watching my wife through her open office door. Can there be a more peculiar sensation? I was handled no differently from any other seedy scribe. Made to wait until two-fifty if the meeting was at two. Handed the obligatory coffee or Evian, then planted in a corner to gather dust until somebody remembered to water me.

These were strange hours, the ones spent slumped behind a *Hollywood Reporter,* trying not to stare at my "better half." The sight of her sharp, Dunaway-esque features, framed in that shock of silver hair, held me rapt. She'd scrunch in grim concentration over her stack of scripts, one hand cocking receiver to ear, the other scribbling furious little notes to flash at her wistful helpmate—things that absolutely had to get done! The whole little docudrama evoked the oddest sensation. This is my wife, I'd think, but why? Twenty minutes skulking and staring, and I was asking the receptionist just where that elusive men's room had got to. Because there was something in there I just had to take care of.

This was a pattern: As whatever producers I was slated to meet harrumphed or checked their Rolexes, I'd be hunkered down in the power bathroom, daintily arranging my needle, spoon, and wadded plastic-wrapped chunk of heroin on the slab of paper towel I'd arranged, like some tiny narcotic picnic blanket, on the floor before my feet.

I remember my first or second shift at MTM, seeing the clean white linen tennis shoes I recognized as Mister Zwick's, doing the men's room dance from sink to urinal,

urinal to sink. While I, on the other side of the stall door, clenched that sleeve in my teeth and softly, lovingly, secretly, eased the needle into my throbbing vein, watched with awe and reverence as the blood from my own body flowed back and up the blessed needle. Then I pressed down gently, shoved the poppy nectar, now stained red, slow as glacial erosion into my bloodstream and off on its holy journey north to heart and onward, upward, to the waiting portals of my brain, where the high priest waited, welcoming the latest flagrant sacrifice to the God of Solitude, the God of Strangeness, the God of Sweet and Terrifying and Secret Ecstasy. While Ed Zwick shook his dick and hummed the theme from *Exodus* three feet away. (At least I think it happened—but I was on drugs.)

I can't tell you the feeling of walking back into that office to see rabbinical Marshall and his partner, no-nonsense Ed, already seated with their pads on their laps, waiting to see what I could do. Because the real rush is not just the pleasure bomb behind the forehead. It's knowing, as you stare into the unsullied eyes of your compadres, that every cell in your body is screaming either "Hallelujah!" or "Kill me now!" as you sit and listen to workaday badinage with an expression of interest willed onto your face.

My script, entitled "Born to Be Mild," concerned the efforts of much beloved Hope and Michael to get away for a "fun" weekend. The first time (here, as we industry pros like to say, is the kicker) these two upwardly mobiles have been able to get away since the birth of their beloved Janey.

They decide to give their friends Elliot and Nancy the responsibility of taking care of the little tyke. But when those two come down with the flu, Ellen and Woodman, two lovebirds who are spending their first weekend together—housesitting at Hope and Michael's, get it?—are suddenly saddled with the task of taking care of l'il Janey.

Needless to say, it's network hellzapoppin'! The high point, for me, is when Robin Leach gets to pop in a fantasy cameo and give the guilt-ridden Hope and Michael the Worst Parents of the Year Award. Do you think Mister *Lifestyles of the Rich and Famous* knew he was mouthing smack dialogue? Do you think he'd care? Does being a horsehead, while we're on the subject, count as a "lifestyle"?

The night before we moved into our dream home, Sandra had to work late and I was under yet another deadline. I decided this would be a good time to spend some time in the new place. I figured I'd head over there, get loaded, and do some scriptwriting.

There's nowhere I like better than an empty house. Here damage has not yet been done. Completely devoid of effect, my new home invoked that place in me that only drugs can ever touch.

Once there, I go directly to the Beany and Cecil shack in back. Failure breathes all around me. I unearth a battered black end table, a rusty folding chair. All I'll need for the night. Then I stand outside, beside the prehistoric cactus. For the first time I see its strange white flowers start to blossom. Waiting for moonlight.

I grab the chair and table and drag it upstairs into what will be our bedroom. I set up my little workstation. Portable typewriter plunked on the skinny black table. Chair unfolded in front of it, facing the window.

I take the typewriter, fumble for an outlet, hit the switch. But the power's off. Nothing for it but to sit down. Don't need electricity to run a book of matches. And there's plenty of water in the pipes. So I measure out water in the spoon and fire up four matches at once, in the one-handed style I've come to master since drifting into heroin. One hand to hold the spoon high and steady, the other to fold and drag the matches across the striker. Then I lift up the roaring flame and hold it an inch or two underneath. Heat it up to but not beyond a bubbly boil. Don't want to cook off the good shit. No. . . . The smell smarts in my nostrils. It's the stinging prelude to the main course. The scent of burning earth and metal.

I swirl the now chocolatey spoonful back and forth, to mix it up, and set it gently on the hand-me-down table. The syringe—a new one, for the occasion, jaunty orange cap still wedged over the needle—has been tucked into my sock. I've got a Q-tip in my pocket, too, and dig that out to pluck a fluff of cotton off one end and roll it into a tight white ball. Drop the cotton in the spoon—sans Q-tip, belly button lint will do—blowing like a careful mother on her baby's soup, and watch the compressed wad expand with the stuff I need.

Why take off my belt? I'll just rip out that Smith-Corona cord. It's useless anyway. Wrap the white plastic once around my arm, stuff the plug in my mouth, bite and pull.

There is no pain. Easy as a knife in warm butter. I draw back the plunger, and even in the waning light the furious scarlet of my own blood seems to glow. Alive with promise. Now I sigh. Take a long, deep breath—just like yoga—exhale in time to the slow, downward thrust of my thumb on the flattened white top of the tube.

You don't exactly hallucinate on smack. But you do see, when the first, fast rush courses north to glory, the smiles of all the unseen beings in the world nodding in the shadows. All the benevolence hidden in the universe makes itself known. The spirits reveal themselves, because they know, when the rushing stops, and the gush wears off, you'll forget all about them. You'll see the world then in a different way: as an awful, hateful place, where every breeze that blows is like the hateful breath of Moloch on your flesh.

I sit there, staring out over the swaying palms, over the rooftops, to the red sun sinking in the far-off ocean with a hiss whose steam I feel across my flesh.

I don't think I knew what was going to happen in that home: how I'd blow my marriage, be brutally strung out, barely escape murdering my own baby through sheer narcotic carelessness. . . .

But I knew, as the sighs of a city full of troubled sleepers gathered in my heart, that there would be life here beyond what I imagined life to be. That the charged peace I felt within these four bare walls would be the last peace I felt.

Soon the furniture of my new life would be delivered. The stage would be set for my high-priced demise.

Not that I didn't try to change. There is, in the shell game that passes for drug treatment in America, a "solution," as it turns out, that drags the desperate shooter deeper into the very shadow-world he or she ostensibly wants to escape.

We're not talking about "rehab" here. At this point, aware of the abyss but not yet cognizant of either its quicksand depths or sheer and gripless cliffs, I still thought there was an easy way out. I thought I could sort of ease my way from hell into at least some non-narcotically tormenting purgatory. I thought I could go on methadone.

I've since learned if you want to find out where to cop, the best thing you can do is let your fingers do the walking: track down the methadone clinic, hit a cash machine, and show up at six in the morning when the hard-core clientele is on hand to gulp its dose and tend to the business of securing its own various and sundry chemical inventory for the rest of the day.

It's not like the stuff exists as some kind of cure. In a truly arcane bit of pharma-coincidence, my stints on jungle juice represent one more brush with the spoors of Nazi-dom.

Methadone, see, was actually invented by Third Reich medicos. Looking for a cheap way to numb the pain of injured Aryans, Hitler's research team came up with this morphine substitute. They called it "dolophine," in loving tribute to Adolf himself. As if every pain-racked amputee could ease his agony with the juice of *der Führer.* It's truly heart-warming. Except, on its transfer from the Fatherland to Marlboro country, the swells in charge figured even junkies might balk at swilling eau de Adolf on a daily basis. So they came up with "methadone."

The actual trek down to the legal dopehouse necessitates some advance work I've been trying not to think about. I can't just hop out of bed at the crack of dawn and disappear without *some* sort of explanation. I always said, by way of squirmy humor, that I stayed with Sandra because she had my favorite quality in a woman—complete apathy. But even apathy extends only so far.

I remember I had to shoot a little heroin to inform my wife of my problem shooting heroin. How could I not? And I remember the pained silence my announcement received. We were in a sushi bar.

Well, thank God for sake! In the lull between my bombshell and any kind of reaction—stunned, furious, hurt, depraved or otherwise—I had time to down an entire vase full of warm and soothing rice wine. Between pre-restaurant bang and in-restaurant guzzling, I had enough artificial nerve padding to handle the anticipated explosion of grief and recrimination.

Sandra's good manners told her to wait until our server, a nicotine-fingered Osakan named Hiro, backed away with our soiled wasabe plates. Then, with a steely self-possession that simultaneously scared and gratified, she put together her clipped response.

"Fine. If you think that's the right thing to do, that's fine."

No "How could you?" No "You fucking loser." No "What's wrong with your head?" Not even a "How long do you think I'm going to stick around for this shit?" or "How much is it going to fucking cost? . . ."

Which made the whole deal more tolerable and infinitely worse. I felt like a salamander wrapped in human flesh. My own breed of Jewish sushi. This wasn't how I'd imagined it would go at all. I'd pictured my doe-eyed lifemate breaking down and me leaning across the table, possibly singeing my soul patch on the restaurant candle, and offering dollop after dollop of brave and admirable rhetoric. "Baby, I know I done wrong, but together we can work this thing out, I'll make it up to you, you'll see!"

Her response left me utterly tongue-tied and unable to shut up.

"Sandra, listen, it's not you, you know. . . . I mean, what I do, this fucking dope, it's got me. . . . I just can't, like, I can't handle it, everything that's going on. The TV, the money, the house, the marriage. . . . I mean, it's good, it's just, my own luck scares me. . . . It fucking scares me, I mean, I don't know. . . ."

Sandra just stared. The expression, on those thin ruby lips, hovered somewhere between heartbreak and morbid fascination.

The dim lights, the mirth and frenzy, the fast-chattering Japanese and the knives dicing fish on the butcher block, all sang and whirred around us.

I waited for Sandra to look at me, give me some kind of a sign, but she never did. She wasn't cold, she wasn't warm. She just wasn't. Our eyes didn't meet the rest of the evening.

The clinic was a concrete bunker tucked off Olympic Boulevard, innocuous as a radiator repair shop, consisting of a single, stained linoleum-floor waiting room with funky metal chairs lining either wall and a wire-mesh dispensing cage at the far end. Mimeographed AIDS and TB warnings curled off the peeling yellow walls, flanked by drab etchings of syringes and coffins over a splash of Spanish even I understood. *PROBLEMA CON DROGAS?*

Right off, what you noticed about the people waiting were their tattoos and their eyes. The green jailhouse ink and the hard dead stare of the majorly incarcerated. It was like we were all sitting on a giant bus to nowhere. Blacks, Anglos,

Latinos . . . all washed up on the shores of maintenance. Staring at nothing in the dingy waiting room.

A white guy beside me, a rangy greaser with arms emblazoned by a crude maze of spiderwebs, barbed wire, naked pouting ladies and, inscribed lovingly across the back of his neck, *100% PECKERWOOD,* eased sideways on his plastic chair and started to chat.

"Fucking methadone, that shit's sick!" He kept his bear-greased pompadour—done up in the Chicago Boxcar style I hadn't seen since my youth in Pittsburgh, high on the sides and flat on top—aimed straight ahead. Looking at the wall opposite. He kept his voice low, too, and talked out of the side of his mouth. "Shit gets me off the stuff, okay? But when I'm off the stuff I start shooting that damn 'caine. And I don't even like 'caine! Damn 'caine makes me crazier than I was on stuff. I was a pussycat on stuff! Plus I put on twenty-five pounds. Man, you ain't supposed to gain weight on 'caine. Somethin' wrong with this shit, brother. Gotta get back to the joint, lose some of this fat. . . . You wanna buy some 'caine?"

A battered door just left of the dispensing cage led to a pocket of offices and a pair of toilets. There were no men's and ladies'. Due to the traffic necessitated by piss tests—a way of life for parolees and methadoners—there was a constant, resentful parade in and out of the restrooms.

After a minor wait, a sullen Latina in a lab coat handed us each a page of forms to fill out and indicated the high school desks we were to sit in while we labored over the Q&A.

My own desk was graced by a baroque and lovingly carved message in the Formica: LA VIDA LOCA.

How far I'd come. . . .

DO YOU USE HEROIN EVERY DAY? YES__NO__

DO YOU REGULARLY USE WHEN YOU WAKE UP OR WHEN YOU GO TO BED? YES__NO__

HOW MUCH DO YOU USE? BEST ESTIMATE:____

HAVE YOU EVER OVERDOSED ON ANY DRUGS? YES__NO__

HAVE YOU EVER BEEN IN A JAIL, HOSPITAL, OR DRUG REHABILITATION CENTER BECAUSE OF YOUR USING? YES__NO__

IS YOUR DRUG USE MAKING LIFE AT HOME UNHAPPY? YES__NO__

DO YOU EVER QUESTION YOUR OWN SANITY? YES__NO__

DO YOU HAVE HEALTH INSURANCE? YES__NO__ (please list)

I breezed through the questions, stumped only by the "how much" number. I bought by the dollar. I hadn't hit either the by-the-gram or the balloon stage. Still, ever the diligent student, I checked and double-checked my answers. I don't know if I expected an "A" or a full scholarship to Dope School.

My fellow testees, a couple of Latino sweethearts so young it looked like they cut geography to sneak out and hit the clinic, huddled together over their forms, dark heads almost touching. They muttered quietly in Spanish. The young girl, dressed identically to her boyfriend in giant plaid flannel shirt and baggy khakis, reached occasionally across her own desk to wipe her strung-out Romeo's sweat-shiny brow. He was obviously on his way to a full kick. And the possibility that some wrong answer might veto liquid relief clearly tore at him.

The same time I finished my form and pulled myself out of the chair, the Cholo slammed down his ballpoint. He laid his head on the desk, crying, so that the tattooed angel on the back of his neck spread her wings for the ceiling. I wanted badly to say something—fill the damn thing out for him if I could—but he and his girl were too lost even to notice me. They were alone, the way addicts without the drugs they need are always alone. No matter who's around. No matter who isn't.

• • •

Dr. Farrell, the man in charge of screening, turned out not to be bored so much as perpetually overwhelmed. "I see all kinds," he muttered when I walked in and took a seat. "All kinds." It was a minute or so before he looked up, and I'm not all that sure he was even talking to me.

That moment of awkward silence gave me a chance to take in the cubicle. There wasn't an inch of wall space not covered with posters. Sports posters, from Magic Johnson to Franco Harris to Darryl Strawberry. All African American, all up there, all beaming down. Confronted by the daily parade of sick and suffering supplicants, the man wanted the permanent benediction of all the healthy, functioning, blessed individuals he could cram onto the plaster.

"Gram and a half," he mumbled, reading from my application and still not looking up. "Used a couple of years . . . married . . . employed . . . college education"—at this he paused, but not for long—"no warrants . . . no record . . ."

When he finally stopped and raised his head, the action seemed to cost him enormous effort. "Okay," he sighed, regarding me with all the interest of a street sweeper for last week's comics, "let's see the arms. . . ."

Now, at least, I had something I could be proud of. I was packing a healthy stretch of Amtrak from the crook of my elbow north and south toward heart and fingertips. In those days I was still shooting righty.

"Um-hmm," the doctor said. "Um-hmmm . . . now the eyes."

He didn't use an examining light, didn't even lean across the paper-strewn desk. For all I knew he just wanted to see if I knew how to open my lids. "Um-hmmm," he said again, "how's the heart?"

I told him the heart was okay, what was left of it. But this bit of nervous humor went right by him. Nervous humor wasn't going to make his day any better.

"Blackouts? Fainting spells? Blood in the stool?"

I gave him the answers, and he gave me the form back, with his notes on the bottom, and told me to leave the whole deal with Carmen, the staffer who'd ushered me in. "She'll give you a TB test," he mumbled, "lots of TB around," then he went right back to the next sheet on the endless stack before him.

That was it: no counsel, no communing, no more interaction than you'd get from a toll booth attendant. "We'll put you on twenty-one-day detox," he said as I hit the door. "Start you at eighty milligrams. Tell Carmen to send in the next one."

Back to Carmen, who pricked me on the inside of the wrist—the test left a mark like a snakebite—then laid out the rules of the clinic like a bored waitress reciting the daily specials: hours five to nine or two to six, seven days a week, once you pick your shift, you can't switch, no sunglasses when dosing, urine tests on demand, three dirties and you're out, pay by the day, by the week or in advance for the whole series. . . . "Take a seat and Julietta'll call you for your first dose."

Over and out. I took my seat back in the waiting room among a whole new batch of juice victims. Ironically, the latecomers—we're talking after eight now—looked less penal than the beat-the-rooster crowd. In fact, they were indistinguishable from any cross section of Jane and Joe Workadays on their way to punch a clock. Here I discovered one of the less-known, wholly unexpected secrets of Big League Geeze-dom: junkies are early risers. Unlike most little birdies, they have to get the worm before the worm gets them.

By the time I heard my name mispronounced from the overlarge lass behind the wire-mesh cage, the surly Julietta, I was already wishing I'd gone ahead and arranged a wake-up to tide me over. By accident or cruel design, the voice from behind the wire sang out, "Mister Stale? Mister Gerald Stale?"

I bolted out of my bone-mashing seat. Instead of a holy chalice, I was handed a paper cup. The blood of Christ was Day-Glo orange and warm as piss.

The seconds prior to actually imbibing my first slurp of Nazi juice, I had all manner of second thoughts. (Would Eichmann be chuckling from beyond the grave?) But once I gulped my gulp, I knew I was on my way.

The methadone didn't hit till I was halfway home. When Sandra walked in I was still sitting there. Not so much on the sofa as part of it. Whatever was in that paper cup had made me furniture. The whole day, my cat, Jackie, simply sat at my feet and stared. At some point she simply reared up and began clawing my pant legs.

It must have thrilled Sandra, seeing that the alternative to a husband spinning on the needle was a husband zombied-out on what passed for the cure. But she didn't stay to tell me about it. She settled in with the telephone to make a few evening calls. While I continued to hold down cushions every bit as animate as me.

Next sunrise I was off again. Nobody fucked with me; I spoke to nobody; and, on Day Three, one teased and eyebrow-plucked *chiquita* gave me the are-you-man-enough eye on the way back to my Coupe de Ville. I wasn't, of course, but I was certainly capable of appreciating the option.

Occasionally I'd try to write, then zone out and come back to find I'd been sitting with a pencil in my hand, still as a stage prop, so locked in the neck and lower back that only the fact that the dead don't feel rigor mortis kept me from screaming agony.

Just shy of three weeks into methadone, I made a move

that would warp my life for some time to come. I'd almost completed my twenty-one-day detox.

Since Day One, I'd seen the pockets of wholesome clients huddled together in the clinic parking lot. It didn't take the DEA to know they weren't swapping baseball cards, but, drawn as I was, I knew better than to just stroll over and invite myself into the action. Basically I kept my mouth shut. Held my mud. Nobody hassled me, but they weren't exactly inviting me over for cheese 'n' crackers, either.

Until one overcast seven A.M., as I was preparing to hit the ignition and swing into traffic, I happened to turn my head and caught a vision from hell, a smiling monster, looming in my passenger-side window.

"Yo, brother," said the bobbing monster whose face pressed into the glass. Without thinking, I hit the autolock. The first glimpse of him scared a bucket of adrenaline into my bloodstream. An outsize skeletal cranium, full-boned Cro-Magnon brow and prognathous jaw like the retarded giant in a Diane Arbus photo, all dominated by a glowing strawberry-red birthmark that spilled out of his hairline over his right eye, down past his nose, and over his knife-scarred cheek to taper off over the jail green ARYAN BROTHERHOOD tattoo and disappear under his T-shirt. Sixteen years inside, twelve on methadone, lent that white skin a pallor that set that red stain off like Christmas.

I didn't know what the hell this geek wanted with me. But I'd seen him around before and didn't want to risk running over his toes, then having to come back tomorrow and face whatever weird wrath he'd deem appropriate when I stopped in for my dose.

"Name's Gus . . . Big Gus," he said, sticking a hand the size of a pie plate through the window. "My people call me G."

I switched off the ignition and shook his hand. "I'm Jerry."

"I know that. Got a broad inside." He winked. "You know what?" He made a show of looking behind him, at a gaggle of black junkies on their haunches just beside the parking lot fence, then swung his massive face my way again. "You know what? I'd rather sell to my own people. Fuckin' niggers put a stink on their money. I put it in my pocket, and all day I gotta sniff nigger-stink. Too much nigger-stink, you gotta burn your damn clothes."

I agreed. Like nigger-stink was something I had problems with myself. Like me and him, we were two of a kind. I didn't like myself for this. But you slide past a certain point in life, self-loathing comes easy. No harder than breathing. There wasn't a whole lot of chance I'd stand and deliver an impromptu Brotherhood of Man rap. The closer he loomed, the clearer I could see the faded, flaming swastika tattooed on his forearm.

Big G slipped a hand in his stonewashed jeans. Pulled out a prescription bottle. He held it out, like he wanted me to take a look, then pulled it away quick when I reached for it. His laugh sounded like grinding metal.

"Interested?" He closed his fist, rattled it in front of my face.

"I guess so," I stammered. A part of me might have wanted to hold out, but I knew any resistance was pointless. Face-to-face with this live wire, I just wanted to say the right thing.

"You guess so? Damn straight! You guess so, shit, you know what's in here?" He growled even louder. "Do you know what's in here?"

It was impossible with G to tell a friendly gesture from a threat. Conversation, even under the numbing influence of methadone, was a draining experience.

"Check it out, slick." He flipped the lid off the bottle with one hand, shook out a couple pills, and slid them under my nose. They were tiny as old-fashioned saccharine tabs.

"You know what you're lookin' at? You're lookin' at the best dope in the world. Dilaudids, man. You can't get this shit on the street anymore. Two for fifteen. Honest to God—you find 'em any cheaper tell me and I'll cut the balls off the motherfucker. How many you want?"

Luckily, I had money. I would have bought them if they *were* saccharine. Something about a pumped-up ex-con Nazi with electric pupils didn't brook much quibbling.

"Gimme four," I said. Staying cool as I could. I started to pull the cash out of my pants when the same hand clutching the pills squeezed shut and landed on my shoulder, pressing hard.

"Not here, man. Not here. You wanna go down or what? Rollos all over the place!"

That he'd been standing there, wagging triple-script, federal-regulated pills in my face for the past five minutes didn't seem to matter. I was the one uncool. And I apologized.

"That's all right," he said. "That's all right. Drive around the corner."

With this he hopped in the car, slammed the door behind him and shouted "Go! Go! Go!" like Daryl Gates was hanging on to the bumper by his thumbnails.

"All right," I shouted, picking up on what I believed was his panic. Except the second I floored it, that meat-hook grip was back on my shoulders. The freak show mug looming hot-breath close to my own face. "What the fuck are you doing?"

"What?"

"Slow the fuck down! You want the cops to stop us? You crazy? Don't drive so fucking fast."

"But—"

"Shit!"

The outsize sneaker jammed down on the brake the same time as mine, mashing into my ankle. The car jolted to a halt.

A truck behind me honked, brakes tearing the air as it jammed to a screaming stop. The guy blasted his horn and I started up again, this time at a moderate pace. As if nothing had happened.

G pounded the dashboard. "All right! That's it!" He buckled forward and whipped his head back and forth in a gesture I hoped signified delight. "All right, cool, a little excitement!"

His laugh was crazed, and he nudged me in the ribs. "Hey, you're all right." He grabbed my hand and shook it in one of those complicated street shakes I could never get right.

I'm embarrassed to say how much I loved having this psychopath ex-con accept me. Big G leaned close, pulled a crumpled paper bag out of somewhere, and pulled out a syringe. The thing was still factory wrapped, clear plastic on top, white paper underneath. Standard flu-shot size. Though it had been quite some time since I'd held my arm out for a flu shot.

G tossed the rig on the seat. I tried to keep steering.

"Figured you might want to start out fresh," he said, gazing out at a Mexican corn-on-the-cob vendor pushing his battered metal cart across the street in front of us. He swerved to miss a homeless lush sprawled across the sidewalk on a patch of cardboard.

G hummed to himself, rocking slightly in my Cadillac, my much-loved land yacht, for all the world like a tourist enjoying the sights. "Check it out," he said, nudging me, nodding toward the facedown alkie as a pair of Koreans stepped out of a grated storefront and over him. "Fucking drunks, they got no self-respect. Bet we could take off those dinks easy as shit. Five'll getchoo ten they got last night's take in the briefcase. Whattya think, they got eggrolls in there? This time of day all the cops are sucking doughnuts. Think they wanna move their fat asses? Tell you what, bro, dope fiends don't piss themselves like wino's. Fuckin' aye! So, you ever run Dilaudids before? Ever do a cold shake?"

I said it had been a while, though the truth is I'd never done it.

"Okay, the deal is, you don't cook these little fuckers. You shake 'em. That's why they call it a cold shake, get it? You're a smart guy. You gotta score one of them little cocaine jars, put in a spoon of water, throw in your pills, then shake the shit till it dissolves. Then you just drop in your cotton, draw it up, and—bingo! So where's the fucking money?"

"I gave it to you. Remember?"

"Three bucks for the pencil," he barked, then grinned.

"Three bucks?"

I wasn't arguing, just trying to make sure I got it right. Whatever mild-ass buzz I'd copped from the fucking methadone, a few minutes in the presence of Big Gus neutralized it.

"Okay, buck and a half. Hey, you're a white guy, right? Us white guys gotta stick together. Give me three bucks anyway and I'll bring you another spike next time I see you."

There was no question that I was going to pay. No question I was going to hop right on the shit again the second I got home. Just holding the rig, feeling the tiny bump the pills made in my shirt pocket, set my heart pounding and my guts churning so severely I had to concentrate on keeping my foot light, not speeding up so I could drop G back off at the clinic and shoot back home to try the stuff out.

I signed on at the methadone clinic to quit, and stumbled into even weightier narcotics. It's enough to make a guy believe in fate.

It's going to be a race. I can feel it in my bones. Between finishing this thing and going out, doing dope again. Every day it's a struggle. I have to say this. It can't be a coincidence, that writing this makes this itch so much itchier . . .

The other morning I was having breakfast with Desiree, the woman I've been seeing. She's what they sometimes call an AMW: actress-model-whatever. Except she does act. She does model. I don't know about the whatever. . . . Anyway, she's blond and tall, beautiful, in a Rams cheerleader sort of way that I'm not used to. What I like about her, as much as anything, is her brain. The unlikeliness—function of my own prejudice—of walking into her pad the first night, seeing her sitting there in a pink lace teddy, reading Céline's Death on the Installment Plan. *It's like seeing Jayne Mansfield on* Meet the Press.

Anyway, that's not what I want to talk about. What I want to talk about is the itch. Yes. How, the other morning, a Sunday, the two of us drove to breakfast at the Pacific Dining Car, near downtown, on Sixth Street. It's a dicey neighborhood, dopewise. And, in the middle of it, here's this holdover from a former era, a nest of genteel dining tucked amid the narco-squalor.

So we finish eating, I'm driving back toward Hollywood, when my car, as if of its own volition, swings right, up

Union. Sixth and Union, for you nonprofessionals, is yet another hub of smack activity. A reliable corner, in a pinch. And at that moment, I felt pinched. Felt driven to use. Driven to cruise by the homeboys squatting on their haunches with their bandannas pulled low over their eyes.

"What are you doing?" Desiree says. She's also, you know, an ex-customer. Though her choice of poison differed from my own. "You're not going to score, are you? Christ!"

"Chill the fuck out, okay? I'm just looking."

"I can't believe this!"

She's not thrilled, needless to say. But I think, at that moment, I think, like, it's okay. That I can handle it.

"It's been a fucking year," I say. "All I'm talking about is a taste. . . ."

"Jerry!"

But I don't answer. I don't even hear her. I'm already out there, projecting myself onto the street, sussing out which homeboy I'm going to saunter up to. The car, I swear, is about to pull over to the curb all by itself. I'm just along for the ride. But I've got the taste now. The tainted metal in the back of my throat. The silverpolish drip.

I'm already reaching in my pocket—thanks to my book deal, I've got a little disposable scratch—when I feel something thump onto my lap like a dropped cantaloupe.

"What the—"

"Fuck you! Just shut up! Shut up!"

It's Desiree, her voice muffled, due to the fact that she's speaking into my crotch. Mouthing her words into the cavern of my open fly as she unzips me.

So there we are, pulled over to the curb in dopeville, and this blond head is bobbing up and down while I'm dreaming of heroin. Until, by sheer will and skill, the dream has been sucked out of me. The itch drained. And I'm just sitting there spent.

Thinking: Is this how it works? Every time you crave "A"

you manage to get "B" instead? Is that it? Life as a process of substituting fixes?

Well, all right, I think. I can live with that.

But now we have to get the hell out of there. I've been so lost, I didn't see the little crowd. The Cholos seemed to like the show. But Desiree, despite her act of love, is no longer speaking to me.

It's all getting edgy. But I haven't scored, that's the important thing.

I drive away, if not happy, then, at the very least, saved.

For now.

Had I known that the stranger with the strawberry-stained face would soon loom so large in my future—larger than love, God, or dignity, the way only a dealer can—had I know that, *can I honestly say I would have done any differently?*

You may think you don't want to throw your life away for mere fleeting euphoria. But, once you get a taste, it doesn't feel so mere.

From then on the planet becomes a waiting room. The rest of your life devolves to no more than the time between highs.

The first morning, tapping the Dilaudids in my shirt, I spun home like a bulimic with the keys to Twinkie-ville. I knew I was "cured." I was no longer strung. But what did that matter? I had eternity in my pocket. The best shit in the world and a steady connect. I was like a man who bent down for his morning paper and found a diamond mine.

Back at the house, Sandra was still sleeping the sleep of the just in the upstairs bedroom. While downstairs, methodically as any hack director bringing his storyboard to life, I set about, one more time, giving flesh to the vision I'd had the very first time I'd set foot in our not-yet-bought abode.

The bathroom was small and white except for the faded blood spray on the ceiling, a flower of pale scarlet I reminded myself constantly to wash off, and rarely did. Once the stuff was in me, a gorged bull moan oozed out of my parted lips. It echoed in my lolling head, and I forgot all about the blood.

Because Dilaudid was a cold shake, you could get careless. You didn't boil anything. Didn't even use a spoon. You found something suitable, ideally one of those little screw-top cocaine bottles. You plopped in your pills and water and just shook until the tiny white pills dissolved down to powder and the powder into dusty fluid.

Now you could have boiled the water. You could have used distilled. All of which I did, for the first week or two, until the impulse to hygiene surrendered to the drive to just get high. Slime that I was, I didn't even have a cocaine bottle. Sometimes people would toss in one of those little spoon-chained-to-the-top coke jugs when you scored the shit off them. But every time I had any cocaine, I always ended up throwing the damn thing away after I used the shit. Telling myself, of course, I'd never do that again. Never. Until, of course, I had the money or the jones, whichever came first. . . .

Instead I used a sake cup. Somebody had given Sandra a little rice wine table set, four tiny cups and one of those miniature urns that fit in the hand and feel warm as life itself when you pour the stuff out. The china was hand-painted: tiny blue-and-green trees swaying over a foaming sea.

This was my ritual, worked out the first day I rolled in from meeting G by the McDonald's. First I'd stop in the kitchen, run myself a tall mug of bottled water from the Hinckley & Schmitt cooler by the fridge.

While gulping, I'd stop to stare out the window over the sink. Just beyond the window stood a twisted apricot tree. Clusters of lush, testicular fruit dangled from leafy branches that kept half the yard in shade. The tree was beautiful to look at, the apricots plump and mouthwatering, even if Malathion made so much as a single bite tantamount to swallowing rat poison. Beyond the toxic apricot, that prop-like R. Crumb cactus rose twenty feet out of the earth, bearing its own strange growths: prickly red orbs that looked like a cross between red peppers and hand grenades. Flaming pink bougainvilleas and heartbreak blue morning glories laced through the fence in back, fronting wild red roses and bright orange birds of paradise. A neighbor's banana tree arced over the blossoms, the first bunches of fat yellow thumbs showing throughout the waxy leaves, its branches heavy with budding nanas.

Anytime at all, you'd spot a pair of emerald hummingbirds, a dozen plump and buzzing bees. Syringe in hand, looking out over my little kingdom, I still couldn't believe the glory of that garden. So much lush splendor. The outsize tropical flowers, the ferns the size of small dinosaurs, like transplanted prehistoric fauna that neither smog nor bad taste in architecture could discourage from blasting out of the earth everywhere you looked. This was life in the urban oasis. . . .

Once my mind snapped back from the garden, I'd pluck one of the sake cups from the nice display on the windowsill. Rinse out any dust or residual goo. The painted china looked nice up there. Sandra had a way of arranging things, making everything elegant and easy on the eye. Everything about our house was spare but tasteful. Her father's charcoal etchings of musicians hung on the walls. A blue marble table, propped on its black pipe sawhorses, graced our dining room. Her gift was for creating an elegant environment. Mine was for destroying it.

Back in the bathroom with my eighth of a sake cup of distilled water, I'd close and lock the door. I'd take off my shirt and pop the plunger out of the syringe. It was always a problem keeping a supply of rigs, and sometimes you had to use the same one over and over, long past its intended life span. Mostly they got sticky, jammed up when you fixed, so you'd have to bear down like a jackhammer, risk having the thing pop out and waste the whole hit. Other times the plastic pusher curled sideways from boiling. The hot water would half melt the thing, and you'd have to pluck it before it curved into a C. Because they weren't made for reuse, they weren't made for boiling. But because you reused them, you sometimes had to.

Everybody had their own way of maintaining works, but my favorite, the one G told me they used in jail, was the ear-wax lube. To keep the action smooth, you'd rub a little of the old gold aural muck in there. That kept things nice and slidey. "Stuff comes out your own body," like Big G said, "how bad can it be?" And so ecological, too!

I'd draw the water up the syringe, drop in two or three pills—that was in the beginning, before I made the leap to thirty—then set the cup down on the sink. After that I'd aim into the cup and squirt the pills point-blank with Hinkley & Schmitt bottled water. By now, like a bartender who could pour an exact shot glass in his sleep, I knew how to use no more water than the syringe could suck back up. Shooting the liquid right on the pills helped break the things down.

After that I'd swish the water around in the cup for a while, trying to work a crumble. And then, when the whole deal broke down to a few stubborn lumps and I couldn't wait anymore, I'd just pull the damn plunger out of the syringe, flip it over, and use the tiny flat part on top, that white plastic disk, in a kind of makeshift mortar-and-pestle deal.

Smashing it could be a messy business. You'd end up splashing your fingers a little; then, in that insane drive to waste absolutely nothing, you'd scrape your fingers, throwing God knows what shower of detritus into the soup and thereby back up the needle and into your veins.

For a while I was only shooting up in the toilet, pants around my knees, sometimes timing the rush to coincide with a healthy bowel movement. I wasn't getting much sex then, needless to say. I wasn't getting much of anything, except a few moments of twisted heart-stopping release, and then that hollow feeling of disappointment, weirdness, and massive, suppressed panic before the sudden jolt to artificial well-being. A state that could last anywhere from minutes to hours, depending. Between the rush and the second stage bliss, always that lake of clarity to be crossed. The thoughts that won't go away. *I'm a guy with his pants off and a needle in his arm. . . . That's how they'll find me. . . .* Lenny Bruce died that way, which is about all you can say for the situation.

But that first morning, experiencing the inner tickle, the self-destructo thrill of knowing you've managed to climb all the way back to the top of the roller coaster, you've finally kicked, you've managed, against all odds, to get off heroin, off methadone, and earn yourself a shot at something like a non-strung-out, non-fear-pain-shame-and-(admittedly)-occasional-bliss kind of existence, and here you fucking go all over again.

The mere thought of my wife, more often than not the bane of my existence, when high filled me with a Hallmark-worthy warmth. In my thoughts she was now adorable, a lovely creature. I couldn't wait to fix her a tray of tea and toast, butter and jam in little jars on the side, just like your finer restaurants, and run it up the steps two at a time just to show her how much I cared. It's as if this saccharine-brained romantic lay dormant inside me, and all it took was a bang of hard narcotics to kill the whiny, out-of-sorts version of myself and bring on Julie Andrews.

"Good morning!" I sang to my just wakened spouse. Her morning face, which sometimes scared me—almost as much as my own—now seemed to me the most appealing visage in the world. I might even have slid back in and held her. That would have been a little extreme for us, but I wouldn't put it past me. There was all kinds of love floating around inside me, but it took the dose of opiates to let it out. On the other hand, what I was feeling was just as likely completely fake: product of triggering busloads of synthetic endorphins to my joy-starved brain, a state that would just as easily have had me loving J. Edgar Hoover, in his secret muu-muu mode, or a bust of Nehru, as the blinking, diminutive, somewhat perplexed, somewhat pretty young silver-haired woman who happened to sleep in the same bed I did.

"Here you go," I said, setting the tray on the bedside table beside the silver clock radio we used to listen to NPR on. "I brought you tea."

"You did?" Her mind could still not wrap itself around the concept of my Jeeves-like attentiveness, my newfound affection. "What's wrong?"

"What do you mean, what's wrong. Nothing's wrong. Can't a guy bring the love of his life a little treat? Here's the jelly you like, Trader Joe's boysenberry. I didn't make the toast too black, did I? I know you like it a little burned, but not too much. . . ."

"Jerry . . ."

"Wait. Let me take the teabag out. It's Earl Grey. That's what you like, right? Earl Grey breakfast?"

"Jerry . . ."

"Hang on, I've got cereal downstairs. I wanted to bring the toast up before it cooled."

"Are you okay?"

"Me? Are you kidding? I'm fine. . . . Be right back. Eat your toast. You want to go out tonight? Maybe go to that Japanese place you like? Invite Janine? Or anybody else? God, you should see how blue the sky is. It's like blueberries in yogurt out there!"

"Jerry . . ." The fluty British tones rolled down the staircase, tickling my ear hairs. "Jerry, are you on drugs again?"

"Of course not. I'm just happy, for Christ's sake. Can't a man be happy?"

"Okay," she replied, and I could almost see the little smile. "Okay, then, bring me the butter?"

"Coming, baby. Coming."

She just didn't trust me—imagine that!—which stung my own dainty feelings so much I had to skip back down and try to squeeze out a third, potent-as-rainwater bang out of the still damp cotton. One thing non-syringe pros don't understand: Once the dope runs out, you've still got the cotton. Which, if you're desperate enough, you'll cook up and water down and squeeze till what you're shooting is basically chlorine. Just to achieve, for that one, endless moment between insertion and injection, the mere possibility of relief. Down the road, this practice would leave me stricken with cotton fever, the hellish, rabieslike condition induced by shooting what boils down to tainted cotton fibers into the bloodstream. It lasts no more than a day or two, but the effects are savage enough to leave even veteran skag kickers chewing the pillowcase and swearing to the strung-out gods that rule the universe they'll never, never ever put a spike in their arm again. Until they do.

By that time, of course, I was probably getting higher from the scent of rubbing alcohol than any residual Dilaudid crumbs. But what the hell? Drug addiction is no different from any other religion. Sometimes the ritual is all that matters.

So what started as a onetime treat progressed immediately to a daily, then twice daily, then ultimately all-day adventure in addiction. I'd begun a pattern that was to define my days for some time to come. Out of the house at daybreak, I'd shoot down Rampart, cut over to Western, then south through Koreatown, past all the beat furniture stores and plastic pod-malls down to skankland. With every block, the clumps of well-scrubbed Latinos at the bus stops— the only people in the city who actually seem to work for a living, cleaning up after all the Anglos who just make money— gave way to smatterings of winos passed out in doorways, then to muttering crackheads, head down scuffling up the filthy sidewalks, vainly scooping the dogshit and broken glass for the one lost piece dropped in the street, compulsively rifling their own shot pockets for the morning hit that could make their hell-sparked circuits hum smoothly for a minute or two, cool out that blast furnace melting all the wires in their eyeballs.

South of Washington Boulevard, just up from Venice, I'd pull into a still shut strip mall parking lot and kill the engine in front of *Bride to Be,* a discount wedding-wear outlet. Gazing at the white-gowned, smiling mannequins—their painted eyes seemed to be telling me something, but I was scared to find out what—I'd wait for Big G's bust-out '76 Bonneville, a rusted baby blue barge, to come lumbering into the lot beside the McDonald's next door. Within a week of meeting G, I was fully Pavloved. I'd see that low-slung Pontiac, and the vultures in my heart would stop circling and start to coo.

It took a week or two before I graduated from parking lot lurker to member in good standing of the Crack o' Dawn Narcotic Breakfast Club. Towering G, see, held court over his own window booth in McDonald's. You have to wonder if Ray Kroc ever knew how much his Golden Arches meant to America's most strung-out citizens. In truth, I've never hit a city where at least one House of Big Mac didn't also boast a booth where locals dished out balloons of smack or linty chunks of crack. If he did know, the late Ray might have at least offered some kind of Drug Abuser Discount. Half-price Egg McMuffins, say, for anyone with track marks fresh enough to bleed.

Every morning G and his regular table mate, Clarice, and eventually me, would sit at the booth, bickering over pills and dollar bills at a table strewn with Egg McMuffins, gummy pancakes, half-gnawed breakfast biscuits, and great piles of abandoned butter pats, nondairy creamer, and cast-off sugar packs. G himself started the day with the giant coffee with five creams and ten sugars, to wash down the half-dozen Valiums that kicked the methadone in.

By the time my two- and three-pill-a-day jones jumped to half a dozen and up—a fraction of what it would be, but still enough to mean heavy, dependable dollars for G and Elmo, his connection—G started shooing the nickel-and-dime customers away, and I ended up joining him and his main partner, Clarice, every morning in their booth. Clarice was a big, shapeless black woman, flesh so puffed by diabetes and methadone she seemed to be melting from the top down, like a bowl of mocha ice cream with eyes. She wore her hair pulled back in a tight bun on her bullet skull. But her features were buried in that mass of bloat. Until she spoke, or burst out laughing, it was hard to tell if she was even conscious, or just a blob that stared.

"Elmo be dying fast. His skeleton be dancing inside his skin, jus' waitin' to hop in the damn grave," she whispered when we first started talking. Elmo, see, had terminal stomach cancer and got the pills from the V.A. Clarice shimmied and made her eyes go wide the way she did when she really had some news about somebody. I saw her make the same face after I was out the door, leaning across the table to tell some other customer about White Guy Me. You really didn't want to know what these people said or thought about you. You wanted to believe they were your friends.

On the home front, Sandra was still heading off to work every day in our new Acura, holding down the fort at Bedford Falls. I hadn't yet signed on board at my TV gig. So every day, for me, was about getting up and tooling down to Mickey D's as fast as I could. I knew G wouldn't roll in till 7:15, but the wait was unbearable at home, and besides, there was always the chance he'd roll in early. Every day, for G and Clarice, was about getting dosed at five, then cutting over to Mickey D's to scrape up a handful of V's to wash down with coffee so they could make it through the rest of the day. Sometimes G had purples, thirty-milligram time-release morphines used mostly for kick pills. But beloved, for some reason, by the mountainous Clarice.

None of the other customers batted an eye at the action at our table. G did not have the kind of face you wanted to risk a wrong look at. He had more ink than Satan: calves, neck, and arms a near solid catalog of tattooed Aryan brotherhood icons: Swastikas, Iron Crosses, barbed wire, doe-eyed naked beauties astride S.S. lightning bolts. Aside from a few sleepy-eyed souls stopping in to get McMuffins to go on their way to work, most of the booths were full of jumpy customers like myself and their various connects, all working their own life-or-death negotiations.

Clarice said G paid the manager off to leave us alone, but I doubted that was ever necessary.

As the weeks rolled into months, my habit once again hit the out-of-control phase. I came to see my time at McDonald's with Clarice and G and whoever else happened to slime by as the only time I could actually feel at peace. Our table was always the hub of commercial activity. Assorted tattooed and jail-hard dudes and their girlfriends with washed-out eyes would sidle up to get what they could from G, who was always on the prowl for Xanax or Valium. No small amount of fury was sent my way, in the form of glares and mumbled threats, over the fact that I bought up the guy's entire inventory on a daily basis. I was, however, G's boy. He even arranged it so that I sat on the inside of the booth, near the window, though whether that was to protect yours truly from the wrath of less fiscally empowered junkies, or to keep me from dashing off without paying, was never entirely clear.

I got to know about G's family—his four kids, two full-blooded Cree by his wife's first husband, who died in a Bakersfield barfight, two of his own—his parole gig in a bakery on Ninth and Vermont. And I learned about Clarice's life as girl cousin to a couple of sixties Motown acts; her stint in a couple of "soul revues"; her three husbands, four daughters, and the son shot dead by the police; and her ongoing battle with diabetes, welfare, warrants, and our mutual friend Gus.

On some level, of course, the social distance was astronomical. It boiled down to that dirtiest of words in American culture: class. Here I was up for a job that paid $3,500 a week, in the world of screenings and dinner parties, trendy restaurants and white ambition. An L.A. as foreign to my narco-breakfast crowd as the survival-level reality of G, Clarice, and the rest of the breakfast denizens was alien to the likes of Sandra and her cohorts. So many of the people I met in Hollywood had money when they got there. Daddy money. Family money. Whatever. They needed it to cover the years of so-called struggle until they hit, in whatever realm they were trying to hit in. Their idea of struggle, compared to the likes of G and Clarice, was absolutely ludicrous, a matter of acne versus leprosy.

Hearing G talking about stealing his boss's wallet, pinching enough to take his family out to Sizzler, where steak dinners cost $6.95, so he could impress his mother-in-law—after I'd slunk through a $100 dinner at Morton's the night before—it hit me somewhere. It was Pittsburgh all over again. White collar at home, blue collar at school. My dad on the news, my friends' dads in the steel mill. Jew to the Christians, outsider to the Jews.

As my habit kicked into overdrive, my night sweats took on tidal wave proportions. Sandra and I hit the sack early. She because she had to get up and work. Me because there was, really, no reason to be conscious. But no matter when I retired, I'd wake up in a sopping wet swamp 'long about two or three, at which point I'd get up to spread a towel over the chilly lake my pores had generated and lie back down again. In another couple of hours the towel would be soaked, and I'd start the whole process over again. 'Long about five I'd give up and get up, then do my wake-up shot, if I had one, or otherwise kill an hour until it was time to shoot down to McDonald's.

Not that I was unhealthy. God, no! I drank lots of water along with that all-important diet of veggies and fruit. Not to mention my rigorous exercise program. I'd shoot up yet another handful of Dilaudids in the afternoon, 'long about five or six, so that I could steam out of the house, run up Coronado, the hill we lived on, and down the back way to Silver Lake reservoir. There I'd jog the three and a half miles around the lake, not once but twice, deluding myself that despite the opiates coursing through my body, with the wind cooling my sweat, my limbs alive with motion, despite so much excess fluid in my bloodstream that my feet swelled from size tens to twelve double E by the end of every day, I was keeping it together. I was, in fact, the Jack LaLanne of junkiedom—even if I did have to sleep with long sleeves on.

My smile was genuine as I shared a little wave with my fellow concerned-enough-about-their-health-to-brave-irate-drivers-and-nose-level-exhaust types. This was healthy California, and I was just another healthy guy. Sure, I'd fixed a minute before dashing out the door. But hey! Junkies could be health nuts, couldn't they? I think they call it "dichotomy." Or maybe the word's "denial."

Once I'd scored, I'd come home and I wouldn't know what to do with myself. Oh, sure, I had gigs here and there. I'm sure I did them wonderfully, just don't ask what they were. It was, at that point, all about what I was "up for." The things I'd be doing soon. Half of being employed in Hollywood is being unemployed between gigs. And I was getting that part down. . . . Back from my morning Dilaudid confab, my loving wife off in her own neck of show biz reality, I faced the hours like any prisoner. Did I want to stay in my cell and read, or did I want to head out to the yard and work out? My confinement was solitary, I just happened to have lots of space.

Some days, with the hours yawning before me, the good shit flooding my veins, I'd drive east on Sunset, then cut up Echo Park and down to Elysian Park. This was where LAPD had their headquarters. It was also where you could run along a dirt path in what felt like authentic East Coast woods. No palm trees, only oaks and maples, trees with leaves. With—and this was even better—a view of the abandoned mills and train tracks down there in Frogtown, along the L.A. River.

On one weird occasion, while running, one of the jarheadesque recruits dropped back and locked in step beside me for a spell of jog-talk.

"See you here a lot this time of day. Guess the acting game's a little sluggish, eh?"

"What?"

I looked at him, to see if he was real. But the junior cop just smiled. He didn't pursue it. His close-cropped red hair and turned-up nose lent him a sort of ur-Archie vibe. As if the comic strip character had dumped Jughead, jumped off the funny pages, and turned up at the police academy to set things right in the world at large. When he caught me checking him out, he stuck out his hand. "Name's Philips," he said. So that we shook on the hoof as we humped up the curving dirt path. Reminding me, for some reason, of those film clips you sometimes see of bombers refueling in midair.

I soon learned that Philips, grotesquely enough, seemed to think my presence on the same running path used by L.A.'s Finest indicated some willingness to sign up.

"You ever"—puff, puff—"you ever think about taking the test?"

Loaded as I was as we panted up the hill flanking the railroad tracks into the woods—as loaded, for that matter, as I've ever been anywhere—the prospect of casting my lot with the Daryl Gates cult never crossed my mind.

So, of course, I had to reply: "I've thought about it."

"Well, you look fit," he said in all sincerity. "You ought to think about it. . . . We could sure use some Jews."

I looked over, but his Archie visage, his open blue eyes, gave me no indication the young man was being anything but honest.

"I'll do that," I said.

"Good deal. . . . I'll see you next time. I got to catch up

with my guys before they think I turned fruit on 'em or somethin'."

"Wouldn't want that," I smiled at him.

"Ten-four, buddy. Think about what I said."

I nodded and waved, watching his snug LAPD-issue shorts disappear up the hill. Wondering if he was toying with me—if he'd seen the bloody tracks I was trying to keep my arms locked tight to hide, or if he was so gung ho he wanted to spread the joy. The odd part is, after seeing him fairly often, I never saw him after that. For all I know they did nail him for a "fruit." Or maybe he had a few tracks of his own to cover.

About this time *Moonlighting* was on the line. Thanks to my old pal Rondo Dicter, whom I knew from my stint in the *Penthouse* den and, more briefly, through our mutual fling for *Real World*, a peculiar humor mag fronted by Alger Hiss's boy, Tony, out of *The New Yorker* offices, I was being invited to try out for still bigger Prime Time torment. Rondo, one of the two or three funniest—and kindest—humans I'd ever met, had at some point made his own move from print to teedly-veedly. Next to legendary plump guy Glenn Gordon Caron, who actually invented the show, Rondo was pretty much "Mister *Moonlighting*." The interview was set up at Jerry's Famous Deli, in Westwood. I'd spent what seemed like aeons rushing off from my first appointment of the day, with stain-faced Gus and the Dilaudid brigade, to my second, with Dr. Wormin in Century City, to try and make some sense of it all.

See, the great virtue of drugs was their capacity to render the mortifying kind of appealing. At least temporarily. With the right petrochemicals, a day job in Hallmark sympathy cards would have been the height of swellness. The real question was why yours truly needed to go this route—to pursue, emotionally and creatively, what he didn't want to pursue; to live a life so fundamentally alienating in all elements that only constant, crushing intoxication made it even halfway livable.

I was excited about my career move, but I knew the career that excited me did not have a whole hell of a lot to do with TV. . . . How better to sort the whole thing out than kick it around with the lovable Dr. Wormin, he of the soft and stocky body, sandpaper complexion, curly just-shaved-off-the-*payess* Yeshiva boy haircut and short-sleeve Penney's sport shirts that showed off flesh so white and fish-like you could have chopped out chunks of his pudgy forearms and used them for barracuda bait?

It was the office that weirded me right out the window. Doctor W. was, by training, a child psychiatrist. His office was stocked with the things troubled children want to play with. Lying back on the couch, I found that my eyes just naturally came to rest on a little playhouse. Stocked with little five-inch action figures of Mom, Dad, Sis and Junior. Mom in her housedress, Dad in his suit and tie, etc., etc.

Each day, when I rolled in, the little Mommy and Daddy dolls would be slumped in different positions in the playhouse. Sometimes the Daddy doll would be facedown in the little living room. Sometimes Sis would be stranded by herself in a bedroom. I couldn't help wishing I could just get up and start playing with them myself. Instead I'd arrive five minutes early, duck in the medical building toilet to fix a shot, and reel into the waiting room and read *Jack & Jill*s until the red light went on and it was my turn to stumble in and stare at the Dysfunctional Playhouse for another fifty minutes.

The dope helped me open up. I'd been to shrinks before, after all. Most of my adult life, in fact. Until then I hadn't made the leap from minor psychotherapy on up to Big League psychoanalysis. This was the real thing, after all. Even if poor Doctor Wormin was an analyst-in-training, and I was well on my way to professional junkiehood.

I didn't ever talk about drugs or my unhappy marriage. I

was one of those patients who expend all their energy trying to convince their shrink how well they're doing.

I was so utterly convincing that at three weeks the man wrote me a prescription for Prozac and told me I *absolutely had* to take them.

"You think I'm depressed?" I asked, gazing longingly at the playhouse, wishing I could arrange little Daddy and little Mommy just the way I wanted them to be. "I don't know if I want to start putting all kinds of weird medicine in my body."

"We should really think about it. We're definitely having a lot of pain." Dr. Wormin always spoke in the first person plural, the royal "we," as if my problems were his problems, too.

"But what"—I remember saying this, and it makes me blush—"but what if we get addicted?"

"There's no withdrawal. No side effects that we know of. Why don't we take them for a week or two, see how we feel, and then we'll make our decision?"

Needless to say, I *was* depressed. Crushingly. But I'd been that way for so long—been, for that matter, raised in a domestic venue where everybody was miserable about just about everything all of the time—that being unhappy was as natural as gravity. I don't even know if I *knew* any happy people, except for my wife. And her emotional makeup, her capacity to actually enjoy life, on a moment-to-moment basis, was so absolutely foreign to me, so alien, I think half my initial attraction for her was just rank curiosity, a desire to get next to a species who breathed an entirely different air from me. What I hoped, I suppose, was that it would rub off. Although, as things turned out, the contagion worked the other way around. She caught misery, and I stayed locked in the same downhill slide I'd started off on right out of the womb.

"What you're saying is, you don't mind being depressed?"

"Well, it's just that I'm used to it. I'm not shouting, 'Thank God I'm a wretch!' from the rooftops, if that's what you're saying."

"We're not saying anything. We're just trying to understand you. Do we remember anything about our floating penis?"

"Excuse me?"

"Your father's . . . you know."

"Oh, yeah. Right."

I knew full well what he meant. He was referring to the first dream I ever had. Also the first I ever told him about. I'd mentioned it my very first visit. A dream—I must have been two and a half, three when I had it—in which I wake in my crib, climb over the wooden bars and down the side, then make my way across our upstairs hall into our bathroom. The bathroom walls, I can still remember, glowed yellow. But the yellow had little red streaks in it, as if someone had painted the room red first, then put on a coat of yellow, like they'd taken out a knife and carefully, slit by slit, cut through portions of the top yellow layer so you could see the original color beneath.

Not until recently did it occur to me this was the first time I saw red on a wall: the leitmotif of my life as soon as I joined the squirting needle brigade. But this was earlier. And what I remembered, as I related to my seemingly rapt analyst—I could tell he was engaged, because his nervous throat clearing, so irritating when things were slow, stopped when we hit a juicy patch—what I remembered was my father, shirtless, bent over the toilet, cursing and hitting his fists off his thighs. *"Goddamn it! Goddamn it!"*

My sister stood on the other side of the bowl, facing him. And, after I shuffled in in my smiling clock PJs, I too stood before the commode and, looking down, saw the object of his wrath. His own penis. His giant red swollen-balled penis, floating on the water. Like a long drowned corpse that had just risen to the surface.

"Goddamn it! Goddamn it!"

That was it: the shining bathroom, the color of bloody egg yolk. My father, seething with muted curses. My sister in her butterfly glasses, absolutely silent. And me, peering over the rim. Afraid to look and afraid to look away.

"As a matter of fact," I said, "I *have* been thinking about that. Sometimes it's all I think about. No matter what I'm doing, inside I'm hearing my father's hiss, seeing the shine in my sister's glasses. Feeling my own mix of panic and shame, fear that I somehow caused what happened and dread that it's somehow going to happen to me."

"Of course, of course," he'd say, and I'd hear the scratch-scratch of his pen on the pad.

The more I attended these heavy-duty sessions, the more I realized they had *nothing to do with my life.* I was shooting up ungodly quantities of narcotics five times a day. I was waking up in a toxic puddle. My feet were swollen the size of Bigfoot's. I hadn't had sex with my wife since Michael Jackson got his nose fixed. I'd just pulled the damn needle out of my vein five minutes before waltzing into the fucking office—*of course I'll talk about my dreams!*

I talked about my *Moonlighting* gig with Wormin before I actually signed on. I had once before, since coming to his office, said yes to a gig I didn't really want. One I thought would look good, if it could just *be done,* you know, as opposed to actually having to do it. Doc W. told me, as they say in the self-help world, that it was "okay" to back out of the gig if I didn't want it. Which is exactly what I ended up doing. He had, in other words, established his credentials as psychoanalytic career adviser. Which made it okay to talk to him about the *Moonlighting* job.

"How much would you make?" he asked when I'd run it down.

"About thirty-five hundred a week."

"Take it," he said, no doubt applying a decade's worth of psychological erudition to the decision.

Which is exactly what I did. But not before the dreaded Westwood deli lunch with legendary Rondo and young Skip Bradley, the staff writer turned exec producer of the Cybill and Bruce show. I didn't know a lot of guys named Skip. Call me deprived. Skips, Chips, and Muffies—even though I'd been shunted to an Episcopalian prep school for a couple of years, I still never glommed on to the big-buck WASP thing. At the Hill School I'd occasionally burn some Grosse Pointe Madras-ass for the price of bogus mescaline, but that was about it.

Now here I was, a hundred years later, waiting at the bagel and poundcake counter in my best long-sleeved junkie duds: black shirt, black pants, black shoes, green skin, to meet with an actual "Skip." To wow him with my ability to take an entertaining lunch. A prerequisite absolutely necessary to land a seat on the ski lift to show biz heaven.

As it happened, I was in the Jerry's Famous Deli toilet when the masters of my fate strolled off Westwood Boulevard to snag a booth and order chow while waiting for my arrival. Which is exactly what I did. I'd already had my McDonald's pow-wow, scored an extra half dozen Dilaudid in honor of the interview, fixed half of those in the shrink's office, a couple more when I got home, and, in a fit of nervous anticipation, the rest right there in the lox-and-halvah-scented deli stall.

By the time I lurched out, past the suspicious glare of the pockmarked busboy sent in by irate bowel-impacted customers who'd no doubt complained that the damn stall had been monopolized for twenty minutes, past the other waiting noshers who now seemed happy as me, I could as easily have lunched with Zbigniew Brezinski and Hank Kissinger, kicking around Cold War anecdotes, as my good pal Rondo and Connecticut Skip.

"Jerry!" I heard a familiar high voice ring out as I lumbered into the main dining room.

"Hey!" I called back, waving like I was standing on the other side of the Grand Canyon instead of two tables away.

"What's the matter?" Rondo asked when I managed to weave between tables, slide out a vinyl chair, and sit myself down. "You're sweating."

"Oh, that," I said, giving a little wink like it was the most natural thing in the world. "I just came from the gym."

Both Rondo and Skip, who looked like a sort of grown-up Dennis the Menace in requisite Reeboks, ironed blue jeans, and buttoned-down blue Oxford cloth, exchanged funny glances. Maybe it was the wink that threw them, more than the copious perspiration. For some reason, when I was high I was always winking. Like me and whoever I was aiming my eyeball at shared some enormous, tremendously private bit of humor. I'd always hated men who winked. It went along with wearing cologne and calling waiters "buddy." But what could I do? Once under the influence, my right eye had an insipid and unstoppable life of its own.

Once at the table, the first order of business was coming off as a "Regular Guy." You know, the kind of fellow you want on staff. An easygoing, "show-up-at-the-*Moonlighting*-versus-*Highway-to-Heaven*-softball game" kind of guy. Since, in the well-known hotbed of "the room," as the place where all group TV writing supposedly gets done, it's important that all parties coalesce to a single, plot-driving, laugh-happy gaggle of young Americans.

First order of business, then, was establishing my Regular Guy credentials. Which meant, among other things, proving I could gobble lunch without turning my lapels into a Jackson Pollock project. See, I've always had this innate fear of meal-meetings. I'm not sure what this stems from. Spending half my life eating standing up over the sink in roach-laden hovels must have something to do with it.

So while Dicter and Skip went the lox or burger route, yours truly made that all-important salad move. The meal that says "Look at me, I'm a health nut." It opened me up for all sorts of good-natured ribbing. The kind vegetarians in a meat-eating cosmos are open to. Which was fine with me.

Since I'd much rather take shit for my broccoli than my bloody veins.

Young Skip was quick to hop on the veggie-bashing bandwagon. And Rondo D. was right there with him. Me and Rondo, see, went back a little. In fact, the last time we'd even seen each other, years and years ago back in Manhattan, was in a Times Square strip bar after a meeting with the go-go literary crowd up at *The New Yorker.* Not that either of us had any deep love for such joints, we just needed to soak our brains after so much gentility.

"Wow, man, I don't think I've ever had a fruit-and-nut eater on staff before. Is this, like, a moral thing? Like, Oo-wow! I won't eat anything that has a face!"

"Fuck that," I said. "I'd shoot a cow just to watch it die. I just don't want to eat it."

"Heavy," he said.

"Go ahead and laugh, man. I once did a magazine piece on the hormones they put in beef and chicken. They put so much estrogen in cows to fatten them up, you could end up in a D cup just from eating a cheeseburger. It's like the Butterball turkey thing. When you chow down on a Butterball, what you're chowing down on is a giant tumor."

Of course it was a lie. I hadn't exactly done a story on beef raisers. I'd done a paragraph blurb in *Hustler* about ten years earlier—when I'd first gotten to L.A. and run their "Bits 'n' Pieces" section—on this new strain of chickens that laid garlic flavored eggs. But what the hell. I'd been in Hollywood long enough to know that there's nothing your TV and movie guys respect more than "real writers." A motley category that includes everyone from newspaper hacks and feature magazine scribes to actual sit-down-and-grind-out-a-novel pilgrims.

"So," said the chipper Skip, tamping his pampered WASP lips the way they train you to do back there in the wilds of Connecticut. "What do you think of the show?"

I have to admit for one bad moment I forgot what show

they were talking about. I was obsessing on potential elbow drip, the velvety blood droplet I imagined worming south down my forearm, over my wrist, and onto my palm like a sudden stigmata I'd have to explain by saying I'd just, that morning, found out I was up for sainthood.

"What I mean," Mister Skip went on, mistaking my confusion-induced silence for strategic thoughtfulness, "do you think last season had the same freshness as the original year? I mean, some of Rondo's stuff, like the Shakespeare show they did? That stuff was so creative, it's like people tuned in every week to see what we were going to be next."

"Exactly," I said. When in doubt agree. CAA had shipped over a few *Moonlighting* tapes. I watched part of one, but—don't take this, please, as evidence of anything resembling snobdom or superiority—they were too fucking frightening. I couldn't even look at Bruce Willis without groping for Alka-Seltzer. That whole wink-at-the-camera, look-at-me-I'm-cute thing. Cybill Shepherd, at least, seemed wholly miserable, so uncomfortable, like she was trapped in the TV screen and couldn't wait to get home and take a shower, I kind of related.

"What I think," I said, hoping the dope would mutate, as it sometimes did, into something resembling intelligence as it oozed out of my cracked lips. "What I think is, people want to like the show. You know? They love the characters. They've got a relationship with it."

"But what about their relationship?"

"What do you mean?" The seat was getting slippery, but I did the furrowed eyebrow thing, the concerned gaze I used for magazine interviews when I smoked too much pot in the parking lot and just had to appear *present.* So I could get home and play the tape later just to see where I'd been.

"You know," Skip said, "the biggest ratings boost we got was when they went to bed together."

"Exactly." For some reason I couldn't stop saying that word.

"What we have to do," Skip went on, "is find a way to recreate that tension. The will-they-or-won't-they thing."

"Exactly!"

I could see Skip cast a sideways glance at my benefactor, Rondo. "I mean," I blurted suddenly, "I don't think we have to treat the fact that they consummated their relationship as some kind of problem. I think we can treat it as an opportunity."

"You mean, make the audience see where it goes from here?"

"Exactly."

"You mean," my host fired back at me, "make the people at home feel like they're involved?"

"Exactly."

And so, of course, I got the gig.

As ever in TV, the writer's job is to hash out vast tracts of dialogue so other, more advanced and established chat-hands can take each word and elevate it to their own lofty standards. That was fine by me. All I wanted, tucked away in the grandeur of my pea green, locked-from-the-inside cubbyhole of an office, was to be left alone to inject the brain tonic it took to nullify the shame of my existence in proper, leisurely fashion and still get paid.

By now the schism between those daily wake-up treks to Western and Venice and my eventual studio destination became ho-hum.

After copping, I'd cruise on through those studio gates down there at Twentieth Century–Fox, park my big black Caddy, skip up the steps to our barracks-like headquarters, and wave hello to the nervous prepster who manned the helm there in Bruce and Cybill Central. Skip, as it happened, liked to reminisce about his days gulping Quaaludes on the streets of Westwood. He'd been there, by God! He wore paisley! He was *hep!*

The whole process became so normal, it was only the fact

that I knew enough to keep it a secret that reminded me the rest of humanity might view it as a tad peculiar.

When things started getting out of hand, I tried to put on the brakes. I tried to find some way to curb what was, as anyone who cared to could see, my rapid mental and physical decline. By now my eyes were permanently pinned. I was so far gone on the needle my ribs would have shown through a snowsuit.

Still, I'd manage to arrive at my lovely office a good half hour before everybody else. Just to have the time to settle in, type up a few quick snippets, get high, and make sure the occasional goop that oozed from the crook of my arms did not stain my shirtsleeves. Fervently as Lady Macbeth, junkies spend insane amounts of time just trying to hide their guilty blood.

My *Moonlighting* office was no more than a cubbyhole up a flight of stairs in a long, low building shared by everyone from parking lot stripe painters to studio carpenters, a race of large-bellied, utility-belted fellows bred to hit manhood with a hammer in one hand and a jelly doughnut in the other.

The only way the Fox lot could pass as "Dream Factory" is if your dreams happened to be stocked with Xerox machines, cookie-cutter cubicles and guys who looked like they ordered their hair out of a Hammacher Schlemmer catalog. Of course, there were the odd TV stars spottable in the studio commissary. It packed all the glamour of catching your weatherman at a dry cleaner. *L.A. Law* was taped around the corner, and I'd occasionally spot one of the Big Names, the little gray pear-shaped guy, stepping out of his Acura. There were others of equal renown, mostly little blondes you'd recognize from the TV page, women you never knew were so tiny and had such bad skin until you saw them close up, like they were made entirely out of melted-down Barbie dolls.

When I was loaded and blissed-out enough to actually emerge from my hideaway, I'd skulk around the *Moonlight-*

ing offices. My only friends on staff were the two young guys in charge of the Xerox room. I never got it together to keep a bottle of alcohol in my office, and I was always ducking into their little utility room to borrow theirs, which they used to wipe down the glass top of the copier, claiming I needed it to "clean my typewriter."

I realize now that my fear they'd know what I was really doing—coming back to my office to clean my needles—was completely unfounded. What they suspected is that I was alcoholic, and so hard-core I actually drank isopropyl alcohol to get going in the morning. Don't ask me which is worse.

The dynamics of TV writing are designed to keep creativity at a minimum. Creativity is the opposite of TV. Creativity means sounding like yourself. TV means sounding like whoever wrote the pilot. When you watch a TV series, the characters sound the same week after week. That's why you watch them. Or why you don't. When you're hired, the producers want to know for certain that what you write will emerge as a seamless continuum of what was written before you got there. A really successful series should sound like the same busy soul typed up every syllable.

When it's time for you to write your script, what you do is come up with an "idea." The next step is to "get it approved" by your superior staffers. I don't know why I was amazed at how "straight" all the people on the "creative end" of the show were. On board my season—*Moonlighting*'s fifth and last, though I can't take all the credit—was a worthy crew of gung ho, "Someday I wanna produce my own show!" gals and guys.

Across the hall from me, in a really *big* office, was Miss Linda, a Virginia-bred "Young Adult" novel writer who reminded you of the gentle schoolmarm folks were always trying to marry off in B westerns. She was pretty in a way that made you want to carry her books, a prim, honeyed blonde for whom the words "sensible shoes" seemed to have been invented. In fact, she was already married, in a manner not unlike your humble servant, to an English person who kind-of-you-know-sort-of-wanted to get into the business. Beside me was Tim, a hearty, hail-fellow-well-met kind of Joe who looked like a Jewish Fred Flintstone. A nice guy, Tim was blessed with the kind of extra-large face that made you think he'd say "duh" a lot, even if he didn't. He had a brother in the biz, named Dick, one of the elite group of writers in the TV industry known as "classy," in whose shadow he toiled. Dick, see, penned a legendary, extra-sensitive *thirtysomething* episode dealing with homosexuality. In which he managed to make same-sex relations every bit as headachingly meaningful as the shows hetero Yup-sufferers.

My "concept," as standard TV conceit likes to dub the clichés around which episode once-a-weekers like *Moonlighting* are built, involved an evil plastic surgeon and the bevy of artificially enhanced beauties he killed—or who killed him. By the time my paltry effort was handed over to Skip, the perky Yale man in charge, it was transformed into something I couldn't even recognize.

I'd have probably been hurt, if I could remember what I banged out in the first place. What mattered is that the second I got the go-ahead, I was free to retreat pretty much unhindered in my private shooting gallery.

My particular patch of heaven was the low-prestige, stuck-in-the-corner office. When a "design consultant" showed up and asked how I wanted my room painted, I was actually pressured by taste-master Skip into selecting a color. I had originally said I didn't want it painted, but you couldn't decline. You *had* to make someone come in, paint your office, then give them some kind of shit, say it wasn't done right, and get it painted all over again, a hue lighter or darker.

Skip himself had his headwaiter—I mean headwriter—office done up in a dark mahogany and richly carpeted manner suggestive of Marlon Brando's study in *The Godfather.*

• • •

Moonlighting's esteemed stars, Bruce and Cybill, did not venture into our neck of reality. Which is not to say we did not have the chance to rub up against the Exalted Ones who lent our own paltry existence whatever meaning it had. Quite the contrary.

Not long after the season got under way we little people received word that Cybill Shepherd had invited us out to her Encino homestead for lunch. Need I even mention that the staff was a-titter? Every writer on board was dizzy with anticipation. I would have joined in the general buzz were it not for the fact that I was gripped by all-but-paralyzing shame over my appearance.

So sunken had my cheekbones become, Keith Richards looked like Dom DeLuise by comparison. My neck had shrunk to the size of a Sweetheart straw with a peach pit caught in the middle, my Adam's apple having grown so prominent I looked like the lost offspring of Ichabod Crane and Olive Oyl. Clothes may not make the man, but in my case they might have certainly neutralized his apparent degeneracy.

Might have, were it not for the fact that my taste seemed to have lapsed along with every other link to decent civilization. Exactly what I was thinking when I decided to wear my electric green suit with jumbo lapels to brunch with Cybill eludes me now. As I slipped my multitrack arms into the silken suit sleeves that morning, I had half a thought that I'd so impress the Amazon blonde with my incredibly urbane demeanor and continental attire, we'd both experience a nameless yet powerful connection in the midst of all the introductory chitchat. Somehow she'd manage to get me alone. We'd exchange a few loaded words. Then she'd ask me to stay behind when the others left. Not only would I impress the staff no end, I'd really get to love and understand this powerful-yet-secretly-lonely beauty.

However, there's a completely different reason I decided to "dress up" that particular day. Happenin' Skip had actually issued a memo advising us, not just of the impending date with celebrity, but—even more important—"to dress appropriately."

I arrived at work the morning of our Cybill outing sporting my phosphorescent green suit. I looked like one of James Brown's sidemen.

Skip, when he saw me roll into his office, gave me a look I interpreted as envy. He was forever popping into my cubby hole to grill me on some new band or hooking me into his Godfather suite to slap on the latest CD and ask what I thought. Inevitably, the band or the album had just been featured on some list in *Rolling Stone* or shown up as guests on *Saturday Night Live*. He was that kind of hip. "Are people, like, wearing those now?"

"Oh, you mean this old thing?"

"Yeah. Is that Negro look making a comeback or something?"

"You kidding me? It never went out."

"Huh," said Skip, momentarily at a loss. Did I know what I was talking about? Should he, on his next shopping trip, snap up a swinging iridescent pimp suit? When in doubt, though, counter with your own cool. He stood up from behind his giant Mafioso desk and headed for the door. "Come on. . . . We'll take the new Beamer out to Cybill's. You've got to hear the CD player in that thing. It's incredible!"

It certainly was. And not just because of the ear-tickling bass that wormed its way into your brain despite the competition from the 101 freeway. Skip kept the top down. So not only could we *be* a carful of grossly overpaid TV biz white guys—we could let everybody *see* what we were, too!

Cybill's house was not the Pickfair-like spread we peons anticipated on the way up. By movie star standards, it was humble beyond belief. A mere ranch home, fronted by the tiniest cacti garden and a short walk up from the street. La Maison Cybill squatted at the top end of a crowded cul-de-sac, a standard patch of suburban heaven, no farther than a few feet from its neighbors on either side. Who'd have guessed the belle of network television lurked just beyond these ho-hum doors?

Once inside I asked discreetly for the whereabouts of the "restroom" and disappeared like Sherlock Holmes on the trail of Professor Moriarty.

What fueled my investigative itch, if the truth be told, was Madame Cybill's recent marriage to her chiropractor. I love the way show biz people are always marrying the most practical employee they have. My next favorite case was Annie Lennox, late of the Eurythmics, who found true love and happiness when she tied the knot with her vegetarian chef.

Uncertain as to whether chiropractors could write prescriptions or not, I felt duty bound to find out. I found no pills, but at least I could hold my head high and know that I tried.

It was then I had a minor accident. One knee on the sink, trying to get my entire face in the cabinet and check those vexing behind-the-aspirin stashes, I somehow slipped, setting off a loud, clattering crash that must have sounded like the Allied Invasion from where the regular folks all sat 'round Ms. Cybill's sunken sushi pit.

The whole sushi pit situation was another nightmare. No sooner did I lumber out of the bathroom, explaining the distant ka-boom with the somewhat vague and ludicrous explanation "My knee gave out"—followed, when the celebrity hostess looked at me as if to say "Is he a writer, or did you pick him up hitchhiking?" with the even more absurd "It's an old football thing"—than I was faced with the awful specter of removing my shoes.

It was part of the whole Japanese/raw protein motif. And scarier to me than if our hostess had asked us to recline on a bed of nails. By now I was already starting to suffer the condition that was to plague me throughout my career as junkaholic: the curse of disappearing veins.

The technical term for those collapsed vessels is "sclerosed." It's like they've turned to dough. You can't connect, so you keep gouging yourself and bleed all over the place. Or worse, you hit an artery, and the dope, instead of racing heartward, goes the other direction, down to the nearest extremity.

Bad news! While you watch in horror, your hand turns lobster red, begins to burn horribly, and mutates to a huge fleshy mitt. In seconds you can't even bend your fingers. Your wrist is the size of your calf, and all you can do is fight the urge to tear at your own flesh, trying to scrape out the awful, burning tingle and squeeze your digits back to something resembling normal size. It's like the longest bad dream in the world.

That morning I had not been able to hit my usual spots. I'd had to go to the next best place: my feet. But no matter how much I squinched my eye and aimed for the dainty vein in my ankle, I couldn't hit it.

All of which shakes down to the fact that it's one thing to bloody your own bathroom, another to leave flaming red corpuscles in a TV star's commode.

Just to make things truly bad, I had white socks on. Don't ask me why. They didn't exactly "go" with my Motown Soul Revue suit. Had I been thinking, and anticipated the whole bloody foot fiasco, I'd have gone with boots. But who said planning is a big part of junkie life?

The upshot of the whole nasty business is that the tension about those telltale bloodstained sweatsocks was enough to counteract the high and set me a-twitch and a-twitter all over again. Happily, none of our little party, near as I could tell, noticed anything, absorbed as we all were in creating our own stellar impressions. The only witness to my Achilles-area bloodletting turned out to be a small unsmiling woman who just seemed to hover behind Cybill in the manner of a royal food taster.

There seemed to be no less than half a dozen helpers, introduced variously as driver, chef, nanny, and a few others. Each twin had their own nanny, as did an older daughter from a previous marriage. Strangely, star-mama doted on the boy twin like a loyal Tibetan fussing over the next reincarnation of the Dalai Lama, while the little girl, for no apparent reason, was shunted out of the room entirely.

The hawk-eyed woman turned out to be nanny for Cybill's *tres* adorable male toddler, Zak. As opposed to "not-Zak." She shot me a disgusted look. But junkies are used to disgusted looks. The beauty part is, at that level, there operates an inherent assumption: If the Mistress Has Invited You, You Must Not Be The Human Scuzzball I Can Tell You Are Just By Looking At You.

I squirmed through the rest of the sushi fest with relative ease and concentrated on the chance to observe that most observable of species, *Blond-us Moviestar-us*. More surprising, Cybill was great. She was real as sweatpants.

What set the tone for the event, unfortunately, was young Meister Bradley's earlier directive, shunted our way along with the "appropriate dress" missive. That we not, UNDER ANY CIRCUMSTANCES, discuss story ideas for upcoming shows with Ms. Shepherd. That darn Skip!

When it became clear, after our initial intro, that the one thing the actress *wanted* to talk about, her roles in the upcoming season, was *not* going to be talked about, a sort of chill fell over the proceedings. You could almost hear the sound of raw fish being digested.

Once it was established we weren't going to discuss *bidness,* her manner softened. Sitting across from this big-boned gal in funky sweats, her hair up, with no makeup and fresh baby puke on her sleeve, you could easily forget who she was. Ms. Cybill's on-set behavior, after all, was the stuff of legend. We'd all heard of her past run-ins with Glenn

Gordon Caron, the show's creator. The most famous one had Cybill popping into his office, sticking her big, beautiful face right into his own pudgy mug, and shouting at him, "Listen, you son of a bitch, I have a gun and I'm not afraid to use it!" That's one way to handle line changes.

None of this was in evidence. Instead, she came across as self-deprecating, possessed of an ironic sort of wit, and, most surprising of all, genuinely funny. As the rough-edged little lunch rolled on, the southern lilt in her accent became more and more pronounced. She told a story about Peter Bogdanovich. A story about coming to Hollywood. And, my particular favorite, a story about Marlon Brando. Cybill, you have to understand, just loves to talk. "Motormouth" is too negative, so let's stick to "animated." Besides, she's so entertaining, you don't mind. Unless you're Marlon Brando, and you're sitting beside her at a dinner party, and you can't get a word in edgewise. Which, according to the lady herself, is exactly what happened at her very first Hollywood dinner party.

"Finally," Cybill laughed, a raucous, unladylike guffaw that would have made you follow her anywhere, "finally Marlon just lost it. He stands up, picks up the wine, and says, 'I don't know who the hell this girl is, but if she doesn't shut up right now, I'm going to hit her in the face with a bottle.' "

Another tale of our genteel industry, and one that endeared me to this supposed queen bitch of a TV star no matter what they said about her. She didn't give a fuck what anybody thought. And if we weren't going to give the information she wanted, she wasn't about to ruin a meal already under way with some kind of hissy fit. She talked nonstop, entertaining herself and disarming everyone else. On top of everything else, she didn't even make fun of my shiny sideman suit. For which I'm forever grateful.

Meanwhile, my habit, fueled by the astronomical sums I was hauling home each week, had launched me into nonstop shooter status. No longer content to fix once in the morning, once more in my post-McDonald's shrink session, and once more at Fox, I more or less kept up that rigorous pace dawn to dusk and back again.

One particular morning, after I'd geezed a sixer of Dil-Dils and collapsed in a heap of sweaty beneficence behind my desk, Tommy the Xerox Boy knocked on the door—I did not, needless to say, receive many guests; most of the other staffers regarded me with all the suspicious esteem of a Quasimodo who lived in a small office instead of a bell-tower—and burst inside with a truly baffled sigh.

"I don't understand Skip. You know, I knew him last season, when he was just a writer, right? Before they put him in charge? I mean, he wasn't, like, what you'd call a regular guy. It's like George Bush, he's always trying to act 'regular,' but it doesn't work. I mean, he's from *Connecticut*. . . . But even that was okay. At least he wasn't a total dick. Now–forget it! It's like he's a completely different person. Now he's important, you know? Everybody knows he got the gig 'cause Rondo didn't want it, but so what? Now he sends back his lunch if there's too much mayo on his sandwich. I really hate having to bring him his lunch. It's like he's doing me a favor, letting me go out and get him something to eat. Like we didn't even know each other before. The drag is, I actually like the guy. . . ."

Never one to miss the chance at firing off some bogus compassion, I offered up the predictable. "Maybe he's a little insecure. . . ."

Tommy raised his head up out of his hands, where he'd buried it, as if to block out the vision of moneyed prephood who made his life hell.

"Well, you never had a job like this before, did you? I mean, are you any different than you were before?"

"It's different with me," I said, "I started off a complete creep. Now I'm just a creep with more money. I'm a creep with hundred-dollar bills falling out of my pocket."

"Jesus," he said, regarding me with the mixture of pity and confusion such utterances inevitably elicit. "Jesus, Jerry, why do you always say shit like that? You're not a fucking creep. You're fucked-up, when you come out with crap like that. But, come on, you never asked me to get your lunch once. . . ."

Mostly what I remember is the way things looked sometimes after I'd push down the plunger, sometimes when I got so high so fast I couldn't even take the needle out of my arm. I just sat back, head lolling on my shoulders like a balloon on a string, and everything, walls, carpet, couch cushion, my own hands, broke down to swirling molecules, reassembled as a million other things, and danced before my eyes before arranging themselves once more as reality. The endless cycle, that dance of molecules and their return to something solid, left me as drained as if I'd flown around the sun with veins for wings.

• • •

One morning I stumbled out of my office, totally loaded on thirty-milligram morphine pills. When I opened my door, there she was, inhaling a Merit. This grande dame of the theater, Colleen Dewhurst, in a shapeless brown housedress and scuffed flat shoes worthy of a trailer park widow. She wore her hair pulled back tightly off her face. Without any makeup, the wrinkles showed all the miles. But her crow's-feet, to me, lent her an almost unspeakable beauty. A sort of dignified gravity. A spiritual presence.

I knew nothing about her. Yet I immediately felt a connection. As if her very presence were evidence of all a soul could survive and emerge with their grace intact, if not enhanced.

The actress's eyes looked somewhere between bloodshot and boiled in peanut oil. But so piercing, so loaded with all she must have seen in her life, all she herself must have been through. . . . When they met mine they held an extra moment, and I had this jolt of weird recognition. *She's been where I am. . . . She knows. . . .*

Not that there was a sign on her forehead. She was having a conversation with Skip. He appeared less than thrilled that I kept staring at her. They were discussing her stint as costar. "I think you're gonna really love this role," he tittered. "It's cute, but it's not cute-cute. There's really a lot to it. . . ."

As he talked he danced about her like a small terrier waiting for someone to toss him a biscuit. Had he broken into a series of high-pitched yips I don't think either of us would have been surprised.

When I finally stumbled into the bathroom I realized that what I thought was spiritual communion might well have been something else altogether. Ms. Dewhurst was staring, it was true. But, poised before the dust-streaked men's mirror, I stared at myself and saw what she must have seen.

For a full minute I stood and gawked at myself the way, seconds before, I'd stood and gawked at her. It hit me, with convulsive horror, that she might not have been staring at my eyes. Just as likely she'd been gaping at the spreading flower of scarlet in the crook of my sleeves. I hadn't expected to shoot that day and so had not worn my usually requisite black shirt. I had on a faded blue jersey, not nearly dark enough to hide the evidence.

When I lurched back out of the men's room, I bumped into her again. This time it was the legend herself who spoke.

"My boy, what are you doing here?" Her voice was a ravaged whiskey drawl, like a soft saxophone filtered through gravel.

"I work here," I sputtered. "I'm one of the writers."

"I know, I know," she said. "TV is where you make the money, baby. But you don't belong here."

"Well, you know how it is. . . ."

"Oh, I know all about it." Once again her eyes sucked me in. Those eyes looked like they had seen a few things. Like maybe she'd been around a few corners herself. Even as she spoke, her gaze was saying something else. *"I know you, Sonny Jim. I know where you live. . . ."*

"We've got to be careful what we do," she continued, with the weariest smile in the world. "Do you understand what I'm saying?"

"Well, yes." And I think I did. So many odd things happen when you're fucked up. You have encounters with people that, even as they're happening, you aren't sure whether they're real. Aren't sure if what you're sensing is what is actually going on. Even as her words left me feeling weirdly chastened, her eyes offered some strange encouragement. Maybe this was an actress's true genius. To convey conflicting messages on two levels at once, to speak eloquently, and to the heart, without speaking at all.

Before she turned and made her way slowly down the steps back out, she reached out with one ancient hand and grabbed my wrist. The look she gave me, there on that dim stairwell, left me simultaneously shattered and hopeful.

Something was about to happen.

This is how I got the news. It's a typical Saturday, I walk in the door from scoring and Sandra leaps off the couch, waving a blue test tube in her hand. She's screaming, "Look! Look!" But I didn't know what it was. Without even glancing at her, I think, "Oh shit, she's found another syringe!" In my guilt, my constant squirmy theater, I slam into an explanation without even listening.

"Listen," I begin, already gearing up. A junkie lies like other people breathe. It's not something you think about. "I must have left it there a long time ago, I was cleaning up, and forgot to throw it away—"

"Jerry!"

"Can't it wait? I'm going to be sick here. I think I got diarrhea or something. . . ."

"Jerry, I got one of those tests. It's positive!"

"For fuck's sake, Sandra!" I stopped and turned toward her. She just stood there; I had to give in. "All right, I give up, okay? What kind of test?"

"I'm pregnant," she said, her voice almost a whisper.

"What?"

"I—I bought one of those kits." She spoke with her shoulders sort of hunched, head halfway averted. As if expecting a blow.

"For home pregnancy. So you can test yourself at home."

My heart sank. Not because I didn't want her to be pregnant. No, what killed was the sense that I had ruined this woman's happiness. Because, God strike me dead, even after I heard, my need was stronger than my reaction. You're pregnant, fine, I have to go get fucking high, okay? *Now leave me the fuck alone. . . .*

"I'm sorry," I muttered. I simply could not *not* get high now. No clearer show of my priorities, the sickness that drove me, could even be conceived of. I gave her a lame pat on the shoulders. She didn't even raise her eyes, just stood there, the sight of her breaking my heart so much I had to walk away even faster. To kill all the feelings I couldn't even feel, numb emotions I couldn't name. To vanquish the rapidly mounting panic that already had my heart slamming at my ribs, like an animal who suddenly realizes it should have fled the cage when it was still open. Who suddenly realizes that now the bars are shut for good.

I tried to blank out the thoughts in my head until the drugs could do it for me. But I had to wait. My hands were shaking too much. All I could do was sit there, on the closed toilet seat, trying to make my eyes go blank so they wouldn't see the future.

Sandra's muffled weeping sounded from the living room. I pressed my hands over my ears. The sobbing grew louder.

Every cry that tore out of her stabbed like an icepick in my brain.

I wanted to cry. My voice strangled in my throat.

I stood up, the needle in my hand, the spoon half out of my pocket. My eyes locked on their reflection in the mirror. But there was no recognition.

Whoever stared back, mercifully enough, had become an absolute stranger.

From that moment forward, every fix became a moral transgression. Relief was no excuse anymore. What saved me doomed another. This unborn creature. This product of my tainted loins. I kept getting high to kill my shame at the fact that I kept getting high.

No doubt my sperm could have stripped the paint off Buicks. I hated even to imagine what was in there: some leprous sludge of methadone, heroin, Dilaudid, cocaine, marijuana, morphine, and alcohol. And yet it had fertilized an egg. Simultaneously poisoned and fertilized. . . . If I was lucky, the thing would be born half normal. Against my better judgment, I told my mother. Crumpled on the couch in my *Moonlighting* hideaway, the belt slack in my arm and my head rolled comfortably back on my neck, as if attached by well-worn Velcro, I decided a little familial connection was in order.

Her voice sounded as narcotically graveled as my own. God knows what private pharmacopoeia she'd been sampling. Call any normal soul at three in the morning and they'd probably sound just like this. Of course, it's closer to noon where she is. But what the heck. . . . *Just a couple of professionals,* I think, *sharing a magic moment* . . .

After the usual horrific stab at chitchat—"What's wrong?" she always bellows instead of hello—I forge ahead, against all instinct and precedent, and cut to the chase.

"Nothing's wrong," I say, cheery as cheery can be. "Nothing's wrong. As a matter of fact, I've got some good news. You're going to be a grandmother."

To which she replies, "Oh, you're going to adopt?"

"What?" For a second I was stunned. Though I don't know why. This was vintage Mom. Still, it took every shred of restraint I had not to blurt out the words that were really burning inside me. *"No, no . . . I CAN DO IT, MOM! . . . I have a dick, believe it or not. . . . WHAT THE HELL DO YOU MEAN, AM I GOING TO ADOPT? What kind of fucked up thing is that to say?"*

Amazing, what a nice call home can do. Eventually we cleared up the whole "your son can actually perform sex" phenomenon and moved on to the usual cancer and cataract update, a litany of relatives and neighbors I'd never heard of who had recently succumbed to Bad Diseases. This was Mom's way of sharing.

(Once born I knew Nina definitely favored my side of the family. She showed up with a unibrow and a moody disposition, two traits of the Stahl tribe since before they were banished from lower Lithuania and shipped in steerage to Ellis Island.)

So my phone rings at six-fifteen in the morning. I'm at my desk, writing. I don't usually pick up the phone, don't usually even have the ringer on, but today, today I hear the ring. I pick it up. Hear my mother, in her disturbed slur: "First National Bank? First National Bank? I can't find my money. . . . You've lost all my money. I have to talk to someone. . . . Who do I talk to? I have to talk to someone. . . ."

"Mom," I say as gently as I can. "Mom, this isn't the bank. This is your son, Jerry, in California. You've called me, Mom."

"I didn't call you. I was calling the bank. Why are you always lying?"

Now the old monsters are stirring. The wounds that go as far back as wounds can go start to throb.

"Mom," I say, but calmly. "You called me up, at six o'clock in the morning, to tell me I'm a liar?"

"I did not call you!" she cries, exuding hurt. "Why must you lie about everything? You think your father committed suicide? Why would your father commit suicide? He was the happiest man in the world. That was an accident. The car was defective. All the windows were open. The door was open."

"Mom . . ."

Is this even happening? It's the day after Mother's day. I don't want to have this conversation. To argue about her husband's peculiar death. But this temper, the one I don't think I have, is banging on the bars of its cage.

"Mom, the man died of carbon monoxide poison." I hear myself speak in a low voice, seething. "My dog, who was waiting for him to get out of the car, my dog, Samson, died, too. Remember? They said he must have snuck into the garage through a crack in the wall. Don't you remember? What do you think, Mom, it was the fresh air that killed him?"

"You LIE!" she screams. Crying, saggy-lipped. Whatever meds she's on coalescing to some horrific, memory-crushing blob astride her speech center. "You always LIE. . . . You . . . You . . . You . . ."

Her voice sinks to a sick growl. I want to shriek. I want to bite the phone. I feel veins begin to bulge in my throat. "Mother," I say, inhaling all the breath in the world, exhaling slowly. "Mother, what I think is this: Memory is a subjective thing. It changes. Your stories change. This is what you believe now. What I believe now is what I'm going to write."

There is a silence on the line. Distant, muffled sobs. "He was happy," she says, pleading. But to whom? "He was happy. . . . Why do you say these awful things? How can you call me up and say these awful things?"

"Mom," I utter, but carefully. I want to tell her she is driving me fucking crazy. She is making me want to rip my eyes out, chew telephone wire. I was fine before she called. "Mom, listen to me. . . ." But I have nothing to say. She has worked herself into violent wailing. And I'm to blame. (Am I to blame? I don't know anymore. . . .) Why doesn't she just yell "Rape!" and get it over with? There's nothing else left. . . .

This is fucking crazy, I say, but to myself. To myself only. I grab my hair and pull. I want to hurt myself. I want to, like my father, put my head through walls. Bloody my forehead.

Punch a hole in the plaster. Tear and crush my fisted knuckles. The house I grew up in was full of shattered doors.

Oh, God, I hate this. "But. . . . Mom," I say, "Mom . . ."

Only now I can't break through. Now she is doing her repeating thing. "Why," in a kind of keening chant. "Oh, God, why why why why why. . . . WHY didn't you take me? . . . WHY GOD WHY OH WHY . . . ?"

I have heard this before. At my father's funeral. When she threw herself on the ground before his coffin. Rubbing her face in the mud. Screaming, before everyone. "David, he wishes it was me. . . ."

Talking about me, her son, her horrible son, in front of a hundred relatives and friends. "He hates me, David. . . . He wishes it was me. . . . Why couldn't it be me? . . ."

I was sixteen. And I told myself, as I had since childhood, as I tell myself now: I AM STEEL. . . . STEEL FEELS NOTHING. . . . PRETTY SOON IT WILL ALL BE OVER. My survival mantras. The ones I have repeated to myself from the pale and frightened dawn of memory. Repeated as I kneeled beside her in the hard dirt and tugged the smelling salts out of my suit coat pocket. Raised the bottle full of green crystals to her nose. Held her head, her slack mouth pressed beneath my palm, like a drunkard's kiss, though God fry me on His holy hot plate, the feel of her wet lips revolted me to death.

And oh Christ, I think, Oh Christ, as I'm holding the receiver, hearing her sob all the way from Pittsburgh. This book is going to kill her. This book is going to push her farther over the edge. . . . But so help me, I don't know what else to do. Not writing it is going to kill me.

So there it is. I'm going to commit matricide or I'm going to commit suicide.

Or both. . . .

"Hey, Mom," I say, and even if I can't muster sincerity, I can, at the very least, avoid meanness, avoid raised voice and curses. "Hey, Mom, I'm sorry if I called at a bad

time. . . . And, please, if you can, have a nice day, okay? Try and have a nice day."

Then I do a bad thing. I don't wait to hear her response. I can't bear it, whatever form the next chunk of pain and accusation will take. I can't absorb any more. I hang up. Rest my head against the receiver. Think: I'm sorry . . . I'm sorry . . . I'm sorry . . . I'm sorry . . .

Talking to no one. Talking to everyone I've ever known. What can I do? I am still sitting here. Still in front of the computer. There is nothing else. I take a breath. I crack my knuckles. Stare through my window at the smudged gray sky above the Silverlake reservoir. It is 6:23 A.M.

Okay, I tell myself, now you will write again. You will. You just have to take another breath. Breathe in, breathe out.

That's what I'm thinking: Be calm. Until, like a blown boiler, I just explode. The words rip out of me like metal shards. Fuck her! FUCK MY MOTHER . . . FUCK MY WIFE . . . FUCK ALL OF THEM . . . !

The dam just bursts. No doubt, at this strange and savage hour, alarming my poor neighbors.

But I can't help it. I can't stay silent, can't protect anyone, anymore. Including myself. Most of all myself. I am a thirty-nine-year-old male human, and this is what I feel—even as I am ashamed for feeling it and ashamed for admitting that, too. Shame is, I know, what I was trained to feel, what I'm supposed to. . . . That's why I am so good at it.

But I am sick of sticking so close to my lessons. Sick of being the good little boy. . . . I have done everything, from slashing my wrists to shooting heroin, to stay the good little boy. Because, I see now, on some cringing level, that's all being a junkie was.

Forget being cool, forget being underground. It was a way of staying ashamed—of trying not to ever say the words that have, just now, come boiling out of me. . . .

That's the shabby truth. I ought to thank this poor old woman for her insane call. Just as, it now occurs to me, I ought to thank my wife for her convulsive threats to sue if I so much as refer to her. For screaming over the phone—yet another delightful chat—that this book will mean horror and professional pain to her, not to mention an eternal plague upon our blameless daughter. (All this, as she tells me, for no more than the millionth time, that she wishes she'd never met me, wishes I would just go die. . . .)

The usual whisper, the usual scream. Sandra was last night; Mom was this morning.

It occurs to me—belatedly, as the obvious so often does—they might as well be the same person. Maybe they are *the same person. "I Married Mom!"—now there's a sitcom idea! Starring Oedipus the Jew and his little dog, Doormat. CAA will drool! But how can I say that? Well, listen. . . .*

This is what I think: If you had the nerve to live what you lived, you should have the nerve to write it.

Unless writing is harder than life. Which, if it is, just makes the task more necessary. Because I am scared, I must not stop.

The truth is chillingly simple. I am sick of the madness that drives me mad. And if I toast in hell, so be it. It's nowhere I haven't been before.

The doomed, I think, as if the phrase has been inside my skull all along, echoing, and I just now hear it: The doomed cannot be hurt. . . .

I know that, at this moment, as well as I know anything. I know, without having to think about it, because I am one of the doomed. So I must write. I must have done with shame. Even if I die of fright in the process.

At least—if nothing else—it will be a different death from the one that awaited me until now.

There is, really, nothing else to say. Except, perhaps . . . thanks for calling.

What stuns me—and stunned me then—is that I *did* love my wife. I *did* want a family. A home. A place to be in the world. I craved the legitimacy, craved the security, craved the *normalcy* of it all. Yet even as I was on my way to having these things, I knew I was on my way to losing them. The nearer I came to authentic fulfillment, the farther I drove myself to needle-induced despair.

Perhaps, underneath the Bill Burroughs facade, was a Dick Van Patten dying to get out. Which is much scarier than the worst down-in-the-hood, spike-in-my-arm, three A.M. nightmare. Along with all the jangly memories are the simpler recollections. Like playing Scrabble with Sandra. She's a few months pregnant. We're lying together on our bed. I rest my head on her swollen middle, feeling the endless Sunday afternoon wrapped around us like the arms of a conventional God. Thinking: "This is it." I *like* being married. I've made it. Against all odds, I have a chance to make it out of the hell in which I've sunk my life. . . .

"*Adjal,*" I say, looking down at the board, eyeing the word with which she's blown the game wide open. A triple-word score. "What the fuck is that?"

"Adjal." She smiles, as if it's the most normal word in the world. Her face relaxes for once—an occurrence so rare, I forget how pretty she can be. How pretty she is. "It's Indonesian. It means the hour of your death."

"I didn't know we were playing Indonesian Scrabble."

"It's a good word. They believe the hour of your death is predestined. When you die, everybody just shrugs. 'There's nothing you can do when your *adjal* arrives. . . .' "

She sees my expression, and she smiles again. This is as close as we get. It's hard, for both of us. Two nondemonstrative types. *Adjal.*

This, it hits me, is the real Sandra. The sweet little girl within the woman. The one I'm slowly strangling even as I choke whatever's good in myself. There is a softness in her, a playfulness, as she jots down her score. And as I watch her, my fingers caressing the swelling bubble of flesh our own strange future occupies, my heart simultaneously swells and breaks. I am bewildered by contentment. I want to kiss her. I want to kill myself. I want to take my child to the circus. Want to spend the rest of my life in a shooting gallery, where I don't know night from day and everybody's dying in their own shit.

I touch Sandra's hand. It feels tiny as a doll's. She looks at me. Expectant. Expecting. . . . Light streams in on the breeze. Palm trees sway outside the windows. The sky's so blue it hurts. One of life's dizzy wonders. "Sandra . . ."

"Yes?"

My lips remain parted, but only silence exits. The words don't come. I want to say "I love you," want to say "I'm sorry." Want to live a life where the two are not linked like Yin and Yang.

"Sandra . . ."

"What?"

"Sandra . . . I think I have to go downstairs for a minute. I'll be right back. . . ."

"Oh."

Our eyes meet, and I'm the first to look away. She knows, I think. She knows everything. And the thought rings so powerfully, I can't stand another second. "I have to go," I say. Wondering, as I slide off the bed, as I race down the stairs, if I create happiness just so I can kill it. If I need this pain in my heart to justify using. Or if I use to justify this pain.

"Jerry," I hear her call from our bedroom, "Jerry . . . *please*. . . ." But I pretend like I don't hear.

Pretend I can't.

I don't know what else to do.

Moonlighting gave us a week off for Thanksgiving. Most people left town for the holidays. Not me. Feeling all the self-love you'd expect, I had my five-months-pregnant partner drive me to the hospital. To Cedars-Sinai Chemical Dependency Wing. To kick.

The ride to the hospital was the longest in the world. I couldn't look at Sandra. She was pale, she was scared, and she was probably furious. But she was not crying. We hadn't discussed the decision. I'd simply announced this was something I had to do and let her know I was going to do it. If I'd asked for sympathy, tried to explain what kind of fucked-up sense of worthlessness drives a soul to such a thing, perhaps things would have ended up differently.

Sandra didn't come in, just dropped me off in the parking lot, at my insistence, and drove back the way she came. I stood and watched our black Acura disappear up Beverly Boulevard before making the long walk. Knowing a life I might have had was disappearing up the road along with it. Luckily, I was once again too sick to consider the implications of what was happening. That was the one virtue of overwhelming physical pain. It took your mind off your real problems. . . .

No more than a few weeks previous, we'd been here for Sandra's ultrasound. This process whereby the parents-to-be, seated next to the doctor-shaman, watch as he runs what looks like a bladeless Norelco shaver over her melon belly, revealing all the nooks and crannies of the baby's topography on a grainy screen. There's no question that in my weakness, my crippling fear over what the future had in store—not to mention the present—I'd upped the narcotic ante just to keep from imploding. If I had to stick a needle in my arm just to unload groceries, there's no need even to mention what I had to do to sit through a session of electronic entrails reading. (And if there's any more corrupt sensation on the planet than attending Lamaze class high on heroin, I don't know what it is. INHALE. EXHALE. *NOD.* INHALE. EXHALE. *NOD. . . .*)

Our last visit to the hospital, it took all the chemical strength I could muster not to simply run screaming onto Beverly Boulevard, gasping apologies for everything I've done, for all the hell my toxic past would continue to cause even if I took the cure that minute and never got high again. That was the horror of it. I'd set something in motion that existed on its own momentum.

The mere fact that the baby was in there, growing, was more than my quivering brain could absorb. I simply did not have the nerve to endure the process.

"It's a girl," the doctor had told us after that last, prekick Cedars visit. At that moment the abstraction became flesh. And my first reaction, odd as it sounds, was relief. My ongoing panic was matched by almost indescribable relief. Unlike every father-to-be I'd ever known, the last thing I wanted in the whole world was a son. I was as grateful to hear the baby would not be born a boy as I was to hear that it didn't have Down's syndrome. What the hell would I do with a little version of me? I wanted to love my child, not feel sorry for it.

Along with gratitude, though, came *the Voice.* The eyes from above. In the same way, in the weeks and months after my father died, when I was sixteen, I could hear him speak to me, could sense him gazing sadly down as I continued to live my wretched life—I could not smoke a joint, masturbate, or cheat on a math test without knowing Dad was up there, watching with downturned lips and disappointed gaze—I began to sense this little creature, my unborn baby girl, taking me in. *"Daddy, why?"* I'd hear, as I slumped on the edge of the bathtub, blood dripping on my shoes and the needle loose in my hand. . . .

As I took those last, leaden steps from the outside world, from the hospital parking lot up the path to the steel-and-glass Schumann Building, through the lobby onto the elevator and up to the seventh floor, to the Chemical Dependency Wing, I couldn't shake the sense of this child, this hurt and confused and wondrous child, seeing me in my moment of deepest shame, deepest grief, and asking in a pure and tiny voice, *"Daddy, why are you doing this to yourself? Why are you doing this to me?"*

And I couldn't bear it. The import of that question, whether sprung from my unconscious or broadcast from some cosmic, prenatal beyond to which only demented dads-to-be are tuned in, bore down like a rain of lead on my skull. I knew I was beyond saving. And what I had to do to stay alive—somehow get off the shit—felt like it was going to kill me.

What haunts me even now is the desolation of that first morning in Cedars-Sinai. The howling silence. Newly alone in a hospital room. Two single beds. Nightstand. Linoleum floor. They tell you to taper off before you check in, but of course you don't. You do twice as much. Because as much as you want to stop, you also want to do more. And this may be your last chance to do anything at all. So that when you get there, and you start withdrawal, you end up kicking twice as bad. What I didn't know is that most people make sure to get high the morning they enter the hospital. Since the stuff they give you to relieve the pain doesn't kick in for hours and hours.

Moron that I am, I went in straight, sustained only by the

elephant-size injection to which I'd treated myself the evening before. Which was already fading fast.

There was a discussion with a nurse. There was protocol. I would stay in the detox section until I was well enough to participate in rehab. This was a thirty-day program, though I'd signed in for four days only. Long enough to kick over the long Thanksgiving weekend. Then go back to work clean and free at the other end. Of course it didn't work the way I planned. Forty minutes after walking in I wanted out.

As I gazed out over the parking lot below, I thought, for some reason, I do not want to land on a Honda.

While the thought of hurtling into space was something I could live with—was, in fact, wildly appealing—the notion of landing on one of those Civics made me queasy.

They'd given me Tegretol to counter convulsions and spasms. They'd given me a little Darvon, for the joint pain, the instant ersatz rheumatoid arthritis that turns a junkie in withdrawal into a whining invalid. They'd given me Clonidine to lower my blood pressure. But none of it kicked in. By nightfall, curled into a sweating, wretched fetus on the sagging bed, I made no attempt to hide my tears from the nurse who popped in on his rounds to see if I was having a good time.

"My knees," I pleaded to the nurse, a tiny, perfectly formed man named Jinx with a startling resemblance to Willie Shoemaker. "You've got to give me something for my knees."

"I can give you Tylenol," Jinx told me, without a trace of the smug grin I was sure would be there.

"I'd have to eat the bottle, and I still wouldn't feel it."

"I been there, babe."

Jinx twisted his well-formed head to blow smoke toward the door as he spoke. "When I kicked it was the back of my neck and the backs of my knees."

"When you kicked?" I managed to lift my head off the pillow, where it seemed to have been glued. It hadn't occurred to me that the people who worked in this unit had all been there themselves. In spite of the invisible piranhas gnawing my bones, I was interested. Was, in fact, enthralled.

"Demerol, babe." He blew the smoke out of his mouth sideways. "Oh, this boy used to love his Demerol. Matter of fact, I used to get it right here in this hospital. I worked in E.R. Had a key to the cabinet, you know what I'm talking about? Things were always so crazy, I'd find a way to sneak in and steal all the good shit I could shove down my pants. In those days you could still get those nice glass syringes, too. None of these damn disposables."

By the time he left, some of the meds kicked in and I managed to half sleep, half drift in and out of consciousness all night. The next morning, feeling like I'd been dropped out of an airplane, I got a visit from the doctor who ran the unit. A surprisingly baby-faced young man.

Of course, he didn't understand. I was different. I just had to shake this habit, then I'd be okay. I had a pregnant wife, after all. I had *responsibilities.* I didn't need counseling. Are you kidding? I knew what I was doing! I just needed to get through this annoying withdrawal and get back on the job. My arrogance was such that I couldn't believe anyone had gone through the kind of shit I'd been through. . . . That anyone could understand. And again, the doctor turned out to have a story of his own.

This MD, a complete stranger, blew me away, got me through another afternoon, regaling me with tales of his own intravenous history. Revealing, one more time, what a bigot I was, what a close-minded cliché-ridden bo-bo when it came to the matter of Who Got It and Who Didn't in this great big toxic world.

"I used to shoot Dilaudid in my penis," he explained, somewhere between matter-of-fact and amused. "When I was in medical school."

"No way!"

It was too bizarre, hearing this from a guy who looked, for

all the world, like he'd stumbled out of *GQ* into my hospital room. The man might just as likely have launched into a lecture on polo-wear as penile opiate injection.

"There's a decent vein down there," he continued, idly tuning his stethoscope to my chest as we chatted. "I'm not going to tell you where it is, let's just say you had to know what you were doing. You had to be good. Which I was. As a matter of fact, I was Intern of the Year."

"Intern of the Year? Jesus!" In spite of my own predicament, once again, I was hooked. Elevated out of my own self-destructo story by the wholly radical details of someone else's. . . .

The doctor checked my eyes as we chatted. He glanced over my chart, tapped my sternum, jotted down some notes. "I had a system. I'd shoot speed and do rounds for thirty-six hours, then slam Dilaudid to come down. But I had to inject where it was impossible to detect."

"How long can you keep that up?" I asked, too gone even to comprehend my own pun. "I mean, didn't they catch on?"

"Well, it worked for a while," he said, eyeing me meaningfully now, since I'd just been regaling him with my own have-to-get-high-to-write, have-to-write-to-pay-for-the-wife-and-baby myth. "What you find is, once you admit you need help, people are more than happy to give it. People you wouldn't expect. . . . I went into a chemical dependency program, and while I was in there I decided this was what I wanted to get into. Back then, the field of addictionology was really just starting up. I realized, once I'd been through it, that's what I wanted to do with my life. . . ."

"In your dick," was all I could manage to say after the doctor had opened up to me. "Right there in your *dick*. . . . Jesus Christ!"

"It gets better," he said.

Except for the first night, when they knocked me out, I did not sleep at all my entire stay. By the last day or two the awareness of what had been so obvious all along—what I'd had to get higher and higher to suppress as it grew more and more apparent—flashed on and off behind my eyeballs like the neon of a cheap hotel.

Every day the doctor would stop in and ask if I'd made the decision to stay, and every day I'd try, as jauntily as I could, to say that I had not. "I can't let you out until you get a night's sleep," he finally told me. So that, by the evening of Day Seven, I'd steeled myself to the prospect of staying perfectly still, despite the ache in my joints, despite the screaming voices, despite all the hell I'd engendered and stored inside my head like nuked-up waste at Three Mile Island: hopelessly contaminating everything behind the concrete walls, but visibly harmless to anyone who happened to pass by. At midnight, three, and five the night nurse popped in, and each time I concentrated. Kept my eyes squeezed shut, my body still. So that when the doctor inquired as to whether or not I'd managed to sleep—thereby proving my worthiness to reenter the world—my lie would be backed up by evidence of those on patrol.

The last morning, as it happened, the nurse on board was one I hadn't spoken to before. Her name was Myrna. She was a tall, incredibly skinny, black-haired woman who, despite her skeletal appearance, gave off an air of enormous, almost intimidating strength. She might have been thirty-five or sixty. I couldn't tell. But, halfway through stripping my bed, Myrna simply stopped. When I looked up, she was just staring. Shaking her head from side to side, she cast a sorrowful, infinitely knowing glance my way.

"You'll be back," she said finally as I made a show of stuffing those ludicrous TV scripts back into the bag I'd arrived with.

"I will?" By then I was so racked with fear and fatigue, I couldn't even fake blasé anymore. "How do you know that?"

"You know it, too," she said. "You're white-knuckling it.

I've watched you since you got here. You think you know what's going on, and you don't have a clue.

"I've seen you before," she said. "A million different versions. Sometimes you make it back, sometimes you don't."

"I'll be okay," I said, as much to calm myself as reassure her.

"Honey, you're going to die," she said softly. Without a trace of malice. With nothing, really, but a kind of overpowering weariness, a fatigue so palpable it seemed to shimmer in the tiny blue veins around her eyes.

"I had a boy, younger than you, and he died. He died of cancer. It was in his bones. He couldn't help it. But you. . . ."

"I'm sorry," I said, but hoarsely. Not even knowing why I was apologizing.

Myrna just smiled and went on about her business. "That's all right," she said. "That's all right."

I was still standing there, now fully packed, when the doctor sauntered in, looking fresh as always in crisp striped shirt and tie. "I understand you slept last night," he said. "They said you were out like a log."

"Right," I said, my own voice echoing from a planet I'd never even been to. "I'm ready to go."

"One more detail," he said. "Just to make sure."

"Right."

He knows, I thought. He knows I'm faking.

"Gerald," said a nurse. "Gerald, I don't like this pacing. You look very agitated. You look like you're going to vacate the premises and use."

"Who me?" I was actually offended. "My foot went to sleep. I'm just . . . full of energy."

"Maybe. But you really should think about staying with us until you're ready to go."

In lieu of keeping me physically inside, the doctor had come up with al alternate proposal. TREXAN. World's first and foremost oral opiate blocker.

"Okay, roll up your sleeves," said the doctor, reaching in

his bag for the still-exalted object of my dreams. If I even entertained a notion I was over my addiction, the effect the mere sight of that needle still worked on my psyche should have hipped me otherwise. I was, to the roots of my hair, as much a fetishist as a man who fondled women's shoes or worshiped rubber.

Mister Addictionologist waited patiently while I calmed myself down. "You know," he said, completely deadpan. "I think maybe drugs affect your memory. I must have explained this to you five times. We have to give you the Narcan test before we can get you on Trexan. There can't be even a trace of heroin in your system."

"What if there is?"

I watched while he injected me, easy as a conductor punching a ticket. "Just hope there isn't."

Even as he said it, though, I felt the creeping dread. I'd faked sleep—had I faked straight, too? Was I really clean? It had been so long since I'd made any move that wasn't sleazy, in my fog I actually wondered. . . .

The doctor must have seen the fear on my face. He gave my shoulder a squeeze, moving his snappy paisley tie out of the way as he did so. "It takes a half hour. Hang on."

"Doctor, I think I . . . *I think I feel something.*"

Narcan, see, is a drug that squeezes opiates out of your system. If you do have a habit, you'll go through withdrawal on the spot. Imagine every nightmare symptom you can imagine compressed, the poison wrung right out of you in a single agonizing blast. . . . They give it in ODs, and they give it, in situations like mine, when the shaman in charge wants to make sure your carburetor's absolutely clean.

In three minutes I was sweating, in ten I was hunched down on the bowl with mainline diarrhea.

"Nerves," the MD declared at the end of my allotted trial time. "You're clean."

He shook my hand, then put two large orange tablets in it.

"Here's the procedure. You come to my office twice a week, and you'll take these there. My nurse will give them to you."

"She'll like, watch me gulp."

"She'll watch you gulp."

"Come on, Doctor."

"Let me tell you something," he said. "I had a patient, a very rich, successful man who came in because his girlfriend was going to leave if he didn't get off drugs. First we let him administer himself. After he tested dirty half a dozen times we knew that wasn't going to work. So he swore up and down he'd get serious, and I had him come into the office, take them in front of Harriet."

"Harriet?"

"My nurse. She doesn't miss a thing."

"Except?"

"Except this guy had so much money, he actually went out and bought a machine that stamped out pills that looked exactly like Trexan. One day Harriet must have turned her back and he slipped a jar of look-alikes on the shelf. So after that he's coming in twice a week, he's even taking the pills in front of me, and his girlfriend swears up and down he's still fucked-up. When I tell him, this guy says to me, 'She's crazy. . . . She's completely paranoid. Now you see what I'm dealing with!' Make a long story short, I finally spring a test on him, and the guy's pissing pure heroin."

"You think I'm going to run out and get a pill machine?"

"I think you come in like everybody else and dose in front of somebody. That's the only way."

"But Doctor," I began, sweating like a malarial swine, "what about car accidents? Say I get pinned under a bus or something, they won't be able to give me anything for the pain. I mean, that's, like, awful. That's, like . . . that's *dangerous*!"

He let out a patient sigh. "Well, if you're still conscious, call me, okay?"

"But what if I'm unconscious?" I blurted, feeling as if I'd

won my point. Like maybe he'd let me stay a junkie. "Then what?"

"Then you're in luck," he said. "If you're unconscious, you can't feel any pain. See you in my office."

So, did I stay clean?

The answer is yes. For the whole cab ride home from the hospital. I actually resolved to do better. *I'll be a good boy, Mommy!* No more draining money that should be going to our child to feed my arm. No more sneaking off every morning. No more hurting and scaring and betraying on a daily basis.

I arrived home, still reeling from how blue the sky looked. One look at Sandra and it was over. In the hospital, in those endless hours wafting in and out of consciousness, I'd found myself lingering on memories—half fantasy, half real—of this once happy-go-lucky, petite and pretty, brilliant young woman I shared my life with. I remembered her face when she laughed, the way her eyes crinkled, the way she tossed back her amazing hair.

But when I walked in all I saw was the horrified victim of life with a dope fiend. The sparkling eyes now weighed down with bags that would make Santa Claus buckle at the knees. Her lips now fixed in a grimace of permanent despair. She flinched at the mere sight of me.

All this was infinitely amplified by the fact that Sandra was weighted down with five months' worth of baby. I walked in as she was in mid–prenatal yoga session.

"Don't let me interrupt," I said, with the sickening attempt at pleasantry to which I was given in those days. Sandra seemed incapable of even saying hello.

There was nothing for it but to sneak into the backyard shed, where I'd generally kept a stash of something, roll up a stick of bud, and smoke away a little of my nightmare until I could find a way to obliterate the rest. The very next day, back in TV-land, it was even worse. Somehow, while my physical habit was banished, I just couldn't *be* in my writer's cubicle, listening to the happy clamor of my compadres as they tossed off witty plot twists and repartees for lovable Bruce and Cybill, without absolutely requiring some strain of mental alteration. So I smoked more grass. Against doctor's orders, true, but still hard for me to view as any big deal. Marijuana, after an aeon of junk, was strictly granola to me.

Of course, in no time I made the decision to stop the Trexan and go back on stuff. I was too cowardly to tell the doctor, so having looked up the dope-stopper in a *Physicians Desk Reference*—the addict's bible—I dug up some side effects I could arrange to suffer from as soon as possible.

"I'm telling you," I told him, "this stuff is killing my stomach. I have gas all the time. It feels like I'm digesting cannonballs. It's a nightmare."

Even Sandra was convinced. My flatulence was peeling the wallpaper. Of *course* it was the medication. What else could it be? Sandra was completely on my team about this. She had not witnessed me gulp down five bowls of oat bran in my office, scarf half a pound of dried apricots daily for three days, and guzzle a jug of OJ to wash down the pound of Fig Newtons I polished off in the car on the way home from the studio. I made sure it was a secret. Doctor Dope was about as fooled by my gastro distress as he would be if I'd painted red dots on my cheeks and walked in claiming the stuff caused measles. He let it slide, though.

When I finally called up to explain why I was stopping Trexan, with Sandra by my side at our dining room table, nodding her support, the doctor just listened and told me to do what I had to do. I hung up feeling completely justified. One of the addict's truly amazing gifts is his ability to con himself. By the next morning I'd rung Big G back up and banged half a dozen Dilaudids in the office. For at least half a week the stuff gave me a rush again. Then, just like they tell you on the drug ward, my tolerance returned to exactly where it was when I left off. I still had to do nearly a dozen of the things to know I'd even shot any.

So things progressed in their downward spiral of denial and dread, the birth of our child looming like the shadow of a bomb dropped from so high in the sky, you could pretend it wasn't even there, wasn't even coming . . . until it explodes, and life as you know it will never be the same.

• • •

It's all true. . . .

March 31, 1989, I found myself in the sterile confines of the Cedars-Sinai OB/GYN toilet, injecting a bomb-size hit of Mexican heroin while twenty feet away my baby daughter inched her way south in my screaming wife's uterine canal.

Somehow, cross-eyed and bloody-armed, I managed to scuffle back in time to see the sweetest thing in life shoot out of the womb and into Los Angeles.

The details of that blessed, devastating event—how low I'd sunk, how high I'd come—still burn through memory with the lurid brilliance of blood-red neon blinking in the fog. The new Mom remained strong and noble through it all. I'm the one who wanted the epidural. Fortunately, we'd done Lamaze. But what they don't tell you, in ten weeks of breathing lessons, is that hands-on Dads don't just have to show up and coach. They've got to *take off their shirts. . . .*

Consistent with my Big League I.V. behavior, I'd taken advantage of the lull between insurance form-filling and jolting labor pains to duck in the new-dad bathroom and cook up a shot. But I barely had time to ditch the spoon when I heard my name being hollered. Still reeling from that extra-big welcome-to-paternity hunk of heroin coursing skullward, I stumbled out of the men's room and off to the delivery. No sooner had I stepped in, however, than Dr. Randomangst issued the dread directive: scrubs.

"Scrubs?"

"You know," hissed the OB/GYN nurse, throwing me the sterile birthwear, "take your shirt off. . . ."

"My shirt? But you don't . . . I mean, I—I—I—I . . ."

"Take it off, NOW!" came the scream from that bed of pain. Even knees up, bucking out new life and basked in primal sweat, Sandra rose to the occasion, slipped into her associate producer mode, and got the job done.

What could I say but "Yes, dear," meek as Dagwood Bumstead forced up off the sofa to mow the crabgrass.

To this day, just writing this, I have to fight off the urge to lie down and cover my head with dirt. I mean, the look that doctor gave me when I pulled off my standard long black sleeves and squirmed into that puke green, short-sleeved germless hospital garb. "Jesus Christ!" he glowered without even moving his lips, his eyes burning two new holes in my already well-ventilated arms. When, in some pathetic sham of innocence, I looked down to see what he was looking at, I was more horrified than he was. This being a special occasion, I was not merely showing tracks—I was really *bleeding.*

Chernobyl pond scum, at that moment, loomed five flights up from me. Would that I could banish all memory of the telltale ruby trickle that ran wristward from the bruised, banana-black inner tubes that by now passed for veins.

But there was, for better or worse, time for no more than a token cringe. By now the joy of my life was already heading south, working her way out of Ground Zero. And I was *there,* I hope you believe this, despite the dope. Despite the shame, despite the life lived lately like a man doing laps in the gutter, I managed to coach the female cursed enough to have me as her daughter's father through a long and painful and successful delivery. Sandra swore she would not agree to a cesarean, and in those moments spent helping this tiny, determined woman absorb her pain and fight to bear her child as nature intended, I probably learned more about courage than I'd learned in a lifetime previous. All the character I lacked seemed, in those howling minutes, to be manifest in her.

Not until the flesh of my flesh was actually out in the world, and Nurse Rictus handed me scissors to cut the umbilical, did the king-hell predelivery hit of heroin kick in like a car accident.

Suddenly, with those scissors in my hand, I was as high as I'd ever been. My knees went watery. My eyes crossed and my vision doubled. For all I knew, I was drooling. High as I was, though, I had no choice. I aimed the blades the nurse had handed me and lurched forward, nearly slicing my child a third nostril, all but lopping her nose off entirely, barely managing to sever the cord without falling forward and giving my poor wife an impromptu postpartum mastectomy.

There are some travesties, I'm afraid, for which they still don't have support groups.

Part Six

HUGGIES 'N' HEROIN

The next week, high on smack and dadhood, I was back on the job. By way of prime-time congrats, a couple of staff caballeros offered me a few lines of coke. As usual, I declined politely. There was nothing I wanted less than a snootful of fancy milk-sugar with a batch of sweater-guys. I didn't tell them I preferred to shoot the shit. I just said "No."

I was weirdly glad to get back to cranking out the crap and blather, nestled in my private hellhole, wondering what in the name of *TV Guide* the Gods of Network Perversity were going to throw me next. At least the door locked.

The last thing I needed at that moment was a $1,500-a-week raise. I was already squandering my three and a half G's. I didn't need five. Still, after I'd done my part to shut down *Moonlighting,* the hard-core success-mongers at Creative Artists Agency had me primed for new horizons. They got me an interview at the Cannell company and sold my unworthy bottom.

That's Stephen J. Cannell, producer of small screen gems from pubescent snitch-fest *21 Jump Street* to highbrow lead festivals like *The A-Team.*

Give me a sitcom, or some chuckly drama, and I could get loaded and grind out something amusing. But the world of *Wise Guy* and Mister T, that was a stretch for which no known combo of drugs and caffeine existed. The whole towel-snapping, mondo-jocko, my-gun's-bigger-than-your-gun brand of testoster-tainment just wasn't me. But you know how agents are. They just want you to get rich.

My meeting with Mister Eric Blakeney, the hearty, pony-tailed swell at the helm of *Booker,* Stephen J's *21 Jump* spin-off, proved one of those instant hit-offs that usually take place on airplanes in danger of going down in the grips of killer turbulence. In other words, we both had to labor over-time against show biz loathing. And, by extension, a certain amount of self-disgust.

A fellow new dad, ex-musician, network-alienated writer, Eric B. had nonetheless managed to carve out a niche for himself in that bang-bang Cannell quarry. Reward for running *21 Jump Street* to the heights of high school triumph, he'd been installed as executive producer for this pretty-boy Richard Grieco vehicle. Also on board was legendary story structure evangelist, John Truby. I mention J.T. because, in the course of endless, prescript days spent kicking around just what Grieco, the hero, would do for his TV show living besides look like he fell off the cover of *Tiger Beat,* John-boy marched out some heavy structure-speak.

And how! The dean of script analysis opined on story arcs, plot cues and secondary-character religious hat symbolism until your author had to plead intestinal treachery and barrel out to the well-appointed Cannell toilet facilities.

No one, in that wild and toxic summer, ever slipped within gasping distance of actually writing anything. And no one seemed to mind. My job consisted of getting blind high and sitting on my ever-softening buttocks while the ascended drama masters declared their intention to revamp dramatic structure, revolutionize TV crime aesthetics, and grant a grateful viewing public the fruits of their philosophical pursuits.

I was making five thou a week and shooting six. The more alienated I felt, the more conventional I tried to become. My main connection was now a doctor's secretary in the Valley named Matilda.

Matilda was the sister-in-law of a fellow junkster, a celebrity trainer at one of L.A.'s trendy-for-ten-minutes health clubs. She worked as gal Friday to a Reseda croaker who peddled herbal rheumatism remedies along with any pill you wanted if you shelled out $35 for a bogus check-up fee. Dr. Bucky actually boasted his own show, on public access, and it was weirdly soothing to hit the remote control and tune in to the proprietor of the Valley's finest script mill on the air hawking homeopathic health tips.

These Reseda trips proved simultaneously toxic and holistic. Sure, I'd lay in my daily smack. But also, when el Doctor was out on a house call, my gal would slip me jugs of the pro healer's own vitamin blend or bend me over and bang a turbo shot of B_{12} in my butt. The B, presumably, was meant to fuel my depleted system, keep me breathing and driving long enough to come back and throw her some more dough, thereby enabling the lovely to keep her own hefty heroin hobby afloat.

My doctor visits comprised the social highlight of my day—though they did make for tons of extra drive time. Squire Blakeney had long since dubbed me the bathroom Bodhisattva. Reference to my constant, often tri-hourly one-man parades past the glaring, praying mantis–like receptionist to my favorite stall to cook more Mexican wonder-tar. Or, if the day's story lecture was particularly arid, a skull-shattering shot of cocaine to lend me some semblance of attentiveness through another forty-five minutes. Until it was time to either aim and fire again or leave entirely. Blakeney, I have to say, while not quite grasping my condition, at least honored it enough to grant me dispensation on the matter of early departures and later arrivals.

"Listen," he'd announce to the assembled staff, "I need all you guys in here tomorrow by eight-thirty."

At which point there'd be a pause, as the others filed out, before he'd lean that patrician profile my way and whisper, "Jerry, man, you can get in here at noon. It's okay. . . ." For which I am eternally grateful, and will always love him like the big, together brother my parents never produced.

So every day, after preschool, my little girl comes over to my apartment. Whatever we play, at some point she wants to watch a movie. The movie. The only one she wants to watch with me. We have Disney films. We have Rescuers Down Under. Beauty and the Beast. *We've got Doctor Seuss stuff.* Hop on Pop. How the Grinch Stole Christmas. *Stuff she used to love. Until one day, when I took her to Crown Books, where I knew they had a few kiddie tapes on sale, and she went right for the one she's been watching ever since. The one called* Big Bird Visits the Hospital.

It's not that long. Maybe a half hour or so. What happens is Big Bird wakes up on his nest one day and his throat is bad. He's got a cough, too, and he feels like he's burning up. Pretty Maria, who I guess is his keeper, or his mom, takes one look at him and announces that he has to go to the hospital. Big Bird's scared. He's never been to one before. But Maria insists. One thing leads to another, and there they are being examined by a scarily middle-aged Robert Klein, in the role of doctor. The graying comedian tells them, among other things, that he has to take a few tests. So Big Bird gets his temperature taken. They take his blood pressure. They send him down for an X-ray, and then, in the part on which my daughter has—there's no other word—fixated, they have to draw some blood. They have to stick a needle in his arm.

That's the deal: Big Bird gets a shot. Is this too vivid? Is it me? Big Bird raises his wing. He asks if it's going to hurt. The cute black nurse starts to say no, then catches herself, says, "Well, yes, but only for a little while." And Maria tries to comfort him as the nurse hoists the syringe before the camera, takes hold of the feathered yellow extremity, and—Mister Bird meet Mister Burroughs—drives it home.

This is what happens. Every afternoon. Big Bird cries out. Maria says, "It's over!" And my daughter yells, "Plause it, Daddy!" In her excitement—and every day she finds it exciting, as exciting as the day before—she forgets the right word and says "plause" instead of "pause."

"Sweetheart," I say, world's most irrelevant human, "the word is 'pause.'"

"I know." She scowls. "You always say that. Just rewind it and make it stop."

Which I do. Much as it pains me. Much as it, more accurately, weirds me right out the window. For every afternoon, in this most wholesome of parent-child situations, watching a fucking Sesame Street *home video, the two of us sit, enthralled, as, frozen by remote control, Big Bird stands stock still before us. Beak parted in anguish. Eyes wild. And—"DADDY LOOK!"—there's the syringe stuck right where a giant land-bound bird would stick it if he used to do what Daddy did. If he were the kind of bird who did the kind of thing Daddy used to do, the kind of thing this beautiful child should have been too young to remember now.*

"BIG BIRD GETS OFF. . . ."

Christ!

Junkie dadhood packed its own brand of positive logic. My baby and I bonded with a wholesome fervor only a man content to be up and at 'em at two, three, four, or five A.M. could ever comprehend. The thing about being a drug addict is that, if you're in pocket, you never have to feel too bad for too long. So no predawn diaper action was going to bother *me.* I'd hear young doll face crying, gather her in my arms and head downstairs. I'd rest her squirming in her cotton cowboy blankie on the closed lid of a toilet while I fixed a spoon, filled a syringe, and fixed before her wide and innocent and, I pray, uncomprehending eyes.

I know I'm going to toast in hell. But in the end there's no thrill, really, like plucking your crying baby from her crib, holding her aloft, cooing soft and soothing opiated phrases until she's ready to lay her seven-pound-seven-ounce self down and drift to baby dreamland again.

There's no defense, really, beyond the niggling fact that the dope kept Dad's hands steady. It took away the sickness. Enabled the joy and compassion buried under all those drug-encrusted layers of self-loathing to trickle to the surface. If you've been there, you get it. If you haven't, what can I say?

Having shot up at some ungodly hour, the man of the house would stay blissed while he played peek-a-boo with his non-toxic offspring. It was swell.

I don't know what Dr. Spock or, for that matter, Dr. Burroughs has to say about junkie fathering. For me, product of a childhood that evokes but a single, wintry adjective—*tense,* the ability to stay happy myself at any and all hours meant I had at least half a chance of easing my young sweetheart through her crying jag and seeing her crack a smile back up at me. Reward, as any schmaltzed-out pop can tell you, transcending any and all sins.

Maybe I wouldn't advocate it on *Donahue.* But after a day of television hell and an evening of moribund matrimony, a late night of horsehead Dad-bliss packed plenty to recommend it. Right out of the gate, recognizing what a show biz–financed moral leper I'd become, the best I aspired to, child rearing-wise, was to be an entertaining moral leper.

How to capture the exact sensation of slowly killing yourself while struggling to imbue a decent life to the one thing on God's foul asteroid that actually means anything to you? I was determined to raise Nina up. And keep her raised, even though I was going down.

Some nights, holding my still-new-to-the-universe baby to my chest, I'd feel her tiny heart beating against mine and think, "This is it . . . This is life's last frontier." As I felt her heart, no larger than a hummingbird, my contentment was savaged by the realization: *Yes, this is her heart, but the blood that pumps through her tiny veins is the very same vintage that floats in my own.* Distilled from my own mother's blood. Which, God help me, I sometimes thought I shot dope solely to banish.

In goes the good air, out goes the bad.

Except we were talking about blood. The family blood.

Whatever'd come from Sandra, I knew, was fine. Untainted. But what came from me would surely rise up and drown the child if she were not loved. Because Nina was born with more against her, she had to be more adored. And if nothing else, I could do that. Even in my now nonstop ravaged state, I could do that.

As I held her in the deepest night, lifted her tiny, squalling form from her still-warm crib, I redoubled my grasp. Tickled her on the belly. Kissed her behind the ear. Swung her upside down. Tossed her in the air. Sang and jiggled and peek-a-booed her to sheer ecstasy. Took this child from tears to delight, however hellish I might feel.

So that squirming angel, in fact, was my salvation. Not the other way around. *I* was the helpless one. I don't know how I ever lived without her.

It's a grim memory: packing my unsuspecting child, still in swaddling, into a babyseat and hauling her to whatever corner was still open for biz at four o'clock on a Sunday morning. At that hour, the only living beings behind the wheel are either looking for drugs or looking for druggies. Addicts and Heat. No in-between. There were late nights, downwind of Fourth and Bonnie Brae, when whoever I was trying to cop from was shy of standing in the streetlight and beckoned me into some cave of a stairwell or some spot behind a dumpsite, where, prior to fatherhood, I would not have thought twice about following. And where now, child in hand, I still followed.

It wasn't that I couldn't see the madness of what I was doing. It was that I could not let myself see it. You think no one ever gets hit over the head trying to cop? No one ever gets knifed in the back? Or worse? . . .

One 3:00 A.M., gripped by the craving, the drive that's beyond describing if you haven't already died and survived it, I followed a cat-eyed young Latina into a doorway off a street I couldn't even find in daylight, through the cast-iron door of a blacked-out abandoned building somewhere in Pico-Union. Nina asleep in my arms, not even wakened by my nervous sniffling. I stepped down that pitch-black broken-glass hallway, the corners stinking of stale piss, stumbling behind this complete stranger into a candlelit room where half a dozen other lost souls crouched or sat in various stages of junk sickness and junk relief. No one looked up. I gave the homegirl my money, waited in stillness while she made her way across the room to dig up the soiled bag where she kept the balloons. I held Nina in my arms, trying not to look at the face of the nearest figure, a muttering skeleton sprawled by a pillar at my feet. Tried not to think, until the skeleton looked up, raised its arms and, with a mouthful of missing teeth, through pus-blackened lips, said, "Nice baby. . . . Lemme hold the baby. . . ."

And when I resisted, holding Nina closer to my chest, the figure took my silence for rejection, a statement of superiority. Then I realized the skeleton was a she. "Hey, I got a baby, too, motherfucker . . . I know about babies. . . ." When I still said nothing, frozen, as I was, trying to just will myself out of there—*where is that bitch with the fucking dope?*—the specter lit a cigarette. For an instant I could see the running sores on her arms, the sores in the corners of her mouth. "Tell you what, motherfucker, 'least I don't bring no kid here. 'Least I don't drag no baby into this. . . ."

Mercifully, the girl stepped out of the dark and handed me what I came in for. I don't know if I could have stood another minute, standing in front of the mirror that this talking corpse on the floor represented. But she wasn't really my own reflection. She was better. She wouldn't bring *her* baby down into this. And, though I stayed frozen, and didn't say a word, we both knew it. *You are worse than me!* That was the message flickering from those tombstone eyes.

It seemed another eternity, at least, until I could get home, take Nina inside, put her to bed, and try to get high enough to forget the status I'd just verified.

The efficacy of taking along a sweet-faced infant to purchase drugs was proved one Sunday morning at the corner of Alvarado and Sunset Boulevard. In my haste to make it home—I'd already copped, and the homeboy gave me a discount 'cause he liked kids—I drove right through a red light.

Didn't even look. Just zipped on through the Sunday morning deserted intersection and kept zipping.

So absorbed was yours truly in anticipatory heaven, I didn't even know I was behind the wheel. In some ways the best rush is the one the adrenaline gives you when you've just copped and you're heading home. Had someone tapped me on the shoulder and told me I was driving, I would probably have been surprised. Which, as it happened, I *was* when I heard the siren.

I pulled over right away, after blithely ignoring the whirling cherry for three and a half blocks. Letting the black-and-white on my tail slip into pre–car chase behavior. I even elicited that LAPD signature, the rolling PA display, the crack technology that turns every police car into a karaoke-on-wheels. PULL OVER . . . YOU IN THE BLACK ACURA, PULL OVER TO THE CURB . . . Which I also ignored. And not 'cause I wanted to. Not out of some brass-balled, *muy macho,* criminal behavior. I was no criminal type. Despite the tripartite felony I committed on a daily basis: buying an illegal substance; possessing the equipment to use it; and, my own favorite, *just having the substance in my body.*

I wasn't dogging the police. I was distracted. The officer told me to step out of my car, spread my legs apart, and put my hands in front of me on the roof of the car, where he could see them. Even without the benefit of Mister Microphone, his voice seemed to boom into the hollow of that four A.M. boulevard. In Los Angeles the absence of traffic noises is itself deafening, but he was even louder. The baby, amazingly, stayed soundly asleep in her little travel pack.

"Hand me your wallet."

"Okay," I say.

"You could have killed somebody," he said, speaking more softly after he saw Nina.

"You're right," I said over my shoulder. "You're right. It's been one of those nights. You know how it is, the kid wakes up at the crack of three, the wife's still asleep, then you find out you're out of milk, so you have to go get some, but you can't just leave the kid in there squawking. . . ."

"You get used to it," he says, handing me back my license. "I got three myself, so I know. . . ."

He tells me to go ahead, get back in the car, but for Christ's sake be more careful. And I thank him profusely, but not too profusely, as I make a show of leaning over my beatific charge. I'm all set to turn the key in the ignition, all set to go, when, Oh Christ . . . Oh, screaming Christ, NO!—I see the syringe, for no reason at all, just roll out from under the car seat, on the passenger side. Just roll out onto a pool of light the street lamp throws in the car.

I don't say anything. I know he's still standing beside me. One more second, I think, I could have made it. . . . Fuck! He won't find the stuff, I think, because the balloons are in my mouth. I'll swallow them if I have to. But the rig. The fucking rig! I didn't even know it was there. It could, I suddenly realize, with a sinking feeling in my gut even worse than the one I've had already, that I'm *still* having, it could have rolled out with Sandra driving. My God. . . .

All of this flashes by in a millisecond. I can't look up at the man. I know he has me. Nothing to say. But suddenly I feel his hand on my shoulder. The fingers squeeze. But not too bad. Somewhere between authority and pain.

"Look at me," he says. And when I do, the expression on his face is not even threatening. It's the farthest thing from threatening. It's disgusted. It's got *You're pathetic* stamped all over it in a million ways.

Our eyes meet, and he simply shakes his head.

"I'm not going to take you in," he says. "What's the point?" If there were a machine that measured contempt, his voice would break it. He starts to walk away, stops, sticks his broad face back in the open window. I focus on his brush mustache. I don't want to see his eyes. "You sorry fuck.

Wherever you are now is worse than any place we can put you."

I don't even start the car. I can't bring myself to start the car, until he's hit his own ignition and pulled away. Not even in a peel of rubber. Not with any drama at all. I'm not even worth that. Not worth the gesture.

I'm not even worth arresting.

The thought hovers inside my head the rest of the ride home. I try to hold it, in a self-contained bubble, for the five minutes it takes to get to my house. I don't want the thought to escape, don't want to follow it to the next thought, or the thought after that. I just want to pull in, take my baby up the steps to our dark house, here in the moments before dawn, and walk inside like a man with a grip on his life.

I walked up those steps, as I had a thousand times before, feeling the knowing, invisible eyes of all my neighbors, all the neighbors in the world, drilling into my back.

I put Nina down. Kissed her on the forehead. Went back downstairs and prepared my fix as mechanically as possible. Without a thought in my head. Keeping thought down by sheer force of will until the heroin could enter my system and do it for me.

Only once—*I used my own child as a front . . . to save my ass . . . I risked everything. I did that. . . .* Only once, as the plunger was driving home, did I let the thought sneak out.

My sweet and newly widowed mom-in-law, she of the Scottish lilt and blood pressure just south of the U.K. GNP, needed badly to set eyes upon her half-Yankee grandchild. And her daughter, not yet widowed but no doubt crossing her fingers, needed to hop the pond but pronto to see her mum.

Left to my own devices, cut loose to geeze freely with my feet up in front of the VCR, my habit, already way rampant, tore forward like Vlad the Impaler with a fresh pair of spikes. No longer able to feed my jones on my wages as small-screen strumpet, I took to snapping up the future ex's Versateller card. Like many a skulking junkie, I could black out on entire decades but remember someone else's PIN number with a mnemonic flair that would scare Harry Lorraine. To this day my heart goes pitter-pat just motoring past the Versateller there at Silverlake and Glendale. My favorite stop.

By the time our teeny dreamgirl and her mom jetted back to our Silverlake abode, something had changed. And it wasn't just the size of my habit.

• • •

By chance I bumped into an old pal, Dog-Boy, member of a legendary one-hit punk band who used to live in the old Cherokee Building on Hollywood Boulevard. Doggy and I took to meeting mornings at the Happy Day Donut Shop. Second only to cops and retirees, full-time junkies spend a lot of their nonworking day at doughnut shops, mulling over lukewarm java, passing that nondairy creamer back and forth while discussing their *Plans.* (Dog-Boy, weirdly, didn't like the term *dope fiend;* he preferred to call himself a "Heroin Ecstatic.")

Around that time, conveniently enough, Cannell fired my friend and boss, Blakeney. And in an act that looked like loyalty—a trusting employee falling on the sword for his beloved superior—but was actually desperation, I'd quit myself. Even the pretense of work, by then, took too much energy. Which left Doggy and me plenty of time to shoot heroin and talk about our latest obsession—*kicking*. . . .

Doggy lived with a girl named Darlene, a onetime Wilhelmina model who never got out of bed. I'd seen her upright maybe once or twice, when Dog made her sit up so he could get a better angle to shoot her up in the femoral. She was the skinniest human being I'd ever seen, outside of Dachau snaps. Her skin, from never leaving the apartment, was some translucent skim-milk color that contrasted horribly with the bruises the needle left. You could shake Darlene's hand and you'd leave a black-and-blue mark. She was that fragile. Which, since all she did was sleep, actually worked out all right.

Dog-Boy had easy access to the au courant kick specialist, Dr. Mark. The good doctor "cured" everybody who was anybody in the L.A. music scene. Though it was one of his unluckier clients who sent him careening onto the tabloid exposé circuit. A heroin victim named Jason, son of the late Jill Ireland, stepson of Charles Bronson, had done a stint on Buprenex, the doctor's secret ingredient.

Unfortunately Jason ended up dead—and the subject of a cheesy TV movie. But that didn't stop boxcars of moneyed dope fiends from hopping on board. Buprenex is amazing stuff. With enough Betty Bupes in pocket, you can actually get off smack—and not have one iota of withdrawal. I never visited the doctor. Dog-Boy got the stuff, charged me double for my share, which paid for his, and instructed me in the rather arcane manner of its application. Unlike other substances I've injected, this one had to be shot, according to practicing experts, into fat. Not always an easy commodity to find in a junkie, but there you are.

Dog-Boy and I, side by side in his rig-littered apartment—there were so many old balloons on the floor, it looked like he'd just hosted a child's birthday party in hell—squeezed out a fold of cellulite from our respective stomachs until we had enough to poke. You had to break a glass ampule—or two or three, depending on the habit you were trying to crack—suck it into the shooter, and jam it into your bunched-up tummy.

You could absolutely get yourself off heroin and not even crack a sweat. But that was the problem. I do believe the great god of hard narcotics designed the hell-on-earth of heroin withdrawal for a reason. Namely, so you could go through it, suffer until your bones broke, and when you came to the other end, swear to yourself, on the grave of Elvis, that you'd never, never ever ever, never put yourself through that again. It was just too painful.

It was so darn easy to stop, there was no real reason not to start again. Which, genius that I am, is exactly what I did. Over and over. Until, of course, the Bupes dried up. Once Dog got off dope, see, he had another problem. He was bulimic. Tragically, amazingly bulimic. He was, in fact, known as Dog-Puke to those on the scene. The man could purge more in five minutes than most people in a lifetime of pie-eating contests. The only reason he got into heroin in the first place, he said, was 'cause it was the one thing that stopped him binging and purging.

One more time, I was strung out like a lab rat. With nothing to do but keep going. And no end in sight. Once more drugs had created a hell that only drugs could get me out of. Fortunately, Sandra and the baby were still out of the country. That was the one bit of good fortune, if you can call it that, to which I could lay claim. I'd actually completed an assignment or two at work during this time. Most notably, in the grand What-If-I-Hadn't-Fucked-It-Up Department was a script gig for this newfangled new show called *Northern Exposure*. Run by this quirky little bald guy and his quirky partner over there in the MGM Black Tower. I spent fifteen minutes wandering around the Bank of America, wondering why it looked so much like a bank, until I realized MGM was *behind* it. It could happen to anybody.

The *Northern Exposure* guys called a day or three after I turned in the first draft. Left me that classic, "*Gee, thanks, it's everything we wanted. In fact it's terrific. Really! One of the best darn things we've ever seen. . . . It's just, um, I don't think you should bother doing the polish. . . . No need to even come in for notes. . . . In fact, you really don't have to come back to our office at all. . . . PLEASE DO NOT COME BACK TO OUR OFFICE! Okay? We think we'll just kind of, you know, write it ourselves . . . But, hey, thanks . . . you're really terrif! And keep in touch!"* That kind of thing. . . . So there I was, on the cusp of yet another ground-breaking TV moment. Jerry Stahl, footnote to small-screen history. . . . Slipping on down the tubes.

Once Sandra and the baby made their way home, I realized my fate fell in the third of the Eternal Trio of Dope Fiend Destinies. I didn't end up dead. Didn't get busted. No, my future seemed to lie behind Door Number Three: in the The Heinous-but-Undreamed-of column. But by then I wasn't really trying to give it a name. I was too busy trying to get through it. . . .

The two ladies in my life made their way up the steps through our cacti garden—*Doctor, needles are everywhere!*—to a darkened home. Not because Daddy, napping after a hard day at the hack factory, forgot to turn on the lights. Daddy didn't pay the utility bill. He hadn't paid any bills, for that matter. The thing is, he needed the extra $143 that would have gone for heat and light to feed his rabid veins.

What I'd done, see, was pocket the mother of my daughter's bank card. Memorized her PIN number, and from the minute she'd left town become a regular patron of the cash dispenser. But those B of A sharpies had cut off access to that C-note Versateller privilege some two weeks earlier. Caring, involved bureaucrats that they were, they wondered, you know, what my better half's sudden upsurge in maxed-out 6 A.M. withdrawals at their scenic Silverlake facility was all about.

Between us, my beautiful life partner and I could just not figure out who or what accounted for this three-hundred-a-day deal. *"I don't have a clue, hon! Maybe some low-life got hold of your card!"*

In the end, no Sleaze Houdini alive could have wangled out of this one. Bank of America, may it please the court, possessed what I believe is known in the legal community as "incontrovertible evidence." Namely, my heathen mug, in grainy photostat, captured again and again by the snap-happy hidden camera apparently mounted over every cash machine on the planet.

It was perfect! My own status as addict, sleazeball and all-around TV deviate now out of the closet—*on TV!*

Late nights when I had Nina to myself, I would talk to her. Rocking her in my arms, or changing her diaper when she woke up wet, I would talk about my father.

"He wasn't home much," I remember telling her, one 4:00 A.M. As I rocked her in my arms. I used to stand her before the picture window, watching the lone palm tree in front of our house sway in the moonlight. Whispering till my lips tickled her ear, *"He was what they call an Important Man. And it made me feel bad. . . ."*

As I rambled on I'd look down at her tiny, attentive face, so beautiful in its innocent wonder, and I would take her serenity as tacit agreement. Nina wasn't a crier. She either smiled, a gorgeous, oddly ironic smile, or she would just . . . look. It was as if she were commenting on my absurd attempts to treat her like a baby. So that instead, eventually, I found myself speaking to her like an equal. Appealing to her for some kind of understanding.

"You see, sweetheart, I know he loved me, but he wasn't around, you know? Half the time he lived in different cities. And when he was home, he left before I even got up and came home right before bed. One thing, though, every day he brought me a little Golden Book. I used to love seeing him open his huge briefcase, this old battered tan thing he never seemed to be without—it might have been an extension of his left hand—and I'd watch while he fished among the important papers, the stuff you have to have when you're running a city, when you're an important man in charge of important things, and he'd pull out The Little Engine That Could, *or* The Brave Little Toaster. *I used to love stories about feisty little machines or animals that no one liked, that*

no one thought could do anything, that surprised everybody and got lots of friends in the end. . . .

"He'd give me the book and, I still remember, our hands would touch. His fingers so thick, so warm. And I would want, sometimes, to kiss the palm of his hand. Want to hold it there. I don't know. . . . Lots of times he would fall asleep in his big yellow chair, while my mother was already upstairs, in bed, yelling down at him, 'David, come up! Come up! Why aren't you coming up!' He never wanted to go upstairs. Never wanted to go. Instead he'd be down there asleep, some giant brown lawbook open on his lap, his hand hanging over the side of his chair. And I would sneak over, I guess I was walking by then, I must have been, but I don't remember. . . . I would just snuggle over, and I would take his huge warm hand, and I would kiss the heart of his palm. I would put it on my head, and I would curl up like that, beside him, on the floor. . . . Just loving the touch of him. Loving the love I imagined was there, even if he was asleep . . . Even if he didn't know I was there. Even if—I guess this is sad now, but it didn't seem that way then—even if he didn't know he loved me . . . Do you know what I mean?"

And Nina, her sweet little chins tucked on my bare shoulder, would raise her blue eyes up at me. And I swear she would tell me she understood. She would—and by saying this, perhaps, I'm damning myself forever to moral decrepitude and the crime of self-delusion; but I don't care, because I felt it then, and I feel it now—*she would forgive me.*

Whatever else I wasn't, I was *there.* Even if every cell in my body was dying, I loved her. And I showed it. I held her in my arms, for hours at a time, wanting her to store up all the love she could get from me. To give her my love so that she could have it when I was gone.

"This is all I can give you," I'd whisper, trying not to let the tears that rolled down my face drip down on her. *"You are going to know, from the minute you were born, that you*

were loved. No matter what. You were held. And you're never going to think you're worthless. Never going to feel bad about yourself. Never going to feel the kind of shame that was all I ever felt. Do you understand?"

In my opiated insanity, my emotions lived so close to the surface they might as well have been tattooed on my skin. As if the love I wanted so badly to instill in her could be transmitted that way, flesh to flesh, by holding her soft, warm body against my bare chest.

"No matter what happens, I love you," I told her, over and over. Until, I hoped, the words found a safe, untouchable place in her brain. In her heart.

No quantity of love, tainted or otherwise, could stave off the calamity to come. There followed, months after mother and child returned from their transatlantic jaunt, the kind of domestic horror show the Big Three networks routinely squeeze into "Disease of the Week" movies. This weeper featured the soul-seared Daddy's last-ditch effort to kick drugs, yet again, on his own and unbeknownst to the women unfortunate enough to share his futon. What I did, see, was gulp a fistful of chloral hydrates, mild sleep aids my clueless analyst had prescribed to help his troubled patient beat his pesky insomnia problem. The idea, as my blistered brain originally conceived it, was to just go out, power-nap straight through the usual slime-skinned, vomitous, cramp-racked carnival of hell kicking cold turkey inevitably invites.

That was the plan. Except that, halfway to Uncle Snoozey's house, in a scene that has *Tales from the Crypt* slapped all over it, the Maine Fisherman appeared at the end of my bed. Straight up! This burly old salt, in yellow slicker from hat to mackintosh to waist-high waders, loomed hugely over me. Anchovies all but dripping from his thick mustache, he kept asking the same insane questions over and over. "What city do you live in?" "Do you know your birthday?" And that perennial fave: "How many fingers?"

Well, maybe I *had* acted up without knowing it. Maybe I had been spazzing around the bedroom like some junk-sick Jerry Lewis babbling about alien conga lines. I just don't know.

All that's certain is, when the fisherman, who turned out to be a paramedic in full-bore firefighting gear, decided I wasn't a candidate for that forced ride to Camarillo—where they shipped Charlie Parker—my wife took matters into her own hands. Though tiny, Sandra had little trouble slapping a jacket on my sopping back. There was scant challenge getting my quaking, gimpy limbs stuffed in some jeans. Ditto shoes and socks. In no time I was off that sweat-soaked mattress, more or less nonhorizontal, and out the front door with car keys in one paw and sixteen crumpled ones in the other.

Good-bye, family. Good-bye, ersatz straight life.

No more than five minutes after the OD SWAT team reboarded its fire engine, the stirring squeal of brakes still hung in the air, I fumbled with keys to my Yup-mobile and headed off to what's known in the abuse biz as an all-new bottom.

From that moment, shoved out in the street, dope-ravaged, weepy, puking in the car that TV had paid for even as I fled the life it cost, I was a man on roads so divergent they could only meet again in some optical illusion of heaven or hell.

I thought I knew what trouble was. But I didn't have a clue.

I'm always buying Nina things: mostly little stuff, shiny animal stickers, silly fifty-cent plastic gewgaws. . . . Nothing major, except for the occasional videotapes, which we go to Blockbuster together to pick out. Her mother hates all this crap, since Nina's always dragging it home, and her house has become like a museum of under-a-dollar kiddie treats, knee-deep with Mickey Mouse rings, rubber iguanas, broken Batmobiles, miniature Spanish food cans, cheesy tchotchkes of every stripe, but what the hell? There are all kinds of revenge, I suppose, and this had to be the most benign in postmatrimonial history.

I have to say, though, I sometimes lean a little on the videotapes. Some afternoons we just head into my apartment, set up the pretzel bowl, snag a couple of soft-box Treetop apple juices for our mutual delectation and pop right on the couch.

Thus readied, we sit in front of the Madeline tape we've seen fifty-seven times, or Beauty and the Beast, *which we've probably seen one hundred and fifty-seven, or the legendary* Don't Cry, Big Bird, *whose performance count is doubtless now in the thousands.*

A none-too-admirable way to spend time with your offspring. Except, that's never all we do. We rarely watch a movie all the way through. First of all there's chatting. There's a whole world I don't understand, and I have to ask her about it. (Like, for example, where chicken comes from. Turns out chicken comes from under the supermarket, where the checkout ladies keep them in spooky chicken caves—I found that out just last week. Old MacDonald has no farm.)

Then there's the kitty visits. Mickey and Minnie wander in and wander out, stopping occasionally to leap on her lap or try to steal her pretzel sticks. Always a welcome diversion. We have not, of course, even mentioned that impulsive dash over to the computer to fuck around with Kid Pix, to etch something suitably grotesque and run it off the printer, or the quick drop onto the carpet for a session spent with markers, doing some serious coloring. (Kids don't have crayons anymore. They have markers. I don't know what the advantage is, except markers stain the fingers. You can give each other tattoos with them, and that is kind of fun.)

Once in a while we even read books—her fave remains Dr. Seuss: The Cat in the Hat Comes Back*—though shame on me, this does not, as of late, in any way comprise her first, or second, or even third choice of happening activity.*

My own favorite, albeit strenuous, dad-and-daughter thing has to be dancing.

Nina's recently got on this ballet kick. She hasn't had the lessons yet. So far she's just got the tutu. But, still, how better to gear up for future pas de deux, to nurse those nascent pliés, than rocketing around the room with a Rolling Stones record or some insane Coltrane tape—anything, as long as it's fast. Nina's favorite is Miles Davis's "Cooking Live at the Plug Nickel," his version of "Stella By Starlight," and the Stones' "Exile on Main Street." Lately I've had to find faster and faster tracks—madder music—and only last Saturday rediscovered "Rip This Joint," second track on "Exile." It's the fastest rock-and-roll song I can find. She's also got a little thing for Pearl Jam, though they're a little sluggish for her taste.

I live in the tiniest apartment in the world. One room—literally. No kitchen. No nothing, just a bathroom off to the side and a slab of concrete in front that we like to call the "patio." (It's never too soon to teach your child embellishment. Such a handy art. Just look where it got me!)

Somehow, between the bed and the bookshelves, the desk and the door, we spin, we spaz, we jump and gyrate and do all kinds of one-legged moves that have me gasping for breath and begging for mercy after what seem like hours but always, inevitably, turn out to be no more than fifteen minutes.

My neighbors, I'm quite sure, are really happy about hearing the same screaming sax solo or the same Keith Richards licks twenty-three times in succession. God knows I am! That's the only real advantage of the CD, as far as I can tell. You can play the same track over and over without any guesswork. No needle to worry about getting in the groove. . . .

So yesterday, in a moment of inspiration, I dragged myself to Hollywood Toys, on seedy and malevolent Hollywood Boulevard, and bought her blocks.

I asked for blocks, and the friendly Armenian lad behind the counter seemed a little dazed by my request.

"Blocks?" asked the youngster. "Blocks? What kind of batteries do they take?"

He had bad acne and a backward Cypress Hill pot-leaf baseball hat, so I guess he was too young to remember them. The owner, a slouchy older Armenian with a tired smile, had to explain to the Blunt boy what they were.

"Kids. . . ." He shrugged. "If it ain't Nintendo, they don't wanna know. Me, I'll take a good set of Lincoln Logs. It's the parents who go for the high-tech shit." He sighed and wiped his face with a smudged-up handkerchief, then jammed it back in his pocket. "Your little tykes, they still want the fuckin' blocks. What are you gonna do?"

Back at the pad, Nina is absolutely ecstatic at what I've bought. "We can build a home," she cries, and I nod yes. . . . "Yes, we can!" All the while fighting the urge to read into her choice of "home," of all the things in the world you can possibly make with blocks. Once I start interpreting, I can't stop. It's not that different from seeing faces in the paint swirls. . . .

We ended up playing with them the whole afternoon. At first, Nina built her home small and secure, adding on a walled enclosure while I built wobbly towers. But it wasn't long before she had an idea: Why don't we build a path connecting my house with her house, so we can have one home? "That way we can all live there," she said.

"All?"

"You, me, and Mommy. Yeah! And we could build a special little home for Minnie and Mickey. Yeah yeah yeah!"

"You'd like that?"

"We'd all be together. We'd be together forever."

So it works out, each time we knock down what we've built—Nina, being Daddy's little girl, takes every bit as much pleasure in destroying what she's built as actually building it—we're careful to build sidewalks that join whatever we put up afterward.

This is very important. We must connect our two independent castles, to make them one.

At the end of the day, when it's time to take Nina back to her Mommy's house, to HER house, there is always a difficult moment. She doesn't want to go. She wants to stay with me. But she wants to be with her Mommy, too.

She's okay one place or another; it's the transitions that are tough. Mommy in one house, Daddy in another house—this is the conundrum that's consumed this child since she sprang into verbal consciousness.

Sadly, on those occasions when her mommy comes to pick her up from Daddy's humble abode, Mommy does not speak. She barely enters the apartment. Instead, she stands by the door in total silence, vibing the place like an ammonia bomb. Her disapproval is palpable. Her loathing, so elo-

quent in her disturbing silence, confuses the child even more. Makes everyone uncomfortable.

At four and a half the child has yet to see an example of even gratuitous parental affection.

"Daddy," Nina says, when it's time to wend our inevitable way back to Mommy's house, "Daddy, don't knock the houses down when I'm not here, okay?"

"Okay," I say, "I'll leave them up."

"We all live together there," she explains, enlightening me with make-believe, the alternate world she'd much prefer to the one she actually lives in. "We all brush our teeth before bed."

I don't know why this chills me. Why I feel constrained to hold her so, to pick her up and carry her to the car in my arms. She's nearly too old for that.

"Don't worry, kid." I can see it's important to her. "I'll leave everything up."

"That's good, Daddy. That's where I want to live."

And in that instant, as if a curtain were suddenly torn from the sun, I think: "This is why I did drugs. . . ."

I did drugs because there was another world, and I wanted to live in it. Because I preferred this Other World to the one I happened to inhabit. Because I could exist in imaginary circumstances with greater ease than I could in real ones.

I did drugs because I felt the exact same way about my life my little girl already seemed to feel about hers.

"Leave them up," she repeats, raising her small, serious face to mine.

"I will, Nina. Don't you worry."

Stroking her hair, I try to remember the first time I wanted to change my world. And realize, with a shudder, I have never not wanted to. Realize, with something like a crack in my heart, that it really must be the same for Nina. That life, for this precious little creature, has already turned.

"I promise, sweetheart."

I hear the choke in my voice and have the worst thought I've ever had about my child: She's the same as me.

As soon as I think it, I hear myself praying that it isn't so.

Dear God, *I scream inside my head,* dear God, don't let her turn into her father. . . .

I press Nina to my chest for an extra second. Then I place her in the car, trying not to let her see how her words affect me. Trying not to let her see my own horrified tears.

"I won't tear your house down, baby. Never again. . . ."

PART SEVEN

TOXIC EXILE

Not a lot of people sleep in their Acuras. It's not the kind of car you associate with the homeless. A fact that must please the parent company. Fortunately it was not very cold in L.A. In fact, it was ninety degrees at four in the morning. So the big decision is whether to open the window—to risk physical mayhem for a chance at a fresh breeze; or keep it closed—skirt suffocation but stave off invasion. There's a seething nocturnal world out there. When you're on the bottom, you're fair game for the bottom feeders.

Of course, considering my condition, my first order of business was not exactly finding a condo. No, despite the crippling effect of the medication already inside me, I had to score more.

In fact, it was fear that I'd had some kind of stroke that made Sandra dial 911 in the first place. Not till she found it was a drug thing did the panic turn to righteous rage. The chloral hydrate left me hunched and listing to the left, like a combination of Walter Brennan doing "Granpappy Amos" in *The Real McCoys* and one of those people in the Boston marathon who squinch across the finish line, disoriented and drooling, brain damaged for life because, no matter what, they just wanted to say they made it. The things people do to themselves!

Along with thrashing my equilibrium, so that I had to lean

on things to keep from falling, I could not keep my head up. My skull kept lolling to one side, like a broken doll's. I'd also fucked up my speech center. My vision was blurry. This horrible swamp gas sweat kept oozing out of me. And I'd lost control of my bladder. . . .

So this was my wife's last vision of me, for some time to come: a man reeling sideways, foam flecking his lips, fresh pee stains on his pants—in my case canary yellow, on account of my vitamin regimen—protesting slurrily that he was okay and begging to see his child. *"Jush lemme kisshabay-bee . . . I jush wanna kisshabay-bee g'bye . . ."*

In desperation Sandra called her shrink, who'd long since advised getting rid of me. She rested the receiver on the arm of the couch as she negotiated my exit. Even from the front porch I could hear the psychiatrist dictating tinny encouragement. Somehow the static made her words more ominous. At first I didn't see the phone. It was like orders were coming from inside Sandra's head. *"Don't talk to him. Do you understand me? You have nothing to discuss. . . ."*

Half-stumbling down the fifty-three steps from door to driveway, scratching myself bloody trying to hold on to thorny bougainvillea, I finally gave up and crawled. I took the last stretch in a kind of backward crab-walk, humping down on my ass before an audience of enthralled neighbors. When I got to the bottom I could hardly stand up, but of course you don't have to stand up to drive. You do that sitting down. It never occurred to me, before then, how handy that was. If people had to drive standing up, like milkmen used to do, there'd probably be millions less traffic accidents.

In a triumph of the human spirit that still scares the T-cells out of me, I managed to aim my auto toward the Hollywood Freeway and head north to the Valley, for Matilda's house. At one point I raised my face off the wheel long enough to see the logo of a Shell Oil truck looming so close I could see the yellow paint pores. Luckily, it was my left leg that had gone numb, so I could jam on the brakes.

Matilda, whose two-room duplex my habit paid for, was less than thrilled to see me. I didn't anticipate my chilly reception. Knowing my condition might, you know, put her off, I decided to stop into 7-Eleven and pick her up a muffin. Matilda had the classic junkie sweet tooth. She lived on sugar and still weighed less than a paper plane. The 7-Eleven jumbo double chocolate she loved the best.

I'd forgotten that I'd peed my pants, and that I still walked like a man struck by lightning. With my unfailing ability to block out reality, I waltzed into the convenience store like any other Sunday night citizen. The crowd in front of the counter cleared a path.

Along with a scowling Latino couple and a trio of Valley six-pack boys in Hawaiian shirts, even the seen-it-all Sikh behind the register wrinkled his nose. I actually looked over my shoulder—*to see who he was looking at.*

"You—OUT!"

"Who, *me*?"

I was ready to call my lawyer. There was nothing wrong with *me!*

"Don't get your turban in a twist, pal, all I want's a muffin. . . ."

"Out. . . . *NOW!*"

By the time he reached down for his baseball bat, it didn't matter anymore. The squat Spanish guy let go of his wife's arm enough to give me a shove toward the door. The three Hawaiian shirts were panting for action.

"I am just going to get a muffin," I repeated, lurching right through this lynch mob, around the ice-cream cooler, and past the Frito's rack to get my mitts on a gift for Matilda.

The Indian screamed something that sounded like "Heep!" though I can't be sure. "Heep!" then a vast rush of air, a whistling right by my ear.

"FUCK!"

I didn't feel the first blow on my shoulder. The Sikh had

held back, letting go something between a bunt and a full swing.

The second time nearly floored me. The Louisville slugger cracked on my elbow and sent me careening toward the magazine rack. I was still ready to make my purchase, but fate, in the form of a San Fernando redneck, intervened.

"Dude!" said the nearest Valley guy. "Jesus, dude, just go home and sleep it off."

The kid looked over his shoulder, saw that the killer Sikh was on the phone, looking the other way, and stuck a muffin—the exact double chocolate I would have selected—into my free hand. Then he guided me out the door.

"He's calling the cops, dude. Go!"

I drove blindly to Matilda's house. In three blocks my elbow was the size of a softball. I must have peed again. I even heard myself crying but felt no grief whatsoever. Felt nothing except that consuming need. The night had become chaos, a sloppy chaos, within which, like a hard, bright diamond, only my need shone through.

Testament to my complete break with reality, I arrived at the dealer's door convinced I could put a smile on my face, crack a joke or two, charm her into fronting me a couple grams of smack. That's how gone I was.

No more, at that point, than a twitchy, urine-soaked heap, newly homeless and jonesing, I still thought I could work an angle. Clutching that half-squashed muffin, emblem of my good intentions, of all the hope I had in the world, I knocked on the door. Nothing. I knocked again. Waited some more. And some more.

At last, hearing the familiar squeak of her peephole sliding back—I loved that squeak, I could have married it—I sighed with relief. Another second while she worked the top lock. One more for the deadbolt. Then the door will open. She'll smile. Tell me to come in. Offer me a pinch to cook up and fix so I can get well. We'll have a nice chat. She'll—

"JESUS CHRIST! WHAT THE FUCK HAPPENED TO YOU?"

"Matilda?" I heard my voice like a squeak from outer space.

"WHAT THE FUCK HAPPENED TO YOU?"

"I-brought-you-a-muffin," I recited, just as I'd rehearsed in my fucking head.

"You fucking stink!" said the bathrobe-clad figure in the shadows. "You shit your pants or what?" She was, clearly, not about to open the door any farther.

"I-brought-you—"

"Christ!" The figure disappeared, returned in a few seconds. "HERE!" came the harsh, deep voice. With a load on Matilda sounded like Orson Welles. One ratty, terry-cloth arm poked out into the night. "Take this. . . . Come on, I got people in here."

"Matilda, I—"

"You're too fucked-up, Jerry."

"Matilda—" I hadn't even seen her face.

"Jerry!" The door closed to the tiniest crack. "You ain't comin' in here and dying, okay? That shit don't play. I'm sorry."

The door shut in my face. For good this time. For the second time in one day. But I didn't care. I could tell, just by the heft of what she'd handed me, I'd be all right. I'd be okay.

Everything was going to be fine.

Too shaky to actually stop anywhere for water, I zigzagged up and down the Reseda streets, looking for a stretch where no family was having a barbecue, no happy kids were peeling by doing figure eights on bikes. I found a spot, under a giant weeping willow in the far corner of a Von's parking lot. I couldn't count the mornings when, making my chipper way to Matilda's, I'd stopped in at this very supermarket and bought a set of spoons, a couple of lighters, some Q-tips or cotton balls, and a fresh jug of isopropyl alcohol. It would have been bad form to use Matilda's supplies. But this wasn't the sort of stuff you wanted to ride around with, either. Just to make sure the checkout humans wouldn't know the score, I'd round out my purchase with a coloring book or jumbo Huggies, so they'd think the whole deal was baby-related, and therefore okay. It was my way of feeling part of the human race. Which was, at this point, no longer an issue.

All I wanted to do now was get well. But with no water to put in the spoon, I had to use spit. It was a disgusting little process, but there was no choice. Finally, after nearly five minutes of hocking and gagging, I managed to produce enough liquid to cook up the dope. I knew I should try to make Matilda's charity last. This being my first night out in the wild, it seemed wholly justifiable to take an extra-big hit. Hadn't I almost kicked? Hadn't I suffered enough already?

Hunching down in the front seat, I did my best to hold the spoonful of saliva steady. Spit gives off a sick smell when it's cooked. But the chunk was so big, I had to keep circling the flame. Finally the liquid burst into a boil, and I dropped the lighter. With the butt end of the syringe I mushed the dope down in the water. Praying I wouldn't spaz out and tip the spoon, I reached under my shirt and into my belly button for a pinch of lint. Working blind, I dropped the shmutz in the spoon, aimed the point straight into it, and drew in a full rig.

There was no way I could go through the rigamarole of removing my belt, tying off, and fixing textbook style. Instead, still hunched under the dashboard, I just held my breath, made a fist, tried to squeeze all the air into my left arm. Pump it up. Finally, tapping the needle off my flesh like a blind man scoping out the curb with his cane, I found a vein.

Still holding my breath, I worked the dull point inside and slowly, slowly drew back the stopper, plunged it back in, and exhaled. At last, my grateful spirit eased out of the fetid bag of humanity crumpled in that Japanese car, eased out and drifted overhead, until it floated high over the San Fernando Valley, far away from all these people who just didn't understand, far away and high above the awful circumstance of what now passed for my life.

The next handful of days, until my chunk ran out, were spent in much the same way. Get high in the car or a gas station bathroom. Or, if I was feeling peckish, the bathroom of Ships, a Denny's, Canter's, or any of Hollywood's other, equally sterling, twenty-four-hour venues. To this day, should anyone require it, I could give the ultimate toilet tour of Hollywood.

I had friends, or at least an acquaintance or two. There were couches to occupy, roofs to crawl under, pity to be milked. All of which I would, eventually, exploit. Just not yet. Not then. Until after a night spent two blocks away from the same building where I used to earn my $5,000 a week, around the corner from Stephen J. Cannell, Inc., up there on Yucca, I had my moment of clarity. One of many, to be sure, but at the time a first.

In the course of meandering after narcotics, down there in the open-air drug dispensary on Alvarado Street, between Third and Ninth, I made a purchase in a back alley that I thought to be smack. It turned out to be something different. Something at the opposite end of the side-effect scale. It was crack.

What I thought was a clean syringe turned out to be a pipe; instead of a rig they'd slipped me the glass dick. I'd smoked crack before, over at Dita's house. But I'd never gone out and copped it, accidentally or otherwise. Never consumed the stuff without a soothing stash of smack on hand.

After I fired up and sucked in that toxic cloud on the freeway on ramp, I didn't just get high, I got terrorized. Like I'd fingered a toaster with my feet in a puddle—I got a jolt that sent streams of smoke from my hair ends. I don't know how I kept breathing, let alone how I had the presence of mind to drive.

When I finally stopped moving, I leaped out of the car. Hit my head on the door without even noticing. Stood, for one heart-scorching moment, braced against the window of an Italian deli, before careening on down the side street to Hollywood Boulevard. Unwashed. Still stained and sleepless. Staggering in the grips of a flaming internal orgasm that had me simultaneously mouthing thanks at the sky and begging whoever lived there not to let my left ventricle hop out of my throat and jerk down the street under a truck tire.

This was Hollywood Boulevard. This was Reagan's America. There were legions of herky-jerk, piss-legged mental defectives tweaking down the street ranting to themselves. The difference was—*this one was me.* People stared and I stared back, the faces no more real than Gumby's.

I'd never been high like that. So high voltage I couldn't touch myself. It was no more than a handful of screeching moments before the ecstasy would turn to paranoia. I'd twitch into a panic as crackling as my rush was ecstatic. Suddenly I felt a hand on my shoulder. I felt human touch! It had been only days, but I hadn't spoken, hadn't interacted in any way with anyone, except to fist over a few bills and pocket the package that got me in the shape I was in at that minute.

I stopped in my tracks. I spun around, screaming "What?" as savagely as if someone had stabbed me.

"Jerry?"

"Huh?"

"Jerry, you're, like bleeding. . . ."

"What?"

I tamped a hand to my forehead. Sure enough, it must have been the bang off the car door. In my first flaming rush,

I didn't feel it. But now, as fast as that Hiroshima blast sent me stratospheric, I was careening down.

"It's Tina," said the impossibly chipper blond girl in pigtails and Bruce Springsteen T-shirt in front of me. "From *Booker*? I was, like, Eric's assistant, remember? Are you all right?"

"What?"

It was just . . . not . . . real. Not unreal the way LSD makes things unreal. Unreal in a different, more horrible way. Like, even though you're standing there, talking and walking, you're really trapped in a vast, terrifying cavern. With no possibility of escape. Racked by a pain so impermeable that it really doesn't matter if you acknowledge the other person's presence or not. They may be standing there, but where you are is so far away . . . so impossible to ever reach or return from, you can barely hear them. Your own voice is no more than an irritating reminder of how far away you are from everything, including whatever you were, whatever you once were, five minutes, five days or five years ago.

"Do you . . . I mean, like, do you need anything? Did you get mugged?"

"I'm okay. I have to go. . . ."

"But you're bleeding. And your voice, I don't know, your voice sounds funny. . . ."

"I have to go. . . ."

If she touches me, I am going to kill her.

"Jerry, hey, I liked you. We all liked you, I mean, some of the other girls thought you were, like strange, but I . . . I mean, well, it's hard, losing a job and all. . . . I mean—Gee, are you, like, crying?"

Just shut up. . . . My fucking hair hurts. . . . I want to die now. . . . Shut up shut up shut up. . . .

"What?"

At that moment I looked over her shoulder. My gaze happened past the innocent twin pigtails into the window behind, where this bleeding, hollow-eyed monster stared back.

This hunched-up stickman hopping back and forth, from foot to foot, like a kid who has to pee or a man with a lit bomb in his pocket who doesn't know where to blow.

And with more strength than I ever required of myself to do anything, I managed a smile. I saw it in the glass, and it looked sick. Creepy and sick, like something sour had died in my mouth. But I didn't care, I couldn't care.

"Tina . . . It's Tina, right? Um, Tina, I have to go now . . . I have to, you know . . . I have to go, all right? I have to . . ."

Her hand reached out one more time. She took my arm, and I wanted to die.

"Hey, Jerry—"

But by then I'd crashed completely. In the space of five minutes I'd shot from whacked-out-heart-stoppingly ecstatic to beyond devastated, so leaden and depressed, I would have collapsed on the spot if I hadn't been too nervous to stop moving.

And then, in a single, astonishing insight, it hit me: *This is what I am.* I am one of those people normal people see and think *"sick. . . ."* Think *"fucked-up."* Think *"What happened?"* And I didn't care. I didn't care about anything except making it back to my car, making it back down to Alvarado to get high enough to blow all of them right out of my fucking brain.

That moment scared me. I'd seen something I didn't want to see.

That very day, and the days to follow, I tried to do something to slow my fall. I called my old porn partner, Rinse. He was completely straight. Drugs were not a part of his life. When I told him what happened, where I was, hinting and hinting, he had no choice but to ask me down to his loft under the Santa Monica Freeway, way downtown, to try to kick.

That's what I said I wanted to do. Rinse hemmed and hawed and finally said he thought his wife would put up with me; we were, after all, all friends once. Even if I'd never once invited them over to our house. Not even to see the baby. (Sandra didn't appreciate my porno pals.)

For thirteen days I occupied a corner of the one big room Rinse and his wife, Yoruna, lived in. They threw me a blanket and a couple of pillows and provided a screen so I could have a modicum of privacy. For thirteen days I did not sleep. I did not move. I tried to eat but couldn't swallow more than the odd cup of noodle soup Yoruna was kind enough to slide through on a plate with a few saltines.

They offered me Valiums. I could have taken other drugs. But, possessed of God knows what blend of backbone and masochism, I decided if I was going to do it, I would do it right. Fuck the Buprenex. Fuck the goddamn tranqs. I was going to go the John Wayne route. I was going to make it through and walk away clean.

Which, amazingly enough, I did. In and out of waking dreams of Nina crawling toward me with her hair on fire, her crib in flames. I'd reach for a hose and my arms would flop like overcooked noodles, or my arms would work but what came out of the hose was sand, or spiders, or broken alarm clock parts. . . . There was no consistency except my child, burning. And me unable, because of my own all-consuming narcotic uselessness, to do anything but watch her melt, and scream, and die.

It wasn't drugs, was the secret that came to me these endless days and nights, listening to Rinse and Yoruna live their lives all around me, to their phone calls, their comings and goings, their life as they lived it, planning and working and laughing and fighting, doing all the things normal people did. . . . It wasn't drugs that brought me to this place, curled in a blanket in someone's corner, in the home of a former friend; hunkered, at the dim end of thirty, like an incontinent dog that nobody really likes but nobody dislikes enough to actually take out and kill.

Fourteen days after going FDOM—Face Down on the

Mattress—on Rinse's floor, I reemerged, my habit shorn, and stepped outside to resume what passed for a life.

When I ended up calling my record producer friend Mitchell Froom from a pay phone, asking if I could, like, stay at his house for a while—"I'm clean now, honest!"—it was not what you'd call a great surprise. What's surprising, at least to me, is that he let me stay for as long as he did.

In all the years I'd known the guy, since high school, I don't think we'd ever had what you'd call a "personal" conversation. Maybe, considering my personal life, that's why we were still friends.

Mitch took me aside one day on the picnic table in his backyard, beneath an avocado tree so ancient its avocados were the size of bowling balls.

Ever the discreet individual, my friend didn't mention my marital situation until I brought it up. Despite his own disinclination to discuss anything personal, I had no compunctions about parading out my own horror show of a life for anyone who would listen. People on the bus would often change seats, just to escape my pleas for advice. And this was Hollywood!

"I don't know, man. . . . Part of me thinks I should go back, if she'll have me. . . . Part of me thinks I should just file for fucking divorce. But you know, I hate to do that to a kid. . . ."

"Okay," he said, "I'll tell you what I think. I'm not giving you advice, and I'm not telling you what to do. I'm just giving my opinion."

"Whatever. . . . We're not on MacNeil-fucking-Lehrer. . . ."

"All right, then. I think you should be a man."

"What?"

"I said, you should be a man."

"I know what you said, but what the fuck does that mean?"

"What it means is, right or wrong, sometimes you just

have to make a move. Take the responsibility and make a move. . . . She didn't ask you if you wanted a child," he continued, blurting it out with unaccustomed intensity. "Look at you, man. Anybody could see you weren't in any position to have children. You shouldn't have been writing TV. You shouldn't have been married. You weren't fucking ready for the family thing."

"Well, I guess I ought to divorce her, huh? I mean, I don't know where I'm going to go. What I'm going to do."

"I'll help you," my friend said. As simple and crisp as that.

"I don't want to take anything," I continued, somewhere between a whine and a shriek. The momentousness of such a move doesn't come up on you gradually. It hits like a safe dropped from the skyscraper you're standing next to. "I mean, I want her to keep the house, the car, whatever we fucking own. . . . I don't care. I feel like it's all my fault anyway. . . . I guess I'll have to call a lawyer, do the whole thing."

But Mitch wasn't listening. Or if he was, he was doing something else at the same time. He was writing a check.

"You just have to be a man," he repeated, looking up when he was done.

Mitch shot me an appropriately steely gaze when he was done writing. This was, I thought, the side of him that all the stars he works with in the studio must know. Maybe Chrissie Hynde and Elvis Costello were used to those steely gazes. Until this second, I'd never had one turned on me.

"It's the best thing for you," he said quietly. "In the end it's the best thing for the kid, too."

"But what about . . . what about Sandra?"

Mitchell started to say something, then stopped. Once more that legendary discretion came to the fore. "Sandra can take care of herself," was all he said. "If she was strong enough to live with you, I'm sure she can live without you. Believe me."

What could I say?

As if reading my thoughts, Mitch gave a little half smile. "It's six thousand. Use it to get a place and get on your feet."

The birds chirped a little louder. Mitch's own daughter skipped out with a Hula Hoop. Something at the heart of this moment was killing me, and again my friend zeroed in.

"I'll help you as much as I can," he said. "But don't spend it on drugs."

"Hey, man, come on. . . ."

We both stood up at the same time. Mitch extended his hand. I took it and we shook. I didn't buy drugs with the money. At least not right away. I didn't have to, because I was busily stealing the prescription cough syrup—cherry codeine, my favorite flavor—and Percodans his wife kept right there on the kitchen counter, next to the Tylenol baby drops and Motrin.

Mind-boggling to a professional like myself, the stuff actually sat there, unconsumed, for weeks, months, *years* at a time. For as long as I'd known them in that house, the stuff was always just . . . *out there*. Perpetually ungulped. A phenomenon as alien to me as going to bed by nine or paying your bills on time. I mean, her doctors seemed a little sick, but she was remarkably healthy in spite of them.

If Mitch's wife ever noticed my pilfering, she was far too classy a woman ever to say anything. Or else, as I suspect was closer to the truth, she was simply embarrassed that I could be so low—not just to stay in someone's house for so long, but to steal their medicine—and didn't even want to bring it up.

I was, after all, her husband's best friend.

Amazingly, even as my "personal" life was on that fast slide to narco-Nowheresville, my career continued to twitch and slither. It was like some kind of snake that wouldn't die. No matter how much you stomped the thing, how many times you whacked it in the head with a shovel, it just wouldn't bite the dust. . . . Short of taking an ad out in *Vari-*

ety: "STAHL SAYS STICK A FORK IN ME—*I'M DONE!*" I don't know what could have stopped the odd job that still trickled in.

The whole deal just served to confirm my theory that people in Hollywood don't hire you 'cause you're any good—what difference does that make?—they hire you because someone else did. I still got work! Tom Patchett, whom I knew from the *ALF* era, had conceived of a show called *Uncle Somebody.* It was about a man with a problem. A newly insane fellow. The premise involved this regular Joe—played by genius stand-up comic Charlie Fleischer, fresh from his huge splash as the voice of Roger Rabbit—who gets hit in the head with a foul ball while attending a Cubs game and wakes up in the hospital with fourteen personalities.

The network decided that fourteen personalities was too many. "How about nine?" So I wrote nine. After this, in another heady insight, NBC came back and requested four. We tried four. This time the powers-that-be came back and said, Look, we can't be making fun of the mentally ill—no doubt a large and vociferous chunk of the viewing public—let's just make it two. So it happened, what had started as a terrific premise—brilliantly suited to Charlie, whose forte was a seemingly limitless trove of voices, dialect, and character—was watered down to a sitcom about a wacky schizophrenic. Sybil with a laugh track.

In all honesty I did little to help the cause. At network get-togethers I couldn't even speak. Having absorbed so many opiates to calm down, my lips were too calm to move. During one particularly awful morning, I'd had an accident in the bathroom. I'd spilled too much coke in my pre-meeting speedball. Loath to waste the stuff, I went ahead and shot it, thereby delaying the important session a half hour while I waited for the bells to stop ringing in my head. Not that I couldn't fake my way through a story session with Big Ben clanging in my skull. I'm a professional, after all. But it would have been hard to explain why I had to spend the whole meeting on my hands and knees. Since the shot, being so top-heavy with stimulants, left me wholly unable to stand up without whirling right down to the floor again. Strong as the heroin was, all that coke just wrestled it right to the mat.

In the end, rather than just pass on the pilot and completely humiliate a man of Patchett's stature, NBC opted for the "partial shoot." They wouldn't shell out to shoot the whole hour show, but they would cough up enough to film ten minutes. The day they were scheduled to film the selected snippet, in the public park across the street from my old office at the Fox lot, yours truly was too far gone even to show. Part of me wanted to go, but part of me was just too tired of dreaming up explanations for that now-unavoidable greeting from friends and strangers: "What's wrong with you?"

I'd used the flu for our first few meetings, switched to diarrhea to explain delaying meetings with my half-hour bathroom sessions, and was now reduced to malaria flare-ups and incipient leprosy. By this point, at any rate, Patchett had no doubt realized the mistake he'd made in going with me. Not just because he had to rewrite practically every word in the script himself, but because he had to drag my sorry carcass along with him and Charlie to every meeting with NBC.

I didn't bother going to any more meetings once the ten-minute segment had been shot. I was too busy destroying my life to bother with a minor detail like contractual obligation. I had veins to blow. A child to ignore. Friends to rip off. An apartment I hated on sight to pay for and move into.

In short, I had a job to do and I did it.

"This is an apartment I can die in," I remember thinking upon first glimpse of my Laurel Canyon digs.

Never one to care much for appearances—I'd spent most of my life more or less contentedly in dives—I found myself suddenly concerned with the appearance of the place. Knowing, no doubt, how quickly I was going down, it was important that I look like I was headed up. Important to whom, I couldn't say, since by this time I had few, if any, friends left.

Laurel Canyon was relaxing. It was quiet. It was beautiful. It was pot-smoking country.

I hauled my share of horror up to my mountain hideaway like some black-clad Sherpa. The feeling that gripped me after one glimpse at the Lookout Mountain pad—*it's too public, you don't want the landlord living above you, there's no fucking yard*—was instantly overwhelmed by that perpetual, you're-fucked-anyway-so-what's-the-point? sense of doom.

"I hate it!" screamed the voice in my head. "I'll take it," said the smiling mouth slashed across my pasty face.

By now all social interaction was like trying to work the strings of an unwieldy puppet. But I felt I had to justify myself to these complete strangers. To explain, if not my existence on the planet, at least the weirdness I was projecting.

"I've just been divorced," I announced to the florid aerospace man and wife who interviewed me, as if this would explain the greenish tinge to my skin or the constant, twitchy-vibrating flutter of my fingertips.

I hoped the "just divorced" pitch would explain everything. And the power of mainstream media helped, too. Just looking at the household names there on my rental applications: big-gun employers like *Moonlighting, thirtysomething,* etc., and any trifling doubts were neutralized.

"Sure he looks a little weird, Marge, but he wrote *ALF,* for gosh sakes. . . . *He must be okay!*"

The very first moments alone in the expansive, exposed front room of my two-room pad, I had that slow, sinking feeling in the gut, that visceral "uh-oh" that manifests itself in a shuddery hiccup of dread and excitement and all-around liver-quaking panic. The apartment was unlike any place I'd ever occupied. The bottom half of a beautiful house on the corner of Laurel Pass and Lookout Mountain Road. The main room, which jutted toward the street like the prow of a square white ship, had floor-to-ceiling windows on three sides. "Airy" is the word my tiny, aerobicized landlady kept mouthing under her hairdo. Airy and flooded with light.

This marked a radical departure from the wholly subterranean aesthetics I'd clung to my whole life. My idea of the perfect apartment was Hitler's bunker: windowless, soundproof, absolutely free of anything resembling outside life. When you live the drug life all humanity is an intrusion.

I felt naked, just standing in the living room. But wasn't that the point? How else to change your rotten old behavior than dive right into something new? That was my bright idea. And the results speak for themselves. . . .

I don't know exactly how long it took for this airy hermitage to mutate to a sodden cave. For my air-thin intentions to "change my life" to degenerate to a full-time struggle to obliterate it. One minute I was gazing lovingly out my sky-high windows, the next, it seemed, I was crawling past them on hands and knees for fear of all the cackling blood drinkers beyond the glass who *WOULD NOT STOP STARING.*

In other words, I switched to cocaine.

Oh, it was difficult, sure. I still had the dope cravings. But then, I didn't stop heroin entirely. Let's not go overboard. No, I just decided seeing where my MO to that moment had taken me, it was time—no pun intended—to switch tracks.

In the beginning, it was tame enough. I had a connection in Echo Park, a chatty Dominican ex-con by the name of Jésus. Jésus never left his apartment, except when screamingly drunk, once a month or so, and then just long enough to pick up another DUI. At which point he'd come home again and get to work on scaring up another fake ID to feed into the System and stay out of jail.

That morning coke whiff could get me over the initial Oh-

Christ-It's-Another-Day dread. The two or three joints that followed might even spark that temporary relief into even more temporary creativity. But it was tenuous, to say the least. For a while, I started each day by scurrying out of bed for a constitutional in the nearby nature reserve. Once or twice I even saw my burly landlord and his wife—her Dinah Shore flip, I noticed, intact and stiff by 7:15—thrilling myself with the thought they considered me such a wholesome tenant.

Upon moving in, I'd made a huge to-do about my baby daughter visiting. And Mr. Dietrich, the owner, went so far as to install a chain-link fence, at his own expense, to make my little patio "toddler safe." Whenever we bumped into each other he'd ask when the little girl was coming over. But it wasn't that long before they stopped asking.

Part of my Whole New Life plan was to start doing some Serious Writing. As opposed to the seriously lucrative, seriously stupid kind I'd lately engaged in. This was the New Me: I'd write meaningfully or not at all. Problem was, not writing was such hard work. You could really strain yourself, spending time not doing something as difficult and soul-wrenching as meaningful writing. Throw in the fact that, along with all the arduous amount of not writing I was doing, I was not using heroin, and you had yourself, by the time noon rolled around, one hell of a challenging day.

Right out of bed, after sitting down from the walk I'd decided not to take, I'd smoke a joint, take a big hit of coke, move to my desk to stare at my Selectric and consider all the writing I probably wouldn't do, which made me so disconsolate I'd have to do more coke, which of course rocketed me right off my healthy-posture chair to start pacing back and forth, tearing my hair out obsessing on how good I was *not* feeling as a result of all the smack I was *not* doing, which justified firing up still another joint, which inevitably set off another round of pacing in the back bedroom—the one spot in the place I didn't feel like I was on display. Until, after I'd repeated the whole constructive scenario too many times to count, the coke ran out, and the pot took its toll, and I was simultaneously jacked to the tits and too fuzzy to type my name. At which point I'd break down, rush to the phone, and make my call to Jésus. Just so I could get out of the fucking house and reup again before scooting back to throw more words down the drain.

The apartment happened to be across the street from the Wonderland Grade School. In all the world, I don't think there could be a more demoralizing sound than "America the Beautiful," sung by fresh-scrubbed children, wafted into the locked-door bathroom where I hovered, at eight A.M., to let me know I'd lost another night to drugs, and the day loomed before me like a yawning cavern still to slog through. Those sweet voices echoed in my brain, and their very sweetness stung me to the core of my corrupted soul.

Occasionally I'd still scratch some coke-fueled smattering of brilliance on a legal pad. But since my handwriting, on cocaine, was harder to decipher than Sanskrit, these rarely amounted to much. I was, miraculously, still laying off heroin. I might have even escaped the needle if Jésus, displaying the customary good sense and helpfulness of his kind, had not mentioned his newfound access to clean works, fruit of a new customer who either dated a diabetic, was diabetic himself, or killed somebody who had diabetes. The truth was somewhere in there.

Jésus, after all, had all kinds of functioning and not-so-functioning types dependent on his well-stocked larder. On any given day, at any given time, you'd be likely to find a smattering of gaffers, lighting guys, sometime actors, truck drivers, or writers—all in between gigs or on their way to one—all hunkered on one of the ratty couches arranged around the overflowing coffee table. Jésus' big-screen TV had no off switch. I know because, at some point, I crossed the line between occasional and full-timer. Which meant I found myself spending more time in his stuck-in-the-seventies dope pad, high or trying to get higher, catching the Shopping Channel at nine-thirty in the morning, staring glassy-eyed at a Discovery Channel special on otters, or wholly enthralled in some similar offering. All the while promising myself I'd leave in another fifteen minutes, another hour, right after the next hit or the next one.

Once I began shooting the coke, there were periods of time when I never left at all. I couldn't. Of course I still had a daughter, of course I still had something to do . . . somewhere. I just couldn't keep the needle out of my arm long enough to do it.

Those rare occasions when I did make it back to my ex-house, to spend an afternoon with my little girl, I'd find myself so jittery, it was all I could do to keep my hands from shaking right off my wrists while I held her, or played peek-a-boo, or tickled her tummy. My great fear, at that time, was that the first words out of my daughter's mouth, when she finally uttered a sentence, would be "Daddy what's wrong? . . . What's wrong with you, Daddy? Daddy, you're sweating like a pig. . . ."

Weirder still, in my newfound nonstop customer status, I got to know Jésus. For he was not what he appeared to be. But because he never judged—or complained about the blood pools in his bathroom floor, the pockets of scarlet in the corner I'd neglected, or been too fucked-up, to clean—I in turn refrained from judging him. So that the first time I dug into his closet, to find a towel after showering off the coke sweats while he was out on a run, I said nothing when I found his secret stash.

I'm not talking about drugs. Drugs were never secret. No, I mean, and it still twists something in my stomach, I mean when I accidentally knocked over his secret stack. His pile of *Buster Boy* and *Camper* and *Young'uns.*

When I picked up the first magazine at my feet and saw the glossy of a freckle-faced ten-year-old boy holding his still hairless penis erect and shiny for the camera, when I dropped that one, picked up the next, only to find two more grotesquely wholesome-looking youngsters, bent over, their buttocks to the camera, a towhead spread-cheeked side-by-side with a curly brunette, I remember thinking: "This ought to mean something. . . ." But it didn't.

I found myself skipping the pictures, focusing, with morbid fascination, on the text. *"Tommy and Timmy like to mess around when Tommy's Mom goes shopping. . . . Boys will be boys!"*

In my stupor, truth be told, it was the peculiar text, more than the import of what I'd found, or the glossy photos themselves, that held me frozen over the magazines. "One wrong move," I heard myself mutter, in the grips of a six-day coke binge, *"and I end up writing this shit. . . ."*

Jésus came home to find me shivering on the carpet in the back room he let me hide in. Not an unusual posture when you've been awake for almost a week. One glance at me, another at the closet that I'd jammed back shut, and he *knew* his secret was out.

"So, what?" he said when he went into his walk-in closet, rattled around, and came back out again. "So, do you think I'm sick? You think I'm fucked-up?"

"I don't think anything," I said. "I don't give a shit. Why should I? For Christ's sake, look at me."

"That's right," he said, fighting back tears, "look at you. Some guy who had everything and couldn't handle it and sits in a room blowing his brains out, in my apartment, with my fucking cocaine, that I fucking sell him. . . ."

"No argument out of me," I said, and that was as far as it got.

Only one thing, really, changed after I found out my dealer's sexual preference. It was as if, having stumbled on one fetish, Jésus felt free enough to let me in on his other one. The one, oddly enough, he considered his deeper, darker secret.

Forget pedophilia. The real passion for my dealer was

freebasing. The first occasion when he invited me to share his pursuit, I felt every bit as transfixed and terrified as any other novice standing in the open doorway of cultdom.

It wasn't the drug that spooked me, it was the look on Jésus' face.

As I watched him tiptoe about the apartment, ducking past the windows, bending over the stove to stir up the cocaine and baking soda like some psychotic master chef, arranging everything to a compulsive T, the thought jumped up and gripped me by the throat: *He might as well be planning a murder.*

For the occasion, Jésus invited over Felix, a lumbering, jug-eared tattoo victim he knew from the joint. Six-foot-five of solid muscle, Felix was simultaneously frightening and ludicrous looking. It's as if Prince Charles's head had been randomly transplanted on the body of Lou Ferrigno: the Hulk with the face of a basset hound.

Felix, who turned out to be half Latino, did not talk a lot. He didn't have to. You kind of got the message without a lot of verbal interference. Before he showed up, Jésus had told me he collected for a Mexican loan shark on Brooklyn Avenue. He said he was a little strange. "But then," he added in the first hint of levity since we'd made plans to freebase, "so are you, right, amigo? That's why I figured you'd be friends." He figured wrong.

For the most part, between hits—when Felix wasn't pulling out a .357 and I wasn't pretending not to be scared shitless—we smoked and sat, sat and smoked, in complete silence. Occasionally, though, I'd bolt upright, look wildly around me, and slump back down again. I didn't know enough about the drug I was doing to know if no time had passed or if it was the middle of the night already.

Everything that was happening, everything that had happened, had become so frightening, I could absorb it only by sitting where I was, putting my leather jacket on to kill the chill that wouldn't go away, and staying glued to the Home

Shopping Channel. That was, I learned, as much a part of this whole savage ritual as the pipe, the cooking, or the minute-but-powerful minitorch.

Jésus had positioned himself more or less permanently beside his front window. There, every second or so, he would risk a peek, peeling the blind back a hair to glue one eye at the street.

"Oh shit, OH SHIT!" he shouted. "Oh SHIT—THEY'RE *COMING*!"

"Who's coming?"

"The fucking cops man. *Listen*. . . . OH SHIT! Can't you hear? Can't you hear the fucking choppers? They—ARE—COMING! *THEY ARE COMING, MAN!!*"

And I did listen. They *were* out there. Helicopters. I heard them. Lots of helicopters, taking off from somewhere, flying somewhere else. Not here, that was certain. Not descending like an outtake from *Apocalypse Now* to round up Jésus and me. No, I was sure of that. But, because I was sure, I was even more scared. More scared than he was, because I was sitting there in a room, with a guy who *did* believe they were after him. Who believed, after he did enough base, after he crossed whatever line there was left for him to cross, that every footstep, every car horn, distant shout, or flushing toilet—every noise in the universe had a threat behind it. And with enough rock in your system, you could hear every noise in the universe.

How long was I there? I don't know. It would make a good story to say five days. It might even be true. The pipe . . . the pedophile . . . the Home Shopping Channel . . .

Jésus watched the Shopping Channel the entire time, commenting when some particularly remarkable deal flashed by on the screen. I remember him, at one point, obsessed with the need for presidential tumblers. Thirty-six tumblers, one for each of our illustrious commanders-in-chief.

"*Mang*, I have to have those," he said "*Mang,* I got to have those!"'"

I'd smoked myself from nothing to a hundred and ended up at Ground Zero again. I'd had enough and headed out into the murderous daylight. Nothing prepares you for the fucking nightmare of eight in the morning on a normal weekday, a sunny hour in the middle of Life-As-Everyone-In-The-World-Knows-It. Everyone but you, who's been up since the Year One. Who hasn't slept. Who hasn't eaten or showered. Who's hunkered behind the wheel, chewing his lips, while drivers to the right and left sip their coffee and tune in to the traffic reports. They're all going to work, but where are you going? And why does your skin creep with the certainty that they know where you've been?

I managed to steer back across town, up Crescent Heights to Laurel Canyon, up the monstrous hill to my little hideaway. Where, of course, my landlord stood hosing his little patch of heaven. Getting out of my car, that lovely afternoon, I stepped the seventeen steps from parking lot to sliding door of my pad. I waved. I smiled. I made my way into that fetid apartment. Took my hand out of my pocket, where it had been squeezing the bag of cocaine to make sure it didn't fall out. Headed into the bathroom. Intent on taking a shower. But really just dying to dip into that stash.

I couldn't stay upright on the toilet seat. So I just gave up. Got on the floor. Found a rig. Filled a spoon. Drew it up, steadied my hand, and fired. Just one for the road, even though I'd already reached the end of it and made it back again. More or less. Just one shot, which I didn't even complete when that nasty animal, the telephone, started ringing in the next room.

It was a dream, as they used to say, come true. David Lynch—in the form, of course, of "his people"—had called. They actually wanted me.

Well, gee! The message was bubbly as a just dropped

Bromo-Seltzer. Unfortunately, the Jerry Stahl they were calling wasn't around anymore.

Sometimes you just don't know you're dead till they close the coffin. And, at that point, with the lid wide open, I was still under the absurd notion I was among the living.

Luckily it was a Thursday when I got back. This meant I could skip Friday—"Sorry, didn't get the call!"—then get in touch with CAA the following week. David Lynch's minions wanted me on board, or at least on script, for the second season of *Peaks*. Needless to say, I was professional as ever. When the phone rang again I was so far gone it took fifteen minutes to remember where it was. For the first few moments it was all kind of foggy. Until my agent, ever the pro, suggested I turn the phone around. I'd been talking into the receiver. He was helpful that way.

"Are you all right?" he asked.

"What do you mean, am I all right? I'm fine. Are you all right?"

"Okay, okay, just make sure you get there. They want to do this right away."

"I'll be there," I said with that phony confidence that was as second nature as any other lie.

I did show up. Though my last minute, head-to-toe urban renewal program did not exactly have the desired results. Not even my old standby, the shoot-up-and-jog regimen, could whip me into shape. There are times, in the life of any addict—particularly that most deluded, the so-called functioning variety—when he just can't do it anymore. There aren't enough drugs in the world to make it work.

The day of my *Twin Peaks* appointment marked just such a moment. I just couldn't get well. All the coke I'd been doing had done something. I pictured my brain in a sling, sprained somehow, and here I was trying to run a marathon before it was even half healed.

Wholly unable even to drive to the San Fernando Valley

address without stopping twice to fix, I arrived in my now-constant mind-numbing stupor, so soaked in drugs I looked like I'd crawled through some kind of viral monsoon that only rained on me.

The story meeting, once I'd gotten the nerve to leave my car and lug my rattletrap carcass inside to attend it, turned out to be a flat-out dictation session. I hardly had to talk. Lynch's first in command, Mark Frost, didn't waste time introducing me to the other white men in the room. Mark was one of those crisp, competent Anglo-Saxon fellows you had the feeling popped from the womb with a perfectly parted Princeton and white teeth.

From the moment a fawning young hipster led me to the conference room—everybody on the show was so proud to be there, they just assumed you were somebody they should be proud to know if you were there, too—the no-nonsense producer started laying out plot points in such prodigious detail that writing the thing would boil down to connecting the dots.

The same goateed hepcat who'd shown me in even provided me with a mini–tape recorder. I didn't even have to listen. All I had to do was smile, say thanks, and disappear back to my foul lair to fill in the blanks and things would have been fine. But no. I couldn't even do that right. . . . God forbid! Midway through Mister Frosty's spiel, when I felt my chin heading down to my chest as if tugged by magnets, I excused myself to "get coffee." Instead of coffee, though, I ducked into the employee toilet to take another shot.

"Okay, I'm ready!" I blurted, a little too loudly, when I skipped back into the room. I don't think anybody noticed my change of behavior at that point, though I do remember the chilly Mister Frost raising an eyebrow.

He began where he'd left off, a point in the story where a traveling judge comes to town to try a case, when suddenly I heard myself pipe up: "This is amazing! My father was a judge. . . . Of course he was on the federal court of appeals, not like this guy, but still, I can probably throw in a lot of details. You know, like the little leather case they keep the gavel in, how they dry-clean the robes, stuff like that. . . ."

By this time everybody in the room had begun to shift in their seats. Beyond being wholly inappropriate, the timbre of my voice had become strangely high. I realized, when I finally shut up, how grotesque my little outburst had been. But there was nothing I could do to take it back.

Frost leaned forward on his chair, looked from me to the three other staffers in the room, and fixed his face in the cruelest smile I'd ever seen,

"Why, Jerry," he said, his voice just brimming with sarcasm, the contempt so thick it might have burned through the floor where it dripped. "Why, Jerry, you're *sharing!* Hey, everybody, Jerry's sharing a little something personal with us. Isn't that *nice!*"

Had I accidentally urinated on the spot, I could not have been more mortified. Indeed, the coke wore off at the exact same moment my cognizance of what I'd just done finally hit me.

"You think we can keep going now," he said, his voice perfectly even, "or do you have a few more little stories for us?"

The rest of the meeting, of course, passed in a furious cloud of shame. My ears burned a flaming scarlet. I believe my eyes even teared up, though I mercifully fought back a complete bout of weeping until it was all over and I was back in the car. . . .

It must be mentioned, if it hasn't been already, that for me the chance to work with David Lynch was as close to dream-come-true as I'd ever hoped to get in this hoary industry.

After that meeting, I hit an all-new level of narcotic dementia. So enfeebled were my perceptions, I thought that only a day or two had passed when the *Twin Peaks* messenger showed up at my Lookout Mountain hideaway and asked for the draft.

To say I was unprepared is like saying the A-bomb broke a lot of windows. The sad fact is, I had spent the previous six days injecting speedballs, obscenely huge cocktails of cocaine and heroin, with such regularity my arms had swollen to the size of Indian clubs. My cerebrum positively reeled from all the brilliant lines I'd type up as soon as I sat down. Which somehow, I never did.

Days flew by. I dimly remember driving down to Jésus' place a couple of three A.M.'s hunkering in the bathroom with my legal pad open on my naked knees, trying to dab syringe blood off the paper without smearing whatever felt-tip snippets of dialogue I'd actually managed to scrawl into a scarlet blur. It didn't matter, though. It was incoherent even before it was illegible,

Next thing I know, I'm sitting in complete panic at my battered IBM, attempting to get something, *anything,* on the page while the sloe-eyed, smirking messenger waited outside my door. I couldn't let him in, of course. My place looked like a Bosnian pharmacy—pillaged and rent asunder.

My fear was that the young runner would simply give up, hop back in the Lynch-mobile, and tell Frost that he'd made a bad mistake. They'd clearly hired the wrong Jerry Stahl. There must be another one out there who knows how to write a script, if not clean himself and answer the door without listing sideways and perspiring copiously. There had to be, because the one they'd hired was absolutely out of his skull. Just to prove it, the courier snapped up my sloppy, blood-sullied stack of pages and brought it back to the producers. How to explain that I'd mistaken seven days for one and a half?

Once the studio gofer grabbed my effort, I was faced with the lovely prospect of waiting to hear how miserable it was. I still remember, sitting there among the crumpled paper, empty Evian bottles, and filthy clothes, the sound of the smirking messenger's car as it motored down the hill from whence it came. It was as if my future had driven off with him.

Dave's office, understandably, never bothered to call back. (You never know if you can catch something over the phone.) I heard thirdhand, *quel* surprise, the *Peaks* people were not thrilled. They were so unthrilled, in fact, that Tony "Son of Judith" Krantz, Lynch's man at CAA, ended up calling my own agent and slicing him a new sphincter for recommending an incompetent skeek like me in the first place. My agent got in some hot water, and another season passed me by without an Emmy.

• • •

It might have been the naked nineteen-year-old, a skeleton-thin strawberry named Ruleena whose mocha flesh blotched up in dime-size scarlet polka dots on account of nonstop scratching, a side effect of ten days on the rock cocaine she sucked cocks on the street to keep in her pipe. Or it might have been the *BOO-YAH!*—that awful, brain-rattling sound of the shotgun just before it blew out the rear window of my Cadillac. For weeks I could not get that blast to stop reverberating in my brain, just like I couldn't shake the hideous image of Ruleena mouthing my penis between hits, like I couldn't control my full-body twitching—borderline convulsions that racked me with terrifying frequency—like I couldn't escape the leering pygmies who taunted me from the corners of seedy motel rooms or the faces in the rearview mirror, cackling shadows who followed me everywhere.

It might have been any one of these things. It's not like you can look back and name the moment when you *crossed that line.* Who can say precisely *what* it was that sent them over the amorphous border that separates Normal Behavior from Insanity, Deviance, Criminal Malfeasance or worse? Or when they knew they'd arrived on the Other Side?

All I can say, with certainty, is that at some point I looked around and realized I no longer seemed to live in my own apartment. Yet I could not have told you exactly where I *did* live. Somehow I'd hooked up with a crackhead named Sammy, a black guy who'd just walked out of County Jail. I knew that 'cause he still had his plastic wrist tag on, the one they give you inside. But I didn't know much else.

I was stumbling down Alvarado one morning when this snaky dude sidled up and mumbled something about knowing where to get the real good shit. Which I guess he did. Because next thing I remember it wasn't morning anymore. It was night. The same day or a day later. And me, Sammy, and Ruleena are sweating in the Cecil Hotel, downtown, figuring a way to get more crack without any money.

Sammy must have said he knew some people. Next thing we're somewhere in South Central, some kid's arm is in the window, I've got a ton of crack in my fist, and Sammy's foot suddenly slams on top of mine on the gas. People are screaming, the car shoots up the street, nearly ripping the kid's arm off, and I'm trying not to smash into any parked cars when there's that brain-shattering BOO-YAH and a blast of splintered glass sprays the back of my head.

After that it's more motels. More ripped-off crack. Coming to with the shakes. Not knowing where I am. Getting fucked-up as fast as I can before I have to think about it. . . . That's what it had come to.

In the midst of this madness I stumbled in to keep a shrink appointment. I'd hooked up with a dope psychiatrist my second time in Cedars, after I'd tried to OD on my birthday. I'd banged seven grams of coke and dope and still couldn't swing more than a headache. Turns out—my bad luck—I had a heinous case of phlebitis. Both arms were the size of fire hydrants and so clogged the powder didn't have a chance to make it brainward.

All I recall about the hospital stay is some John Carradine–like MD looming over the admissions desk, announcing in a voice like a gravedigger that "the arms have to go." Happily, whoever was in charge of amputation changed their mind. I was on the ward three weeks, and when I left I was still able to applaud.

I have no other memories of hospitalization, except for one happy circumstance: hooking up with Doctor Bob.

Bob Jurkovich—or Doctor Bob, as he liked to be called—was a lanky psychiatrist a year younger than me who specialized in dope fiends. He put me on Prozac and doxepin, a last-ditch pharmaceutical designed to restock the serotonin in those with parched and chafing brainpans. In my case, all the neurotransmitters had been burned to a crisp by IV cocaine. But the meds aren't what mattered. What mattered was the subsequent efforts of Doctor B. Somehow, throughout my downward spiral, I managed to make maybe one out of four appointments. Until one session, after relating yet another incoherent saga about motels, Cadillacs, smack, crack, leering pygmies, and the other usual suspects, my friend the doctor simply looked at me, threw up his hands, and offered me his informed psychiatric opinion.

"You're fucked," he said.

Without giving pause to let me dispute the obvious, he laid out the rest. "I see no reason to continue therapy. The way you're going, you're going to kill yourself, kill somebody else, or, if you're lucky, end up in some kind of institution. If you're really lucky," he went on, "it won't be jail. That's why you should go to Arizona."

Somewhere I thought I'd missed a transition—I was missing lots of transitions in those days—but it turned out I heard right. Either I headed out in two days to some place called Progress Valley, in beautiful downtown Phoenix, or I was on my own.

"You mean," I protested, "you want to send me to some kind of halfway house? A live-in thing?"

I was about to complain that that sort of thing was for

complete losers, but even in my current crack-addled state I could sense my rebuttal was a little thin.

"That's exactly what I mean," he said. "Don't tell me you're busy."

He had me there. I couldn't have told you the last time I'd worked. "I think I can squeeze it in," I told him. "How long is it?"

"Ninety days."

"Ninety days in Phoenix? In the summer?"

I heard my voice crack and hoped that he would hear it, too. But Doctor Bob just smiled. He handed me a piece of paper with the phone number already scrawled on top.

"I've made all the arrangements. All you have to do is call."

"Phoenix," I repeated, "*Phoenix,*" fighting off the urge to drop to my knees and blubber on his socks every time I said it.

"That's right," he said, patting me on the back as he steered me to the door. "Phoenix, Arizona, in August. Send me a card if you have a minute."

The first thing I noticed about Phoenix was what people looked like who were flying there. All the men on the plane looked like Harry Dean Stanton. All the women looked dried up. It was as if they'd started out to get tan, fallen asleep, and woken up halfway to jerky. And they all wore cowboy hats.

Unlike Angelenos, who tended to stay out of the UV rays, nobody seemed to have told your Phoenix citizens the sun was bad for you. They weren't just dark, they were leathery. Cured.

I'd loaded up on unwholesome stimulants and analgesics before boarding the plane. I didn't pack any drugs, I consumed them all before takeoff. The fact was, I did want to get clean. But not until I got where I was going. My last fix, I believe, was in the Burbank airport, the Gate Four men's room. I indulged myself in the first—and last—speedball I'd be taking in some time, then reeled out into the horde of leather people in string ties and snakeskin cowboy boots, all milling about waiting for the moment they could step onto the runway and up into the shiny winged pipe that would whisk them from smog-washed Los Angeles and off to their sterile desert home.

The folks from Progress Valley—or PV, as its devotees loved to call it—requested newcomers step off the plane clutching a Bible. It was their version of the red carnation. Those dispatched to airport duty could spot the lifesaving tome, then swoop up the chemically damaged supplicant and whisk them into the van for the trip back to the halfway house.

That's right. It was back to the institutional van. My favorite transportation! I don't know just what cosmic union binds drug-and-alcohol rehabilitation with these glorified station wagons. But you cannot, apparently, have one without the other. I had not set foot, or buttocks, in a van since my last stint at rehab, in a fun-filled shlep from Cedars-Sinai to the Gene Autry Cowboy Museum.

Now, though, I wasn't just visiting the Cowboy Heaven, I was moving into it. For it was clear, even before leaving Phoenix Airport—or Sky Harbor, as the city fathers preferred to call this waterless facility—that the same western sensibility relegated to the tourist trap in the wilds of Burbank lived on beyond any institutional walls here in Arizona. And now, thanks to my own inability to control my chemical intake, I was to become its latest display.

But Phoenix, jeez, there's so much to say about the place. For starters, there's the booming prosthetic limb business. Phoenix stands out as the proud hub of the fake leg industry. You can't go three blocks without passing vast window displays of lifelike hands and calves, world-class artificial body parts of every stripe. That and wig stores. Every other corner boasted a Heddy's House of Hair. Outgrowth, apparently, of its booming cancer populace, the place caters to all your chemo needs. It was a startling vision for a man on the downward slide of hard narcotic addiction.

Phoenix, see, lives on as a popular place to retire or die. It's the site of the world's first fully equipped oldsterville, Del Webb's gargantuan Sun City (affectionately known, among locals, as "Seizure World"). Those who just come to pass the flu season are known as "snowbirds." The latter tool down in their Winnebagos, soak up the sunshine, then plow on back to Minnesota when the yellow snow melts.

Going into a rehab stands out as a kind of retirement in itself. Which helped make yours truly feel right at home. Whether you were a blue-hair, a no-hair, or just trying to shake off a hairy habit, this had to be the right city for you. . . .

The PV ideal was simple: Take your run-of-the-mill undisciplined substance abuser, throw him in this highly structured, not-quite-jail-but-not-the-real-world-either residential community, make him get a job, make his bed, brush his teeth, go to "group," and re-create with fellow fuck-ups, and—presto!—ninety days later he walks out recovered.

That, at least, was the idea. Myself, and I know this will come as a real surprise, I've always had a little trouble with "group" activities. I'd had little experience with overnight camp. I was never Cub Scout material. And I did not serve in the military.

It might have been an ideal situation to help a boy break his drug thing. The problem was, I was no longer a boy. I was over thirty-five, while most of the other guys *were* boys. Whether Doc Jurkovich had been misinformed or he thought the humiliation would do me good, I found myself a sort of senior citizen among the two dozen late teen and middling twenty types who filled the shabby suites.

My first night, as was the custom of the place, I had to stand in the dining room—your basic curdled linoleum, ex-junkie staffed, all-male starch factory—and introduce myself to the other recruits. I don't know what I said, but the main counselor, a self-styled bespectacled "intellectual" named Martin, immediately put me on "joke probation."

"Clearly," he informed me, back in his tiny office during the first of our private sessions, "you use humor as a defense. We're going to have to do something about that fast."

Nobody wants to go through life a deluded smart-ass. Especially if it means they're doomed to an existence as a malcontent, not-quite-clean, not-quite-strung-out drug addict. There I was, in this claustrophobic little non-air-conditioned office, smack in the middle of this strange sobriety compound, listening to this arrogant Barney Fife-with-a-BA type listing everything wrong with my personality. If I disliked him on sight, I realize now, it's probably because, on some level, he reminded me of *me*. But who wants to cop to that? Who wants to admit that the flaws that disgust us in others are really our own?

By way of not saying something I'd later regret, I asked my counselor what was up with all the chess-o-bilia lining his walls and desk. Every available inch seemed taken up with photos of Martin hunched over a chessboard looking thoughtful, Martin hunched over a chessboard looking steamed. Martin hunkered over a chessboard looking pretty darn delighted.

"I guess you play chess," I ventured, going out on a limb.

"Matter of fact, I'm thirty-three points shy of becoming a regional master," he said. He explained that he would have attained masterhood already, but he got robbed in his last tournament. He was, however, ranked fifth in the state.

After boasting some more about his chess prowess, he went back to analyzing my own personality, by way of letting me know why I lacked the self-esteem necessary to live life without drugs. "I had a problem, too," he said, "I'm not going to lie to you. When I was at Oxford"—he made a point of mentioning the Oxford thing, and honked on it constantly—"when I was at Oxford I sometimes lit a joint before I even got out of bed in the morning."

What a wild-man!

"Is it an Anglophile thing," I heard myself ask, "or do you just have body odor? I mean, no disrespect, but the no-shower deal works in England 'cause it's chilly. I'm sure all you Oxford boys were into it. But this is Arizona. It's hot. And you really smell. . . ."

Which he did. But still . . . not only was this an ill-advised, infelicitous remark, it was bound to make my stay on the sobriety campus a less than pleasant one. Which proved to be the case. Though not for the reason I expected.

Part of the PV deal was that you had to leave by eight every morning and look for work. Which meant, despite the three-figure temperature, traipsing up and down the mean streets of downtown Phoenix, popping into car dealers, clothing stores, burger joints, artificial limb outlets, and any place else sporting a shingle to ask if they'd like to enhance their status by hiring the likes of me, a middle-aged rehab resident, toxic perspiration machine, and at that point—by way of special qualification—the palest man in Arizona.

My third or fourth day there, I left the lovely erstwhile motel compound, popped on a bus and, after riding aimlessly for half an hour, straggled off in front of a place called Sims Film and Camera. No sooner had I run a hand over my thatch, tugged my pants, and crossed the threshold, however, than a man I can only assume was Mister Sims began making sideways comments to his assistants—perhaps they were the little Sims, the Sim-ettes—about how, if he had his way, them generals would stop dropping them darn nuclear bombs on the good people of Utah and start dumping them on Israel. Which, for the record, he pronounced Izz-ree-ale.

"Wouldn't be so bad if the damn Izzy-rail-ites started mutatin'. Be a sight better than them poor three-legged sheep they got poppin' out downwind. . . . 'Course with the noses on some of them See-mites, looks like they done mutated already."

Mister Sims cleared a couple of old camera catalogs off

the counter in front of him, then turned to his two assistants with a wink. Oddly, the old bigot, who had to be sixtysomething, sported a full head of curly blond hair, while the two younger fellows were both prematurely wispy.

"And what can I do for you?"

"Um . . . huh?"

As it happened, after his mutant schnoz speech, I'd not only forgotten what I was doing there, I'd forgotten I was there at all.

"Don't tell me, you're one of those photojournalists fellas. . . . There are quite a number of you people in the media, aren't there?"

"Dad," said one of the bald young Sims.

But old Goldilocks feigned no offense. "Just stating a fact, son. . . . So what kind of camera you got, mister um . . . ?"

"Ford," I said for no particular reason—or maybe 'cause he was waiting for Weinberger. "Gerry Ford, just like the president. Actually I was wondering if you folks were hiring. I'm just in town for the summer, and—"

"Rehab," father and son said in perfect unison, exchanging a mutual eye roll.

"No thanks," the younger camera dog continued. "We don't hire rehab people. Tried it once. Didn't work. Thanks for coming in."

That same scene, with variations, met the bulk of my early employment efforts. I had, as you may have gathered, scant experience in the gainful employment category. I was a writer after all. I didn't work for a living. . . .

Finally, after being chastised by Martin, "brought up" before the other counselors for my lack of employment success after being there over a week, my roommate, Buford, offered to talk to his boss. Buford was the oldest-looking twenty-year-old I'd ever seen. A sad round bald head. Hangdog eyes. Skin the color of liver left out in the sun. His MO was nothing but beer and crack, but that was enough. "I knew I done too much when I let my dog run away"—he pronounced it, heartbreakingly, "dowg"—"I just sat there and let ol' Willie go. And I loved that dowg. But I couldn't get up off the pipe. . . . Couldn't get the damn thing out my mouth. . . ."

He came from Baton Rouge, Louisiana, where he'd bussed tables for a living. "Everyone down 'ere looks old," he told me one night when we were chatting after lights out. "There's so many damn refineries in Louisiana, just breathing can make you look like you're fifty 'fore you get out of kindergarten. That's a natural fact. . . ."

So it was I ended up with my first "real" job, at the very same place I used to show up at six in the morning, back in my Big G days. Of course, I had a different occupation then. It was the same outfit, different branch. Thanks to Buford, in other words, I was soon to be a proud employee of Mickey Dee's. That's right. Yours truly signed on with McDonald's.

I did not do well on my McDonald's interview. Wendy Wa, the young Taiwanese woman who did the hiring for the Ninth and Indian School Road franchise, started off questioning with a real poser. "Wha'," she began, "wha' is most important product at McDonald's?"

Now, I'm no marketing whiz. I'm not even much of a burger eater—it had probably been over a decade since I'd sunk my chops into meat, let alone a Quarter Pounder—still, I didn't think it took a Wharton grad to know good, solid hamburgers, decent fries, and thick chocolatey shakes were probably what your average customer wanted when he sauntered in the Golden Arches.

Boy, was I wrong.

"Happy attitu'," she snapped. *That* was what people wanted. *"Happy attitu'!"*

"Well, of course," I said, smiling my biggest gap-toothed smile, just to let her know I was pretty much a "happy attitu' " kind of guy myself.

There were more questions like that. It wasn't about Egg McMuffins and hash browns. No sirree! It was about "being ni'." It was about remembering to "smi'." It was, and always would be, about maintaining that "happy attitu'."

The interview took place in the McDonald's back room, a tidy little spot where employees could enjoy their own half-hour break. (On which, by the way, you were allowed one food item and one beverage. Anything after that was deducted from your pay. Which, when you were making minimum wage, could really take a bite out by the end of the week.) I should have guessed that happiness was the main product. Right up on the wall over the time clock, Ms. Wa had mounted a homemade chart, sort of like the safety posters they used to put on the board in grade school, where a big yellow sun was asking the question "Is your smile so bright the customer needs sunglasses?"

Beneath this was a list of names, all current employees, with a little box beside each in which someone—my guess was the little Leona Helmsley of hamburgers, Ms. Wa—inserted a big smiley face or a big round frowning one, depending on the answer. Buford, I noticed, had a Big Frown beside his name. And I made a mental note to buck him up later.

God knows what would happen if, for want of a customer-blinding smile, she let him go. I had a hunch I'd be out right behind him. Buford, despite his "attitu'" problem, must have really impressed Ms. Wa. Otherwise I don't think she would have signed me on after my weak interview performance. Nevertheless, she went ahead and hired me.

Call me a sentimental fool, but I was positively thrilled to make the grade at the Golden Arches. I really wanted that job. Not just 'cause I was tired of making the rounds and absorbing Jew slurs everywhere, but because it just seemed so fucking wholesome. When was I ever going to get the chance to get wholesome?

Talk about miracles! Two weeks ago I was geezing smack

in an airport toilet. Now I was chatting away in my single bed, across the room from a twenty-year-old Cajun, jumping out of my skin at the prospect of a future in burgerdom. Of someday—call us a couple of cockeyed optimists—opening a McDonald's of our own.

"We'll get our feet wet working for Wendy," Buford enthused, "then we'll save our money, maybe get a scholarship to the McDonald's College, you know? Hamburger U. Then come back and open our own franchise together."

It seemed so exciting! "It'll be great," I cried, sitting up in bed and talking in the dark. "We'll find some city that doesn't have a McDonald's!"

"Hooo-*eee!*" Buford let out an ear-bending Rebel Yell. Outside of the odd *Dukes of Hazzard* episode, I'd never heard one in real life before, and it was quite a thrill. "Now you're talkin', Jer-babe! Maybe I'll even serve catfish on the side. My grandmama used to whip up these little catfish balls that could make your eyes water."

"Can you do that?" I asked. "I mean, if it's a fucking McDonald's, don't you have to serve McDonald's stuff?"

"Well, shoot!" Buford was positively indignant. "It's our fucking McDonald's, we can serve whatever the hell we want!"

"Jesus Christ, you're right!" I said. "You're absolutely right! I mean, what are they gonna do, put us in hamburger jail?"

We went on like that, jabbering excitedly about the fortune we would make, until next thing you know it was next morning already, and the two of us were dressing up in our matching fast-food outfits, setting off from the seedy compound to our House of Dreams.

McDonald's didn't open until five-thirty. But I had to be there at a quarter after to fill out my time card and get my uniform adjusted. The red baseball hat was okay. So was the gray-and-white-striped polo shirt. It was the trousers that needed a little work, the sturdy, elasto-waist black polyesters.

The pants, see, stopped half a foot above my ankles. They looked more like clamdiggers than regular pants. And if truth be told, the shirt wasn't really that hot, either. It was so stretched out, it would have been baggy on a sumo wrestler. But when I presented myself to young Ms. Wa, her own "at-titu'" was less than sympathetic. Nobody, she said, would see my ankles behind the counter anyway. What's important, she said, wasn't the clothes themselves. It was what they represented. Just having the official pants and shirt, however they hung on me, meant I was a member of the McDonald's team. And, blush as I might to recall it now, it had been so long since I'd belonged to anything, I was proud as proud could be to belong to McDonald's. Even if I did look mildly retarded.

Before I could actually start working, it turned out, there was one more step. Orientation. I was a little let down—eager beaver that I was, I wanted to hop right behind that counter and flash my smile—but it turned out there was one more essential step on the road to McDonald's-hood. A ritual, in its way, as secret as any Masonic rite.

Once more Wendy steered me to that little room in the back. This time, though, she gave me a little key on a string. Told me to unlock the cabinet in the corner. I'd noticed it my first time in, when I was busy failing my attitude test.

Turns out, the faux-mahogany cabinet back there was not stuffed with mustard packs. It was full of videos. Cassettes on every conceivable Big Mac–related topic. An entire cachet of *Cinema Burgerté.* All produced and conceived with the intent of training the budding counter-human to become part of the team, feel that fire in the belly, strive with everything in them toward the goal of Hamburger Greatness.

First on the bill was a sort of WELCOME TO THE FAMILY spot, a ten-minute promo hosted by one Bob Beavers, Executive in Charge of Employee Training. Bob's a wide-faced, blue-blazer-and-red-power-tie kind of guy. Ironically, for a man at the helm of McDonald's, he's got hair just like the little Big Boy boy, a perfect Porkchop Hill of laminated black parted on one side and swooped skyward in the other. The resemblance is uncanny! Stick Mr. Beavers in a red-and-white-checkered suit, give him a Big Boy Burger to hold aloft like the Statue of Liberty, and you'll swear he was the logo all grown up and come to life.

Beyond appearance, though, Bob's pitch exists as the epitome of midlevel corporate warmth. Right off, he tells us he'd like to be there in person, to shake our hand and welcome us aboard. But, doggone it, McDonald's has grown so large, that's just not possible. "We were founded in 1955," Bob begins, poised before a sparkling clear McDonald's franchise window, a score of happy eaters visible behind him. There is no hint as to where this is. But it doesn't matter. The place is perfect . . . serene . . . almost—no, it is, it really is—*divine*. We have, clearly, arrived at the Uber Mac. This is Hamburger Heaven, and Bob our Host of Hosts. Hear him, as he spreads his words like stardust. "Since the beginning, one man's dream has brought happiness to millions. . . ."

It's almost too much! By the time Bob walks us through his brief, tradition-laden history of Ray Kroc's tasty dreamchild, I'm so proud I'm ready to go on a mission and convert natives, like some kind of McMormon.

After the pep talk, of course, it's down to nuts and bolts, as Bob lays out some of the requirements that go into making a wretch like me into first-class fast-food material. No detail is too small. From hygiene to headgear, milkshakes to manners, there's a system for everything. "A daily bath or shower, clean hair, and tooth brushing is a must. Anything less is offensive to customers and co-workers."

Well, okay! It's a tall order for a junkie for whom the touch of water is still like burning oil. But, inspired as I am, I pledge silently to do the best I can.

The real thrust of the film, beyond the vast schemata for

the food and customer handling, lies in the intense interemployee competition foisted by management to keep everyone on their toes. It's a theme picked up in the screaming yellow *Employee Handbook* passed out before screening, sort of a "Read Along with Bob" deal.

"McDonald's is number one in the fast-food industry," the budding team member is told, "and we are proud of it." But! "It didn't just happen that way. It took a lot of hard work to become the leader, and it will take even more hard work to remain on top."

That's the reality, the Reagan-esque thrust to Squire Beavers's inspirational oration. There exists, like it or not, an invisible army pledged to dragging the Golden Arches in the dirt. And it's up to us, the troops in the trenches, every last man of us, to see that Good triumphs over Evil. "Millions of dollars are spent to insure that McDonald's products are of the best quality possible. . . . You, as a crew member, will become a very important member of McDonald's quality control staff."

Well, there you are! It's enough to make anyone bust their buttons. Who'd have thunk, back when yours truly was stepping over the flooded toilet, fighting off the stench of grease and feces, holding his breath while he shot Dilaudid in the Venice and Western branch of this very institution, back in the wilds of Los Angeles, that I'd end up part of Team McDonald's.

From the Bob Beavers promo, back in the Big Mac Screening Room, it was on to hoarier topics. For whatever reason, Ms. Wa sized me up as French fry material. So, aprés Bob Beavers, I got to sit through a reenactment of Tom and Nancy, two unspeakably hygienic industrial film performers, on their first day tackling potato duty. Mornings, see, your French fries specialist doubles on Hash Browns. I should say "Brown," since technically speaking it's actually a single coffin-shaped hunk of potato matter, dipped and deep-fried to a grease-encrusted crispy brown, then set to rest in the fry basket till cool enough to slip in its little cardboard casket. Same with your fries, except they're bagged instead of boxed.

The whole process breaks down to a six-step procedure:

1. OPEN FROZEN POTATO BAG
2. DUMP IN BASKET
3. DROP IN HOT GREASE
4. PRESS 3-MINUTE TIMER
5. REMOVE WHEN BELL RINGS
6. DRAIN AND BAG

The hard part, beyond inhaling rancid grease fumes and trying not to scald yourself, was slipping the finished product into the custom receptacle. There was a special tool for the job, a sort of half-scoop, half-trough deal. But, try as I might, I couldn't get it right. Every time I piled fries in the bag, I ended up dumping in too many—to the point where, by way of punishment, I had to stand there and count French fries, making sure to have the requisite twenty-three or risk running the entire company into the ground.

I *could* handle the one duty not mentioned in the handbook or cassettes. That of the McDonald's bouncer, the lug whose gig is to police the men's room, in those crucial early morning hours, and eighty-six any Native American brothers who've somehow ended up crashed out in the stall. After a night of booze, the sons of Geronimo just seemed drawn to curling up in the McToilet. I could relate, of course. For me it was studio men's rooms. Nicely as I could, I'd pick up their pints—usually Four Roses—or their blue-and-white generic brew can and hand it back to them, let 'em finish if they wanted, as I tried to steer them outside without arousing any undue wrath.

They were big men. Some downright enormous—three hundred pounds of lard and acne. But, for the most part, they were benign. Wendy was amazed at the job I did. (Apparently the boy before me got his nose broken, another quit on the spot when a couple of cranky reservation customers cornered and peed on him.) I didn't tell her it was 'cause I knew how they felt.

No, the Indians were fine. It's the white guys that got to me. Specifically, Phoenix's brand of upwardly mobile professionals. You know who I'm talking about. The I'm-White-Collar-and-You're-Not crew. The Hungry and The Smug. . . .

Some mornings, dressed in my Total Loser Suit, the sight of all those young suit-and-tie types locked on the fast track at local hot spots like Motorola, U.S. West, or Allied Signal got to me. I displayed no grace under pressure. Worse than that, I took to shooting death rays at every junior exec who took out his own stress by barking at me, the jim-jim serving his morning cholesterol.

From where they stood, of course, what was I? A chump. A complete moron. Some bohunk one notch up from a WILL WORK FOR FOOD–sign guy, parading around in this ridiculous outfit and handing over their Sausage McMuffins. God knows I tried to cling to Bob Beaver's Gettysburg Address. But it just didn't take. I knew, as Bob so eloquently put it: "Our customers enjoy friendly people, and it's up to you to show your smile and make them feel special." But it was all I could do not to leap over the counter and shove a sizzling hash brown in their eye sockets, let alone fork over their reconstituted lard product with a smile.

What I wanted to do was maim and kill. I wanted to torture these suspenders-clad young professionals, to stick their wingtips in French fry grease until they called me "sir." In lieu of that, I opted for subtler sabotage. For acts of silent retribution, to which only I, until this instant, was a party. (And I realize, by this confession, I am condemning myself to a life of condemnation, to the status of outcast. But I deserve no less!)

My crime was *that foul!* For you see, part of my job involved whipping up the guts of your McFoodstuffs. And God help me, some mornings I spat in the batter. I could not help myself. My heinous expectoration, to my diseased mind, seemed almost noble. A tiny gesture compared to the overweening wrath that burned through my brain like battery acid. Standing in the back, the last snot-bag customer comment still smarting in my soul, I'd dash back to the storeroom with a fresh-dumped vat of processed whatever mix.

For one savage minute I'd lean over the bowl, seeing my reflection in the translucent gunk. A yellow, swirling version of my own rage-contorted face. "All right," I'd mutter. "All right, you want to be snotty with me? Fine. I'll show you what snot is, motherfuckers. Matter of fact, I'll feed it to you. I'll custom-spice your goddamn breakfast, okay? So fuck you and have a nice day." And then I'd do it.

One morning Philipe, a young Latino I'd never even talked to, happened to walk in the storeroom as I was . . . acting out. Now I hardly knew this kid. He'd been working there for years, he had a wife and baby to support. He kept to himself. That's all I knew. But Philipe, who I always suspected had more on the ball than anyone gave him credit for, snuck up behind me as I was adding an exceptionally large wad of saliva into the morning's mix.

Our eyes met. *Mano a mano.* It was a classic moment of truth. And in a gesture so satisfying it still warms my heart to recall it, the up-till-then-implacable Philipe broke into the largest grin I'd ever seen. Without saying a word, he raised his hand to slap me five, then took the bowl with a high, wild whine and ducked into the freezer. Once inside, he gestured with his head for me to watch the door. I don't think robbing a bank could be more exciting. While I held lookout, Philipe whipped out his dick, broke into that high, wild laugh again, and let loose a steaming piss dead center into the egg mix. I thought I heard him say *"Viva la Raza,"* but I wasn't sure. My head pounded with blood and adrenaline.

I don't think Philipe and I ever exchanged a word after

that. Only an occasional nod. We were members of some deep Resistance, guerrillas engaged in our own brand of fluid sabotage. After that, in fact, I stopped my revolting behavior altogether. It had gone as far as it was going to go. Besides which, most of the customers were repeaters. They came here, smirky and gummy-eyed, every goddamned morning. So I was fairly certain I'd avenged myself on all of them—and none had died.

Still, from the moment of my first expectoration, Boss Wa commented on my change of attitude. She said I was finally getting the McDonald's spirit. Treating our customers like the extra-special people they were. I was, by now, really a member of the McDonald's team.

At Progress Valley I got on fine with the other inmates. While I seemed psychically incapable of taking part in softball or water sports, I could always redeem myself by insulting the people in charge. It was high school all over again. The lucky egghead directly in charge of my personal growth, the aforementioned Gamy Martin, took most of our weekly counseling sessions to tell me that he could have been a writer had he wanted to, only he'd wanted to do something meaningful with his life. What kind of people, after all, made a living in Hollywood? Shallow, self-centered people, that's who! *Circus People!*

I almost enjoyed these tête-à-têtes, if only because they confirmed that I still had the power to disturb. I'd been so fucked-up and useless for so long, my self-image had sunk due south of slug. So it was healthy to know that, clean and sober, my mere presence in a room could drive someone to such paroxysms of loathing. A typical session with Martin would start off with something like "So, you really think having your name in magazines and TV makes you something special, don't you?"

"Well, not really, Martin. Most of what I did was complete shit."

"Aren't we fashionably cynical? Aren't we just too too trendily negative? Of course, you've made yourself a hero to these other boys."

"I wouldn't say that, Martin."

"You seem to take great delight entertaining them. Do you really think you're in any position to play role model?"

By now he'd be fully steamed. The pink flesh of his cheeks would glow a mottled red. Half-moons of perspiration soaked right through the blue blazer he insisted on wearing, Bob Beavers style, despite the inhuman desert heat.

To make matters worse, but vastly more interesting, I'd taken to leaving the compound in the mornings to attend an early meeting of addicts and alcoholics a few blocks away, at a place called Central City. This marked a welcome change for me. Something about the physical plant of Progress Valley made me antsy, so I took advantage of the rule that said leaving campus was permissible, if what you were leaving for was one of these support groups. It was a blue-collar group. Terrifically down to earth. Reminding me, for some reason, of the people I grew up with back in Pittsburgh. People just trying to work for a living and take care of their families. That they also happened to be there because they drank or used drugs uncontrollably made it that much more appealing.

One morning, I shared that my PV counselor, Martin, had suggested I might be a "sex addict," by virtue of recent adventures I'd related. After the meeting, as I was scuffling back to camp, a banged-up Triumph convertible pulled up and honked. Behind the wheel sat the one beautiful woman in the group, an athletic-looking blonde named Kitty. "Hey, sex addict," she hollered. "Get your ass over here."

I must confess, I'd tailored my little pitch of the morning to the female contingent. Hoping to stir up a little interest under the guise of scathing self-exposure. Kitty, to my jaded eyes, seemed like the very vision of wholesome, Pep Club

Americana. A bouncy blonde given to short shorts, snug T-shirts, and high-top tennies. That she'd been an off-the-charts Scotch-guzzling cocaine shooter rounded the picture out perfectly. What more could a guy want?

I'd heard her share on occasion and knew she was a foreign sports car mechanic with a long tall boyfriend and a boss given to constant verbal abuse.

From that day onward, the high point of my existence was hopping in that Triumph, stopping off for a chat over doughnuts and java at the local doughnut shop, then riding back beside her to PV to change into my McDonald's suit. For weeks, I listened to her litany of disappointments and crises. Learned that she loved animal and horror movies, that she'd been groomed as an Olympic tennis prodigy, that she'd given that up to concentrate on bowling, ended up discovering booze and drugs instead, and slid down the ladder to college dropout, biker moll, borderline coke whore and live-in companion to a convicted child abuser before getting clean. My kind of girl!

Every detail drove me deeper in love. The vulnerability, the aura of tainted Homecoming Queen, the Catholic school slut spun from sin to salvation and back again. All of it touched me in a way that left me physically dizzy every day when I stepped out of the car and into the compound with a little wave. I knew that she lived with her boyfriend. I'd actually seen him, at a Saturday morning meeting, a tall, strikingly handsome fellow with the kind of shocking blue eyes you might expect in Viking visionaries, sidewalk schizophrenics, or Paul Newman.

Each morning, as our talks got more intimate, the urge to rest my left hand on her gorgeously tanned thigh became overpowering.

It had been so long since I'd felt this kind of longing. This unrequited passion. Nothing could have been more delicious. We both knew it, you see. Yet it was never addressed. I suspected she may have expected me to make a move, but that only made it better. (Not doing something crude right off is about as close as a guy like me ever gets to class.) I was clearly capable, but I was trying to be different, to not repeat the old patterns: the heartfelt aim of everyone in recovery support groups everywhere.

So all we did, every day, was talk intimately, stare and smile at each other over cinnamon rolls. For my part, I was happy just to sit beside this creature. To walk out of a meeting or a doughnut shop beside her. Part of the gift of being clean, of resisting the daily, minute-to-minute urge to get fucked-up again, was that I was losing my paranoia.

One morning, in our first moment of physical contact, Kitty reached out one awesomely tanned and well-toned arm and brushed her hand over my eyes. "You have the most amazing eyebrows," she said, running a finger along the single thatch that runs from one side of my forehead, straight across the bridge of my nose, all the way to the other, as if a furry caterpillar had crawled there, caught pneumonia, and died.

It was not exactly the stuff of Harlequin romances, but it was certainly novel. "Are you making fun of me?" I replied, half joking, half not. "What's next? You going to start talking about my facial moles? How 'bout the fact that I'm missing more teeth than a full-blooded hillbilly? And what about my complexion? You like green, or you prefer your men a little ruddier?"

Fortunately, she took my neurotic response for humor. She leaned her head back on the car seat. Showed that turned-up nose in profile. Laughed up at the sky. Turned back to me, put her arm around my neck, and pulled me close and planted a kiss on my lips like it was the most natural thing in the world.

Her skin felt smooth and firm. Her hair smelled faintly of motor oil. Her mouth tasted like coffee. She was absolutely real, and it was the sexiest combination on the planet.

"This never happened," she said, firing up the engine.

"This never will happen. But if it did, I know it would be great."

"I wish I'd met you when I was still shooting dope." This was my idea of romantic.

"Don't even think about it."

"That's all I think about."

"It gets better," she said.

We drove the rest of the way to my punishment farm in a kind of tingling silence. She pulled up outside the compound. She still stared straight ahead, both hands gripping the steering wheel.

"Jerry," she said, very slowly, very carefully, enunciating as if every word were as significant as every other. "I don't do this anymore. Okay? Every relationship I've ever been in I've fucked up. I've cheated. I've lied. . . . I am not going to fuck up this one, okay?"

"Okay. It's okay," I said, and I meant it. "I'm just happy you even talk to me. I'm not exactly the Prince of Faithful Relationships myself, you know? It seems like the best thing I can do with someone I'm attracted to is not get involved with them. You know what I mean?"

"So we can just be friends?"

"Come on, I'd love to be friends! It would be incredible to be friends."

Her brown eyes smoldered beneath her straight blonde bangs. Her lips parted slightly. In the relentless sunlight, her track scars shone milky white against her strong tanned arms. This was it: *The Girl Next Door Gets Out Of Jail.*

"You really mean that?"

"Of course I mean that."

"Okay," she said, "call me tonight. But hang up if Tom answers."

"What?"

"Hang up. He's a freak when he gets jealous. Maybe we can meet this weekend."

"But—"

"But nothing. We don't even have sex. He's too busy reading the fucking Bible. He calls me Jezebel."

"Jesus!"

"No, Jezebel. I'm supposed to call *him* Jesus. Call me."

She left me there. Standing slack-jawed while her little sports car spat dust all over me. I'd have to dash in and take a shower. Ms. Wa said if she found dirt under my fingernails one more time, she'd let me go.

The very next week, having bonded the way only two ex-dope fiends can, Kitty and I moved on to the next plateau.

What made this, for me, the most extraordinary of affairs—the one, perhaps, genuine love in my life—was that I entered it so naked. Stripped, not just of nerve ends, not just of self-respect, but of the capacity to hide what I really was. The fear that coiled and uncoiled like an opiate-soaked snake in my guts.

We're talking about a thirty-six-year-old repeat offender living in Drug Camp and scrubbing pans at McDonald's. I had a daughter I loved but could not see. A career I'd blown, a talent squandered. A wife, whatever I felt about her, I'd hurt without meaning to.

Our first liaison took place on a Sunday morning. She told her born-again boyfriend she was going to church with her parents. He didn't approve of Catholics, but he was happy she was finally starting "to walk in the path." "Meanwhile," she'd told me, "all he does is walk around naked and watch the *700 Club*. He sits there spooning in Häagen-Dazs and screaming 'Hallelujah!' "

Site of our sin-fest was the Cactus Lodge, a nondescript four-story motel within walking distance of Progress Valley. Sundays were big days back at the ranch. Either we went on outings—back in the van again!—or it was Pitch-In Day. When everybody pitched in and cleaned the place from top to bottom. Not that it was dirty. Part of what your three hundred a week paid for was the privilege of wielding a mop, washing dishes, manning a broom, and vacuuming administrative offices on a daily basis. This was part of rehab. You pay them money, they let you play janitor.

It put me back in prep school, when ducking out at night to smoke joints and hook up with townies made life exhilarating. I wasn't doing the joints, but two decades later, here I was shirking my duties, sneaking out my dorm window and meeting a town girl. In some ways nothing had changed. It was still about ignoring authorities, breaking rules, shirking my assigned duties and sneaking off to meet a bad little local.

The major difference, embarrassingly enough, is that I was now older than the authorities I was busily defying. If I ever needed proof that I was trapped in terminal adolescence, this was it. I'd based my entire life on the premise that rules were bullshit—as were the people who upheld them. The trouble was, I'd never found anything but bullshit of my own to replace theirs.

Kitty was clean two years to my twenty days. Her example brought home to me the possibility of actually putting down the needle. For good. One day at a time. What made this so staggering was that I knew how much she loved to get high. She was as hard-core as I was. An addict to her marrow. She'd been to those places most normal citizens could but dimly comprehend. We were exactly the same. I was so in love that it made my heart hurt.

But, at the core of whatever honesty was left inside me, I hadn't made the commitment to non-drugdom she had.

I didn't like the consequences. I could no longer stand where narcotics took me. But I knew I would go back to them. I was like the battered wife who goes back to her husband because she likes the way he treats her when he isn't killing her. . . .

No matter what I was doing, there was always a part of me in reserve. A whisper that never ceased: *You-know-you-want-it-you-know-you-want-it-you-know-you-want-it* . . .

Some mornings, when Kitty and I would be tooling down Camelback or stuck at a red light on Indian School Road, we'd get wrapped up in HOW IT FELT . . . HOW INTENSE . . . HOW GOOD HOW GOOD HOW *FUCKING* FUCKING *GOOD!!!* Until it was all we could do not to make a U-turn and head to Broadway. Phoenix's narco-sleaze strip. By then we'd be screaming it, teary-eyed, giddy, willfully crazed. "*We need drugs! We must have drugs!*"

The possibility was always there, like a deadly tease. In two seconds we can cop a rig, load up on bleach and cocaine. We can dig up some smack, find a motel and shoot ourselves into sweet oblivion.

Jesus, yes! I would have fixed her. I would have fucked her. I would have licked blood from the holes in her arms. That's how gone I was. That's how we finally did end up in that motel room, on Sunday morning, when she was supposed to be churchbound and I was sworn to hosing down the PV Dumpsters.

It was the strangest foreplay in the world. And it was certainly the hottest. One wrong move and we'd both be stretched out on slabs.

Instead, we were stretched out on a sagging double bed. Still talking. Still pushing the self-destructo envelope. Still working ourselves into that frenzy of desire for drugs. Which we could, with luck and cunning and a perversion so savage it could consume us even as it saved our lives, displace into physical lust.

What we craved was drugs. What we had was each other. And our words fed the craving even as our flesh, however imperfectly, strived to satisfy it.

I can imagine no greater frustration. Nor any stronger aphrodisiac.

• • •

I was already in the hotel when Kitty roared into the parking lot. I watched her from the balcony. She swung the Triumph to a screaming halt. Sat for a moment, in the middle of the empty parking lot, both hands still gripping the wheel. This sprightly blonde with wraparound Ray-Bans and turned-up nose. I could see her working her lips. She opened the door. Started to step out, then slammed it shut again.

This kept up a good ten minutes. Finally, throwing both hands up in the air, raising her face to the heavens, she flung open the door and tore herself out of the tiny car. Dressed for church in a long white dress and an old-fashioned straw hat, trailing pink ribbon down her back. She held a pair of white gloves in her hands. It would have drawn approving nods from the most conservative Mormon. Except for those wraparound Ray-Bans, the whole picture was straight out of Norman Rockwell.

It was no easier imagining the Flying Nun slamming cocaine than sweet little Kitty. Something about that dress, the way it hung on her, a little loose, a little ill fitting, so you just knew she'd made it herself. Knew she was poor. Devoid of big-city style. A small-town, hardworking, blue-collar sweetheart. Fighting the needle, skipping mass, and cheating on her boyfriend.

A couple of just-washed family cars pulled into the lot as Kitty was walking past. Each disgorged a little swarm of Grandmas, Grandpas, Mom, Dad, Sis, and Juniors. They were, I could see, dressed not unlike my girlfriend. One of the old ladies, a hearty blue-hair straight out of Central Casting, Grandma Division, drew close to Kitty, wearing an approving smile.

Kitty, apparently, didn't see her. But she did see me up on the top floor. She raised her arm, shaking a fist in my direction. "Hey, motherfucker!" she yelled. "Get in that room and get your pants off. I ain't had my breakfast yet!"

I stayed on the balcony just long enough to make sure they didn't put down the babies and lynch her. The blue-hair blushed nine shades of scarlet. "Men," I heard Kitty tell her. "You don't put 'em in their place, they walk all over you."

She looked back up at me and gave a little hoot. I walked back into the motel room, dizzy with love.

Once locked in, deep behind closed curtains and chained door at ten A.M. like the dope fiends we were, the showy élan of her parking lot display gave way to a kind of desperate regret. Still wearing that sad straw hat, she threw herself on the bed and buried her face in her hands.

"I can't believe I'm doing this!"

"But Kitty . . ."

"I know, I know, I wanted to come here, okay? It was my idea. I'm just not used to going to motel rooms with strange men. I'm not like you, okay? I don't do this all the time."

"Hey—"

"Oh, what? Tell me you don't have five women stashed around this fucking city already."

Her rage, this tide of hate that roared up out of nowhere and receded as soon as it appeared, was something I came to expect, though I never got used to it.

I stood there, feeling no doubt as dumb as I looked.

Willing myself, I stepped forward and edged down beside her on the bed. Took her in my arms. She was that kind of crazy; you didn't know if she was going to smother you with kisses or jump up and hit you with an ashtray.

"Take my dress off," she cried, turning her head away on the pillow. When I reached for her she suddenly sat back up. "I'm sorry, okay? I'm just scared. I hate this. I mean—" She grabbed me, pulled my face close to her. "I want to be with you. I just hate . . . you know, the way life gets. I just . . . Oh, fuck, I just want to get high!"

"I know," I said. And I did. I'd been devoid of feelings so long myself, the sudden flood of them made the urge to obliterate them all almost unendurable. I thought, Can I love her? Can I really love anyone? Just thinking the words *I love her,* just having them in the head, made me feel ridiculous. What the fuck was I talking about?

This was an emotion. This was for real people. It's just . . . her pain was so much like mine. Her nightmare so wholly in sync with my nightmare. . . . If it wasn't love, it was a process of identification so strong it loomed unlike anything I'd ever experienced. Except for the odd strawberry—when I was, really, more sideline furniture than participant—I'd never been with a woman as fucked-up on drugs as I was. Never shot up together. I knew guys who said fixing and fucking at the same time made them believe in Jesus. And I could believe it. . . .

But this was more intense.

For Kitty and me, that morning, it was precisely the opposite. Dead straight and dying to get high, we were overwhelmed by each other. There was no place to hide. We were in thrall to our sensations with nothing to dilute or alter them.

Kitty curled up in my arms on the edge of the bed. She pounded her fists off my shoulders. "I'm having feelings," she cried. "I hate this. . . . Why the fuck am I still wearing a dress? Why aren't I naked yet?"

"Easy, baby, you were ranting. I didn't want to interrupt you to tear your clothes off."

We tangled for half a minute. The sight of that made-it-myself churchwear still choked me up. By the time we got it over her head, I found myself staring at Kitty's arms. I'd seen them before, spotted her ancient dope scars in the car, but it's different when you hold them. When you run your fingers over the little bumps, touch all the little hard places where the tissue's clogged and hardened, where the flesh had revolted and swelled in on itself, never to go back to normal. My eyes roved from those elaborate tracks to the babyish fold between her legs, where she'd shaved her pubic hair, where the flesh shone smooth and startling, inviting and pink and mind-scorchingly virginal. . . .

Without thinking, I took her arm, raised it to my lips, placed a kiss on the inside of her elbow where the tracks were worst.

"Why did you do that?"

"I don't know. . . . I—I just . . ."

"Do it again."

I did. Somehow my own clothes had flown off in the confusion. So the both of us were sitting there, sort of sprawled across the bed. Kind of making love and kind of not. Every time we'd get knee deep in the preliminaries, one of us would pull back, not from lack of interest, but from, I don't know, from acute awareness. The enormity of all the sensations swirling around, inside and outside our dizzy little skulls.

I had never been with a woman straight. Never. Even when I was a kid, my first time, at fifteen, I was at least potted up. Half drunk. Something. . . . Kitty, I knew, had been with a couple of boyfriends since getting clean. But I also knew why she was with them. Food. Shelter. Security. Not being alone. . . . All the usual reasons, according to her.

Without drugs, for me, it was like simultaneously trying to enjoy yourself and watch yourself blown up to scoreboard size, every little move and murmur exaggerated and blasted back in your face. Consciousness was crushing. I could not stand not being out of my mind when I was out of my clothes.

Tangled together, I slipped my hand between her legs, pressed my lips against her ear as she craned her neck, thrusting her head back on the pillow. She held on to me, squeezing my erect cock as much, it seemed, from confusion as arousal. As if, should she let go for a second, she'd go flying around the room like a balloon with the air let out.

"Oh, God," she whispered, pressing her other hand to my face as she spoke. "Oh, God, do you remember that feeling when you just pushed the plunger? . . ."

"What?"

We were both breathing fast. Starting to sweat.

"You know," she went on, half gasping, accompanying her words with earnest, upward thrusts of her hips. "When the stuff's inside you, but it hasn't hit yet."

"Yes. . . ."

"But you know . . . Oh, God . . ." Her voice sank to a throaty drawl. "But you know it's just about to explode. . . . You've got those first, like, tingles. . . . You know the rush is about to hit. . . . You're holding on, you're holding on. . . ."

"And the light goes funny," I whispered, lips brushing the faint hairs of her ear. "And the paint on the walls starts to pulsate, like suddenly you can see the air. . . ."

"That's right, that's right." With one finger she'd now started to massage her clit, with the other hand she'd begun to rub my dick, to tug the throbbing shaft up and down, up and down, in time to the rhythm of her own frantic recall. "When the shit's, like, inside you, but it hasn't hit, but you *know,* you fucking *know* . . . Oh, fuck, put it in . . . put it in me, you bastard. . . . But you know in, like, three seconds it's going to shoot up your spine, your heart's going to explode. . . ."

"Like Nagasaki," I groaned, "like Hiroshima, behind your eyeballs, inside your brain. . . ."

"And you could die," she whispered, maneuvering, shifting so that she lay poised beneath me, letting go her own fresh-shaved pussy to work my cock with both hands, to open herself and guide me up inside her, "you could die from the pleasure. . . . You want to . . . the coke makes you feel, for one second, for just one second, that you've felt as good as you're allowed to feel. That now you're just going to turn into a scream, a giant scream, to drown out all the sounds that rush inside when you get off, to smother everything outside you. . . ."

"So you boot it," I murmured. "You slide out that shining

needle, you pull back, watch the blood fill up the tube, and plunge back in, shove . . . it . . . all . . . back . . . in . . ."

Our eyes locked. Her fingernails slashed my back. Her sharp teeth tore at my lips. Groans tore out of our throats even as our eyes flooded with strange hot tears. We were more than lovers now, or we were less. We were two souls so gone on loss and panic and flat-out fear, they did not even know if they were making love or dying.

"Oh, God, yes . . . ," I sighed, hearing my voice and not hearing. Rocked with pain and numb with ecstasy. There and not there, fucking her cunt but feeling the needle, making love with my muscles but shooting up with my mind, letting her words, her insane narcotic narrative, lift me out of my body, out of both our bodies, into some savage blend of memory and sensation and crippling, frustrated desire for an orgasm that couldn't come from sex, could come only from drugs and madness and injecting our selves to death. . . .

"Don't stop . . . shove it all the way . . . make me feel it. . . . make me stop feeling . . . make me make me make me make me make me *makememakememakeme* . . ."

By the time we clawed our way to some semblance of mutual climax, exploded and collapsed, I felt like my mind had shattered inside my skull. If I moved my head, I could feel the pieces clank and shift.

Spent and sweating, we rolled out of each other's arms to opposite sides of the bed. This was William Blake territory: "The fiery limb, the flaming hair, shot like sinking sun into the western sea. . . ." That was the only orgasm that mattered: death by injection, overdose, the thrust that ends all thrusting.

I didn't realize how much I wanted to die until the first time I fucked Kitty. Nor how much I wanted to live. Over and over, each time we made love, we repeated this oddly disembodied foreplay. Face-to-face, belly-to-belly, reciting our murmured litany of this-is-what-it-feels-like dope memories, we were at once recreating and banishing the passion that had ruled our lives. We were, in each other's arms, celebrating narcotic ferment and mourning its eternal loss.

Thus was our relationship engendered: two people who based their love on the shared reality that love was something they were both too crippled to do right. At any minute one of us could relapse, one of us could succumb. We could use drugs or we could become them. And use each other. Which is what we did.

We continued, each time we went to bed, to tantalize ourselves with sense-memory of past inebriation. My entire time in Phoenix, I was trying desperately to leave my past life behind, to shake my habit. But for all the meetings, all the counseling and group dynamics, it was Kitty who saved me.

Kitty. Who drove me so deep into my obsession, I came out the other end. Instead of denying my craving, I embraced it. I replaced it with her.

I have never, I believe, loved anyone as much, nor been so utterly incapable of love. I surrendered completely.

As things shook down, McDonald's fired me. I didn't pass that shining smile test and got the boot after my trial period was up. No matter what I tried I just couldn't correct that pesky "attitu' " problem. And Progress Valley, a ninety-day program, threw me out after sixty.

There were a lot of reasons, as you can imagine, but things came to the proverbial head one evening when, after telling Squire Martin and the staff I was off on my new job, serving food to firemen—I don't know where I came up with that little lie, but it sounded good—I got a ride home with Kitty and got a little carried away in the parking lot. The truth is I wasn't working at all. I was hanging out at Phoenix College, writing unreadable short stories in the library stacks.

We started off with a good-bye kiss. We ended up in flaming, legs-out-the-window, axle-groaning, seat-wheezing public fornication. Even now it amazes me. I could barely hold hands in public, let alone attempt intimacy. But that day Kitty'd ditched out of work at the Foreign Car Shop to spend the afternoon at some duck pond, hanging out with me. By the time we tooled into Progress Valley, we were pretty well into it. Knowing Kitty, I'm sure we must have got started on one of her patented remember-how-speedballs-feel? bouts of foreplay. Next thing you know, it was off to the races. And out of Rehab.

Of course, the professional drug and alcohol counselors had to do what they did. Taking me aside, the guy who worked in the kitchen, a rail-thin, ex–New York shooter, confided that it wasn't just lying, having sex, sneaking off the compound, and all the other stuff that got me tossed. It was, he explained, my influence on the other residents. "They see you getting away with this shit, they think they can do it. It takes emphasis off their recovery. You're a bad egg."

The night they gave me the word, Martin assembled a meeting of the entire "community" in the dining room. I had to sit in the middle of the circle while he read off a list of my transgressions. I might as well have worn a dunce cap.

Martin's eyes looked parboiled. Sweat all but steamed out from under the arms of his blue "chess-player" blazer. For one bad moment I thought he might have a stroke just from hating me.

"You . . . you're entirely self-centered!" he sputtered. "Y-you think rules don't apply to you. . . . You think, just c-cause you're from L.A., you're some kind of big-time junkie. . . ." And then the clincher, the one I'd been hearing since I was old enough to be thrown off Little League: "You're just not a team player. . . ."

All more or less right on the money. Still, part of me wanted to launch a scathing rebuttal. To point out that, since *he* probably had less sex than a truck tire—due to the toxic clouds that trailed him like contrails off an F-15—perhaps there was something less than community concern behind his wrath. Perhaps there was a little jealousy. But what the hell.

I was so fascinated by the way Martin's face mottled up like ground beef at the mere mention of my name, so weirdly flattered at my ability to upset this clammy chess whiz, I let it pass.

Just that week, my sponsor in the morning group I attended had given me a word of advice on how to handle criticism. "Whatever people accuse you of, whatever they call you, don't argue," he advised. "Go along. The best way to put it behind you is to just say, 'You're probably right. . . .' Otherwise you work yourself up, you cop a resentment, you invent a reason to go back up and pick up a rig again. We're addicts, you know? We use other people to get what we want. Especially if what we want is an excuse to use. 'You're probably right,' " he repeated, "that's what you say. Trust me."

And I did. When Martin asked, like some B-movie prosecutor, if I had anything to say in my defense, I shrugged and smiled with a grace that was entirely new to me. It was dangerously close to martyrdom but still better than some smart-ass reply.

"Martin," I said with only a trace of Wellesian flourish, "Martin, you're probably right."

And that was it. My finest moment. I stood up amid backslaps, shouts of support, sympathetic kibitzing from my fellow substance abusers. There was Skipper, the obese eighteen-year-old alkie from Minneapolis; Jimmy O'Keefe, the Brooklyn crackhead who got popped in the toilet of his Wall Street brokerage house; Jorge, the definitive rich kid, son of a Mexican diplomat and in for his sixteenth rehab. Even Patsy, the sepulchral, Fredo-like scion of one of New York's Five Families, a helpless sniffer, gave me a timid thumbs-up. This was a lot for Patsy.

I thanked my inquisitor, nodded to my peers, and strode with the noble step of the wrongly accused back to the suite to pack my bags. I still hadn't returned my McDonald's uniform. I was, in fact, intending to let them keep my deposit and abscond with the outfit, imagining it'd come in handy, at a later date, in some as yet unspecified scam. As if, perhaps, there were a future in embezzling frozen hash browns, a thriving market for mass quantities of secret sauce mix. Mmm-mmm!

Alone with Buford, in our snot-colored cinder-block room, I changed my mind. My Louisiana friend was still on board at Mickey D's, so I turned it over to him.

"A grim moment in hamburger history," he said somberly. And I had to agree. "You know why I got thrown out of the Navy?" he asked me after we'd shaken hands and I was about to walk out of his life. "'Cause when they asked if any of us used drugs, I raised my hand. I hadn't got high in over half a year, but my daddy raised me to be honest, so I stuck up my hand. I was out of there by eighteen hundred hours. That's when I knew my daddy was a goddamn fool."

"I understand," I told him, though I wasn't sure I did.

"I'm telling you," he said, "because I want you to know you're not the only one who ever got throwed out of a place. Your buddy Buford's been there, too. Don't mean you're a bad person. Just means the people in charge are a pack of egg-sucking eunuchs."

"Thank you, Buford."

"'S all right," he said. And I actually saw the eyes mist up in that young old man's face. "Afore you, I never even met a Jew. Now I know they're okay. A little ange-stray, but okay."

"Right."

I didn't want to touch that, but I did appreciate the sentiment.

The next morning I was back in Kitty's Triumph. On the way to the airport. We planned on getting back together.

She'd long since dumped her born-again boyfriend. She was staying with her mom and dad till she got a place of her own. Conveniently, I'd been evicted from my apartment before coming to Phoenix and had only the vaguest idea where I'd stay when I got back to L.A.

No matter what else happened, I'd been clean sixty days. I felt renewed. I felt cleansed. I felt like having a drink at the airport and was absolutely smashed by the time we landed in Los Angeles.

A day in bed. Something I never do. Either that, or do all the time, and forget immediately. I don't know. . . . They tell me, what with my ill-used liver in a state of permanent struggle, there will be times when the fatigue just comes on like that. Fatigue and sweat, with headache and complete loss of faith thrown in for good measure. I cannot believe, when I'm in this state, that this is not how it's always going to be. That this is not IT. You don't die, you just stay so tired, you don't even have the energy to commit suicide, were you so inclined.

But maybe it's not my liver at all. Maybe I'm just—dread word—depressed! Depression is the shield I kept raised before me as I slogged through life. Unhappiness was so ingrained, so much a part of my being, that I lived like an Eskimo who, having been cold from birth, simply believes the chill is emanating from within.

But it does not have to be so cold. Come hell or high anxiety, I'm there every day with the well-heeled Volvo-ites to pick my kid up from preschool. Nina bursts into a giant smile and yells, "Daddy!" the second she sees me. She hops right off the swing like the kid in a Kodak commercial and comes running into my arms. Then I pick her up and swing her in the sky for a giddy second before swinging her back to earth again. Now I know what "swoon" means. Because I could almost do it. I almost do.

I hang on these moments when the itch is on me, when the Monkey's on my back with a grappling hook. Like it is today.

See, it's very simple: I choose the Monkey, I lose the Daddy-gig. If it were my last earthly moment—watching sweet Nina hurtling toward me with open arms and a dizzy grin—I'd die happy. On the other hand, a shot of smack wouldn't be too bad, either. Who am I kidding? After all this clean time, that first hit would be unbelievable. With drugs, see, you get to be a virgin again. But why is this even in my brain?

That's the sickness, see. That awful thought, grafted like a diseased limb on the tree of life—there's always drugs. . . . Even knee deep in the familial bliss, the thought persists. . . .

Maybe I'm some kind of sick puke for promoting both notions at the same time. For sustaining such polar opposite options. Unless, of course, they're not really so polar. Unless they're not so different at all. . . . At this point, in all honesty, the major difference is that dope seems like the safer bet. Indeed. Even if Hallmark does not make Happy Heroin! *cards, dope is ultimately cornier.*

What is heroin, really, but every junkie's teddy bear? What makes a soul feel all snuggly and cutesy-poo. . . .

Can you understand this? Shooting dope is all about getting warm and fuzzy. Dependably so. But the Daddy-rush. . . . Forget about it! I've never felt anything so terrifying! It's so real, even the pleasure can break your heart. Which, in the grand scheme of things, is what separates shooting smack from loving your little girl. Heroin may kill you, but it'll never break your heart. Not like a child.

Not like loving a child.

During my first, frantic stab at L.A. clean-and-sober-dom, my day revolved around making it to my daughter's house and back without succumbing. I didn't want to keep using, but I couldn't stop.

Stumbling drunk off the plane in L.A., I made the resolution: new city, new life. I began by fucking up on the airplane. (But no more than five or six times. . . . How many cocktails *can* you swill in an hour-and-a-half flight?) It's not like I was an alkie or anything. Alcohol's for cleaning needles. . . .

"Don't beat yourself up," Kitty said when I confessed over a pay phone. I could tell she was thrilled about me calling her collect at work, but what could I do? This was the addict's forte: putting those you love in tight spots so they could bail *your* ass out. Whining *"I hate myself, but what can I do?"*

"Do you mean that?" I said when she fired her first blast of compassion.

"Of course," she said. "You shouldn't beat yourself up. I'll do it for you, you fucking asshole. . . . You had two months, and you threw it away. . . . Where are you now?" I heard her boss nagging her to get off the phone. He was a freak about personal calls. It was an auto repair shop, but he'd been in the Navy for seven years, and he ran it like a submarine. Like if you even talked above a whisper, the enemy would track you down and drop a depth charge.

"I think I'm in the airport. . . ."

"You think? You're not sure?" Disgust all but oozed out of the mouthpiece.

"I know, okay? I'm in the airport."

"You *are* in California, right? You're not going to surprise me with a postcard from Milwaukee."

"Come on, Kitty."

"Come on, shit. Get in a fucking cab. Do not pass GO. Do not stop and buy a bag of heroin. Go directly to Mitch's house. Unpack your bags and stay there."

Which I did. I stayed at Mitchell the Producer's. I did not use. I did not steal his wife's pharmaceuticals. Although, remarkably, the same pill bottles were still out there on the counter. Amazing! That people could actually keep drugs around and not use them. Not empty a whole jug of Percodans in one crazed night, then tell Doctor Heeby-Jeeb the dog ate them, or they fell in the toilet, and demand a refill for those pesky back spasms—or whatever the hell you made up to snag the shit in the first place.

For an extended stretch, I managed to stay clean and reasonable functional. And, most important, to visit my daughter. This last, for reasons that boiled down to the geographic, marked a crucial, daily test of my determination to walk the walk. To stay clean no matter what the temptation.

The temptation was my old pal Towner. He of the tar and tinfoil. Young Townie, in his diehard HipHop gear, still lived within sight of my bus stop. Which meant every time I rode over to see Nina I had to resist the itch to pop in and relieve my terminal angst. I was dead broke, bumming bus money, living in somebody's spare room, and feeling useless. If I ever thought I needed escape, if I ever thought I deserved it, I thought I deserved it now.

If I could make it to my daughter's house without succumbing, I still had to handle the urge to score before the bus ride home.

My entire life was about not using. I spent every waking moment trying *not* to do something. Had I a form to fill out, under occupation I'd have had to scribble "NON-DRUG USER."

The horrific part about getting clean is that at the weakest point in your life you're required to be the strongest. Your nerves are shot, you can't sleep, your brain's still woozy, your pockets are empty, and some combination of fear and detox and naked, unrelenting pressure still has you sweating buckets and puking on street corners, but you have to be more together than you've ever been. You have no choice.

Not until you finally try to put down the stuff do you realize, with stinging clarity, precisely why you picked it up in the first place. All life, in this freshly nerve-flayed state, boils down to a choice of hells. The hell of being fucked-up on drugs or the hell of being fucked-up without them.

Because I had no place of my own, I had to play with our baby in Sandra's house. Which served to remind me how far I'd sunk, and just how much I'd lost.

Try as I might to just forget my discomfort and *be* with Nina, I could not help thinking of myself as a ghost. And, legit or not, I had the sensation my own child thought of me that way, too. It was such a halfway, shadowy existence, how could she think anything else?

There were so many reasons to feel bad. You couldn't count them. Bad as I felt after a session at my ex-house, the prospect of riding that rush-hour bus back to Mitch's was almost worse. All these people packed in like kipper snacks, and then me. Nobody rides the bus in L.A. unless they have to. Even the people who do it every day have contempt for everybody else who rides along with them.

Standing there, squished among the blacks and Latinos who actually had a reason to be going somewhere, I felt wholly unworthy. I knew what they were thinking: Look at that low-life junkie! Look at that loser! Fucking *puta*. . . .

Days when the bus wouldn't come, I would just stand there, across the street from the Café Tropical, gazing down Silverlake Boulevard at Towner's pad. Knowing the relief that awaited me in the house, if I just strolled on down.

It was bad enough to just gaze longingly at Towner's apartment. But if his truck was there—the truck I used to wait for, to sit in the coffee shop jonesing over when the greeper was starting to squeeze—I could literally feel my adrenals start to pump. It meant he was home. The doctor was in. I could just walk across the street and get my medicine.

I was thoroughly conditioned. At the sight of his Chevy pickup this rat would drool. Skulking there, in the dusk, counting out my bus fare in pennies, I would taste the bitter tar in the back of my throat. My fingers would curl and uncurl. My vision would blur. My prick would stiffen and I'd sweat through my shirt.

I might have made it through that first time. Might have if I hadn't decided to add to the burdens of my modest existence with a wholly ludicrous delusion. What happened—and it still sort of baffles me—is CAA tracked me down. Good old Steve Sticket somehow got my number and gave me a jingle.

"Jerry, babe, how the hell are you?"

I'll never forget his voice. The same old rah-rah. Like it was the most normal thing in the world. Like I hadn't fallen off the edge of the planet, clawed my way into the abyss, and clawed my way out again with my ass in my hand and my pockets full of bloody Chiclets that used to be teeth. . . .

"I'm talking cool TV," Steve chirped. "I'm talking

groundbreaking. I'm talking Wes fucking Craven. Huh? What do you think? Sound hip or what?"

"What?"

My own voice sounded so feeble, only he didn't seem to notice. "How did you find me?" I heard myself whimper. His go-get-'em-ness was truly scarifying.

You had to hand it to CAA. I had a feeling I could have hung myself, just thrown a rope over a convenient rafter and strung myself up, and good old Steve would have sent a messenger to cut me down and arrange a meeting with some bonehead producer who "heard all about me," "really liked my stuff," and "definitely wants to touch bases. . . ."

"Steve," I wanted to tell him, "Steve, I'm *dead*. . . . Leave me alone."

Instead, knowing I was sealing my doom even as I went along, I heard myself giving a half-assed imitation of my old phony-baloneyness.

"Wes Craven, huh? I love him. . . . Sure. . . . Freddy Kruger is the godhead. . . . You bet. . . . MGM out in Culver City. . . . Can't wait."

It was all I could do to make it from Mitch's to my daughter's house without skirting neurological collapse. And here I was agreeing to ride the bus from Hollywood all the way out to Culver City to take a pitch meeting.

All I knew about the show is that it was called *Nightmare Cafe*. That it was Mister Nightmare on Elm Street's virgin foray onto the little screen. That I had more business interviewing at the local Army-Navy store than I did chatting up Big Wes and his cronies. My hands shook so much, I could barely write a bad check, let alone a script.

And yet, in my perma-fog, in my post-narcotic blur, I followed my agent's suggestion the way you'd follow a dead relative in a dream.

All I remember of the bus ride is that I had to transfer three times. And the last one, a straight shot west on Venice Boulevard, was full of black kids who'd just gotten out of junior high. It was the farthest I'd been from Hollywood since coming back from Phoenix. As usual I was dressed in black. And sweating my ass off. So of course a lanky wiseass in the back started dissing me.

"Yo, Elvis . . . Elvis, how you get your hair to do that? Check that shit out! My man looks jus' like Elvis! C'mon, man, you s'posed to be the king! Sing 'Hound Dog' or I'm gonna kick your ass. . . ."

It went like that, all the way from Fairfax out to Culver City. Tough guy that I was, I pretended not to hear. It was all I could do not to burst into tears, maybe tell him my father could take his father. I was so out of it I could not even be insulted.

By the time I made it to MGM's hideous pink offices, a pyramid erected to itself, I just wanted to lie down in the dirt and wait for worms to eat me.

You should not be doing this! screamed a voice in my brain. *You should* not *be doing this. . . .* You *should not be doing* this. . . .

I was still muttering when I went by lobby security. And they were not impressed. "Hey, you . . ."

"I am not Elvis," I called back without thinking.

The pug-faced lobby cop took a second to reply to that. When he did he spoke very slowly. "I'd say that's affirmative, fella. Why don't you tell me who you're here to see, then I'll tell you whether or not they want to see you."

I told him Wes Craven, and he gave that "yeah, right" look. Shot me the smarmy nod studio guards have been shooting Show Biz wannabes from time immemorial. It did not make him happy that I actually had a meeting. And he did little to hide his disgust.

"Third floor," he snarled. "Elevator's to your left. . . . You know how to use the elevator, don't you?"

I can't say I remember the meeting. They're all so identical, remembering one is like remembering a sneeze. I do recall that Wes was a surprisingly delicate little fellow. A slight, graying man in a crewneck. Not the heavy you'd imagine for Freddy's dad. At one point, apropos of something, he began quoting from *Fear and Loathing in Las Vegas*. "We were somewhere around Barstow on the edge of the desert when the drugs began to take hold. . . ." Which impressed me immensely.

Impressed me more than the actual subject of our little get-together. One rule to which I cling, be it small screen or big, is that any show that ends with a wink—one of those big, cutesy, let's-all-mug-at-the-camera deals—is doomed to a hideous death. Sure enough, in the *Nightmare Cafe*'s episode, Robert Englund, a man of infinitely more élan in his Freddy Kruger mode, plays a sort of polyester Mephistopheles. And he breaks into a real nice "It's okay, kids, it's just good clean fun" winker-oo for the folks at home. Bob, see, is not just the maître d'—he's the *Devil!* Ouch!

Are you getting the feel here? Every week characters stumble into this cafe, where—ooogelah, boogelah—instead of a Western Omelet, the blue plate special turns out to be—good guess!—their worst nightmare, served up with special effects of infinitely greater cheesiness than an omelet ever could be. I do recall one line, oom-pahed by our mayonnaisey hero midway through a chase scene. He's on a boat, the villain's trying to hide his Bad Deed. Suddenly, the hero spots a huge barrel. Playing the sleuth, he pries open the lid. Sniffs the contents. Then, in a line of such dramaturgic impact it still has me reeling, he shouts: "Oh, my God! It's Toxic Waste!"

Yow!

To make matters worse, in a post-pitch chat with Wes's first in command, a swarthy prepster in tennis shoes named Meely, I slipped into a wholly inappropriate confessional mode. No one thing set me off. It's just that my defenses were down. Meely was friendly enough, if a tad—how to say this?—chummy.

"You're kind of a big guy." He chuckled, giving me a we're-all-guys-here punch on the shoulder. "You're one of the first writers I ever met who I'm not sure I could take. . . ."

Reference, no doubt, to the newly beefy physique I'd picked up in Progress Valley. Where for lack of anything better to do between getting fired from McDonald's and seeing Kitty, I'd lifted weights and scarfed a lot of peanut butter. Two months off dope, and I gained nearly fifty pounds. Going from a death camp 144 to a burly 190. That proved to be one of the weirder side effects of getting clean. I realized I was actually kind of a *big guy.* Or, at least, not the skinny cheekbone victim I'd seen in the mirror since I'd started full-timing the toxic input back in my teenage amphetamine days.

When Meely asked, as TV preeners are wont to do, where I'd been working last, I made the mistake of telling him. Only instead of dropping, say, a swingin' pilot, a hot mini-series, or even a direct-to-video, I went deep into left field.

"My last gig? Let's see . . . Matter of fact, it was at McDonald's. Making French fries. Doing a little counterwork, you know, 'Will that be a medium Coke, or large?' But I'm not going to lie to you, I was mostly fries. . . ."

Well, one thing led to another. And before you can say "inappropriate behavior" I was spilling the beans on everything. My habit, my rehab, my bus ride over.

It was the bus ride that really shook him. "I can't believe it," said Mister Meely, shaking his head with a sympathy you'd have thought reserved for terminal cancer victims. "I can't believe you had to ride the bus. . . . What's that like?"

He simultaneously stepped away from me and leaned forward as he asked about my RTD experience. He didn't want to miss a single detail, but didn't want to get close enough to catch anything.

"Sometimes it gets kind of rough," I told him, recounting

the time I saw a pubescent skinhead get stabbed in the neck for something he couldn't keep from saying to what looked like an 8-tray-gangster Crip.

"It's not that bad, is it?" Meely chided me. "I mean, L.A.'s not like New York. It's not dangerous or anything."

To which, of course, there really was no response. He wasn't being stupid. He was being honest. And friendly on top of that. In the Los Angeles he inhabited, what he was saying was absolutely true. And since there were countless nice white humans who'd never been east of La Brea Avenue, who lived in L.A. without even seeing what ninety percent of L.A. really was, he was being accurate, too. Of course, this was before Rodney King and the LAPD made their video debut.

I didn't know whether to envy or pity him.

Big surprise, the *Nightmare Cafe* gig was a complete fiasco. But it was a valuable learning experience. What I learned, once again, was that working in television without hard narcotics was absolutely laughable.

Sitting through those endless story sessions, I remembered with awful poignancy why I used to get fucked-up for these meetings. How else to manufacture enthusiasm? How else to keep from screaming?

Nightmare's pilot episode packed all the fury and suspense of a Mylanta commercial. The acting was flat. The sets were hokey. The stories were lame. All in all, it was the perfect job for me. Except I couldn't fake it anymore.

Whatever I turned in was subject to all manner of excess scrutiny and skepticism. Not that it didn't suck. Forget about it! My writing was atrocious. I couldn't even get my margins right. Everybody else had computers, and I had this rebuilt Smith-Corona I bought at a pawn shop. Which was fine, as long as I could write an entire script without *j*'s or *w*'s.

Halfway through my nineteenth rewrite, when I'd spent one more night bussing from coffee shop to coffee shop to keep from disturbing my early-to-bed hosts with nocturnal creativity, I bought a car with my first story money and drove back to Phoenix. I thought Kitty would be good for creativity. And I was scared that having to write was going to send me out again.

For two weeks I drove her crazy, faxing bogus changes to the Meely and Wes back in *Nightmare*-land. Then I decided to head west again. That used station wagon—a diesel Oldsmobile, just what I always wanted—burst into flames outside Blythe, not far from where Hunter Thompson's drugs kicked in. I did some stunt driving for half a mile before getting towed back to Hollywood for a hundred bucks and finishing my "polish" on the front seat of the Triple A tow truck. I sold the torched Olds to the mechanic for fifty bucks.

Back in TV-ville, I began to suspect Meely was some kind of dialogue sadist. The show stank. It was clearly going to be killed by the network. But John-boy, who just couldn't get enough of those spicy bus anecdotes—"What's it like? I mean, really? . . ."—seemed to sense I was desperate enough to keep jumping through hoops. Until one night, after I'd taken a cab to his fucking house in the Hills to drop off yet another rewrite, the Yapphet Koto–like cabbie took one look at yours truly and said, "Man, you look like you need something. . . . Bet you love that rock, right? Why don't you let me cop you some rock. Thirty dollars. Get you tweaked and squeaked. . . ."

Though I'd managed, somehow, to stay clean until now, it still sounded good. *Too* good. Looking in the rearview, I watched my own eyes staring back at me as I uttered the fateful words, "Let's go. . . ."

Next thing I knew I was deep in the heart of Watts, crouched in a taxi next to Jim Gilliam Park, trading hits off a lead pipe longer than my arm with a giant black dude who seemed to grow more menacing with every puff.

One puff and I was fucked all over again.

In nothing flat I'd become exactly what I'd strived so desperately for all those months not to be. It wasn't long before I hopped back to smack and grabbed a habit again. Once I was nicely hooked, I decided that what I needed was a new set of walls. A different environment. Then, of course, I could get straight again.

They call this, in Recovery circles, a "geographic."

My next friend and savior presented himself by telephone. Eric Blakeney, my old *Booker* producer, had been calling me, at intervals, ever since the top brass fired him and I retired in what seemed like an act of solidarity. I never called him back, for the same reason I never called anybody from "my old life." I no longer considered myself part of their world. I left civilization behind when I picked up the needle.

But, with my back to yet another wall, I began to see him as someone I could use. I would have, too, if the man in question had not surprised me with generosity. You can't steal from someone when they've offered you the shirt off their back. And Eric, God love him, had plenty of shirt.

One more time I'd got a message from Blakeney on my faithful Voice Mail. When I called him back, he seemed surprised. "I thought you were dead," he said.

How could I explain that the notion of somebody actually liking me, of wanting me for a friend, was as absurd as an invitation to dine at the White House? "You know how it is," I said vaguely, "Missing In Action."

Much to my surprise, he said he understood. My plan was to chat the boy up, tell him once or twice what a terrific producer he always was—if not an outright unappreciated genius—then tap him for a few hundred bucks. If I didn't have a place to live, I could at least lay in some drugs.

Eric and I hooked up for java at the Onyx, a coffee shop/"performance space" in newly trendy Silverlake. The Onyx catered to the look-at-me-I'm-a-rebel set. The new breed of retro-beats given to body piercing and poetry readings. Souls so hip they do acid on weekdays. It was easy to laugh at the Nuevo bell-bottom crowd. Say what you will, though, you had to respect these earnest hepsters. They were, in their way, committing true Los Angeles Revolution—they weren't writing screenplays. Which was more than you could say about hacks like me and Eric.

They were writers, but their god was Henry Rollins, not Oliver Stone. When I got to L.A. every *shlub* with a felt-tip was penning a "fish out of water" script (*Something Wild* being the archetype of the genre). Now they cranked out "come on my tattoo" poetry. The free verse of the terminally free. *"I am Hate. . . . I drink strong coffee. . . . I hope Mommy dies. . . ."* That kind of thing.

Into this trend festival walked ex-Cannell ace Eric B. in khakis and Reeboks—he'd even chopped off his ponytail—and yours truly, still in the same old black he'd been wearing since the early seventies. Once it was about style. Then it was about hiding blood. Now it was just 'cause I didn't own any other clothes.

Though awfully successful in his chosen field, Eric still hated himself for it. But he looked back with fondness on his days as a starving rock musician in England, where he'd lived for almost a decade. "What am I going to do?" he mumbled into his decaf, which we'd ordered instead of actual coffee, since we were both Yuppie enough to worry about the side effects of that pesky caffeine. "I've got a wife, two little kids, and a fucking mortgage."

What transpired in this simple coffee shop exchange, the mind-set it demonstrates, is crucial to understanding how a man can take himself down, and keep himself there, the way your unhumble author did.

Simply stated: To be treated like I was something other than a complete pariah was more than I could handle. It was just too out of sync with the worldview necessary to sustain a life of prolonged self-destruction.

Over the course of an hour or two we both talked about

how we ended up where we ended up. "I remember once," Eric told me, his juicy tale in remarkable contrast with that genteel polo-shirt-and-khaki countenance, "I remember once, I was working as bodyguard for this guy who was selling heroin to Keith Richards. We went over to Keith's place, and there were these people sprawled all over the floor. They were slurring their words, talking all kinds of shit, and it just struck me, you know, this is the most boring scene in the fucking world. Somebody wanted toast, but the toaster was broken. So I fixed the fucking thing—I think it just had to be plugged in—and they treated me like I was some kind of genius. I mean the money, the drugs, the whole thing, it's like it just made them all so stupid. . . . I couldn't wait to get out of there."

For a long moment the two of us sat there. In sterling silence. While around us, in all their tattooed glory, a younger generation, a new breed in the grips of their own new breed of clichés, lived out their own contempo fantasy. In a couple of years half of *them* would be smacked out. The other half would be accountants.

"Well, you need a place, you got it."

"I don't know . . . ," I mumbled. The usual coy con. The trick was getting THEM to end up begging YOU to let them help you. So you can, in your infinite beneficence, let them do you the favor.

"Look, do what you wanna do. I'm just telling you, I got a place out back. I hardly ever even go back there."

"Well . . ."

I hemmed and hawed. Another minute passed. Eric excused himself to call his wife. I sat there, dreading the moment he strolled back from the pay phones.

Charity makes it so much harder to sleep at night than outright conning.

But now, here I was, being offered food and shelter for which I had to neither lie nor steal nor say "I love you"—and I wanted to pick up a fork and poke my retinas out.

Eric wormed his way past a table full of tattooed poetry victims and sat back down.

"Everything okay?" I hoped maybe his house had burned.

"No problem. I talked to Tina, and she said it'd be fine."

"Well, what the heck," I said.

And that, more or less, was that.

Once ensconced in my new "home," I cleaned right up. A phony Valium script. A handful of Percodans. It could be done. The garage was pleasant enough. A bed, a desk, some books, a window, and the all-important blind. What it didn't have was a sink or a bathroom. A shortcoming that wouldn't have fazed a normal citizen—it was only twenty-five steps to the house. But I was not, of course, a normal citizen. I peed outside.

Afternoons, I did my best to make it over to my daughter's and to dodge the withering glances of my lovely ex if she happened to be there.

Nina, for her part, viewed me as a sort of lovable anomaly. A fun intrusion. She knew Mom didn't like me—kids snag all the nuances—but she and I had such a bundle of laughs, she seemed to love me anyway.

I don't know how long I lived like this. Embracing this shadow life as a sort of permanent transition. The necessary step to get from the HERE of drug abuse to the THERE of recovery. The notion of having my own apartment, making the money to pay for it, living like a Regular Human Being . . . it was no less exotic than hopping a freighter to Tahiti.

I was still muttering when I knocked on Towner the dealer's door. And I was probably still muttering, five hours later, when I stumbled out again, gowed to the tits, plunked unsteadily on the very same spot on Sunset where I'd got the bright idea to do some heroin in the first place. It took half a minute of circuitous reasoning to convince myself that getting loaded was actually a *good thing* for my little girl, that, in the end, I was actually *doing it for her.* I started off on a nice new little habit that picked up speed by the end of the week and had me sweating, half a week after that, if I went for more than two or three hours without taking a hit of tar.

At the Blakeneys I tried to keep a low profile. Ducking out early and coming back late. When I did bump into Eric, I can still recall, all he said was that I seemed a little cheerier than usual. My color was better. I believe I told him I'd started jogging. And that was the end of it.

I still visited Nina. But I took to carrying a can of Right Guard with me. A little something to spray over the stink of melting Mexican tar in the bathroom. I wasn't shooting now, I was smoking—chasing the dragon—and never made a move without lighter and tinfoil. It was disgusting. After that two-week run I was completely strung again and decided to go back to Phoenix.

Of course, I didn't tell Kitty I was using. I didn't tell her that I was coming back to kick. I told her that I missed her. That I had to see her. That I was coming back because I couldn't live without her.

The sick part was, I did love her. Or thought I did. But how much can a junkie, really, love anybody more than he loves his junk?

When she met me at the airport, Kitty was so teary that she didn't even notice I was green. Didn't say a word when I made love with my shirt on. Didn't mind when I came in a minute and a half.

"I guess this means I love you," I said when she was dozing off beneath me.

"What does?" she mumbled. "Shooting your wad in two seconds?"

But I didn't know what I meant, either. . . . I just didn't think my habit was that bad. It seemed, while I was puffing away, to be strictly lightweight. Enough to make me jones, but not enough to kill me. But you never know. That twinkly tinfoil is deceptive.

Halfway through the night the cramps bit into my liver like a shark. I'd already soaked through the towel I'd laid over the blankets. The air seemed to grate on my flesh, but if I covered up, it got instantly clammy. At the first of the body aches I gulped a bunch of aspirin. I started out with four. Waited a half hour. When that didn't work I swallowed four more. By midnight I thought the pain was going to break me in half. I dumped a few more Bayer in my hand and washed them down with warm tap water.

It's an awful thing, OD'ing on aspirin and kicking dope at the same time. The aspirin, when you take too much, causes ringing in your ears. It's like a doorbell behind your eyeballs that you can't unstick. Instead of killing the pain, it just gave everything an echo effect. The sharp pains in my guts were set off by the dull, steady throbbing in my joints. Knees and neck, especially, seemed crushed in an invisible vise.

I'd planned on telling Kitty of my habit. But the notion that I was fucking up her life was too awful to contemplate. I shouldn't have come. A woman who worked as hard as she did to stay straight should not be with a fuck-up like me. It would hurt her, I knew. But worse than that, knowing how much she loved the needle, if I ended up pulling her down with me, it would be the end. For both of us. I'd never known her in her using days, but I had an idea.

When I came to my senses, I was in the bathroom holding my head in my hand, rocking back and forth on the toilet. It took a minute or two to realize I was back in Phoenix, going cold turkey. With absolutely nothing at all to soften the kick.

Peeling myself up off the toilet seat, I opened the bathroom door, stared down at Kitty as she slept on the floor. Her job at the foreign car repair shop paid minimum wage. It was a big deal for her even to have her own apartment. An actual bed was still out of reach. She didn't even have a mattress. Just a couple of ratty blankets piled on the floor. A couple more piled on top.

Kitty was curled up in the fetal position, as always. Surrounded by the same stuffed animals she'd collected as a little girl. Why, I thought in the midst of my drug-deprived madness, *why am I always attracting women who still slept with stuffed animals?*

No time to think about the answer. I still had another minute to get through. It's just, it was so sad, looking at this pretty, hardworking young woman. . . . This creature who deserved so much better. . . . Sleeping on the goddamn floor.

Of course I'd said I would pitch in. The plan was for me to send money, sort of keep the place as half mine so I could fly in and fly out, so we could be together when I wasn't busy burning up the writing world back in L.A. But somehow it just hadn't worked out that way. Big surprise. More than once, I'm mortified to admit, I'd actually called collect to pester her for money. "Just thirty dollars, baby, so I can buy some typing stuff and finish this article. Then I'll make enough to come back and visit. . . ."

Of course, there was no article to finish. And because she was too sweet to mention it, I'd forgotten I'd ever asked for the cash in the first place, let alone what I said I needed it for. No, I arrived in Arizona with a ten spot in my pocket and a spent plane ticket. Financed, as ever, out of someone else's pockets.

Without planning to, so sick now that the perspiration formed a film over my eyes, I took the route touted by more than a couple of old junkies I'd known over the years. Back in my Big G days, copping methadone and sitting around McDonald's with the old-time hypes, I'd heard them talk about the one thing that could get you through a bad kick when you had nothing else, or nothing else could.

"Whatcha do, son, you grab you a woman," I remember one old coot saying, a gentle grandfatherly African-American fellow with a full head of bone-white curls and the mutton-chops to match. G swore the guy had served two dimes in Leavenworth for killing his wife. I can still see him, a withered little man in an oldtime pimp suit. Poly-blend sharkskin. His two twinkly eyes crinkled up to slits when he offered his advice: "You grab you two if you can, mebbe three. . . . The thang is, you jes' fucking grab and you don't let go. . . . That's the onliest way you gonna kill the monkey. That's the onliest way. . . ."

Hubie, that was his name. Hubie the Ice Man. I have no idea what that meant—G said he used an ice pick—but the advice just came back to me. I hadn't even thought of Hubie, or Big Gus, or anything about those old days in I don't know how long. It was still too close. The danger of ending up right back there was still too fucking real.

Kitty's voice sounded full of smoke. "Hey, fish-skin, what are you doing? . . ."

"I was going to shower, but I didn't want to wake you up."

"So you woke me anyway. . . ."

She had me there, but it didn't matter. I couldn't have taken a shower with a gun to my head. The feel of water right then would have sent me screaming out the bathroom window. As it was, I was still ready to jump. Instead I jumped on her, and before she could say anything else I was pressing a clumsy kiss on her mouth.

"Hey—"

"Mmmph . . . What?"

"Are you okay?"

"I'm fine." I worked my hand between her legs. Tried, despite the violence of my shaking, to work a finger along the cleft of her pussy, to get her wet so I could justify what I was going to do. What, I realized, I had to do if I was going to keep from killing myself.

I'd vomited before and wondered with a start if I'd remembered to brush my teeth. Oh, Christ, this was disgusting. I was disgusting. But the second I pressed myself to her I knew I had to do it. Only the feel of her skin on mine, the wordless intensity of flesh and tongue and cunt . . . only that could keep me alive.

"Kitty . . . Kitty, you know, I really missed you. . . ."

"Hey, me too, but—"

"I know you have to work, baby. I know you have to get up early. . . . It's just—"

"Are you sure you're all right?"

"I have to fuck you, that's all."

"What?"

"I have to shove my fucking cock in you, okay? I have to jam it inside you, right now. I have to do it. . . ."

My own sweat tasted like blood in my mouth. It was getting harder to breathe. My lungs felt like I'd inhaled a cheese grater. The bugs were on me, too. If I stopped moving for a second, the little ant-feet would have me screaming. So far I hadn't screamed. So far I'd managed to keep it halfway together. But I knew it couldn't last. I couldn't hold out much longer. I'd tried pacing. Even tried stepping outside, staring at the highway. But there was just too much sky. Too many stars. And all the trucks roaring by stank the air up.

No, it had to be this way.

Kitty took my face in her hands. Said nothing about my sweat. The canned clam feel of my flesh. She put her mouth on mine. She let me, in my crude and shaky way, massage the baby-smooth shaved groove between her legs. Until the lips of her vagina felt almost as slick as my own skin felt from head to toe.

She opened her legs, started to wrap them around my hips. But I held back. Pulled away to keep her from seeing that, for all my ardor, all my protests of *now now now,* I couldn't have if I wanted to. My dick was still soft. It was my mind that needed it. My cock was still useless.

"It's okay," I muttered, as much for my benefit as hers. "It's all going to be okay. . . ."

And, sliding south, I cupped my hands over her ass. I plunged my face between her sex-drenched thighs. Just jammed my face into her. I wanted to die there. It wasn't about sex—it was about desperation.

"Jerry, *Jesus!*" Her gasps sounded far away. I'd closed her thighs on my ears. Held her flesh pressed into me. Let her own warm flesh block out the world. That's all I wanted. To block out the world. I didn't even lick her. Not at first. I just pushed. That's all. I just pushed my face into her labia. Jammed my mouth, my nose, eyes, as much of me as I could, into the wet beyond. Up and down, back and forth, sideways and no ways and inside and out . . .

I managed, at last, to find perfect blackness. Soft, hot blackness, where all I had to do was breathe. All I had to do was move my mouth. My lips. But slowly now. Slowly, almost not at all. Until her fingers were tearing into my hair. Ripping at the back of my head. Pulling. Pumping. Tugging.

Yes. . . . I thought, hearing a distant droning. Some muffled supplication. *Yes. . . . Finally, I'm lost.* At last I'm fucking lost. But, then—OUCH! WHAT THE FUCK?

She pulled my ears, tugged my head back like you would a man who was facedown in the tub. . . .

"MOTHERFUCKER!" she screamed, and I realized she'd been screaming all along. The sound had been muffled by flesh and muscle. I looked at her and blinked. "What?" I wanted to get back there. To get back in, back down, underneath the world, before my pain came back. I'd almost, in that moist labyrinth, I'd almost lost myself, almost outsucked my pain. "What is it?"

I reached for her face. Felt the tears there.

"Too rough," she whispered, her voice scared as a child's.

"Too rough?" For a moment I panicked. What the fuck was I doing? Had I hit her? Do I bite?

"Not you," she whispered again. "Your beard. Too rough. You're scraping the skin off."

"Oh, that . . . ? Sorry. . . . Really . . . I'm sorry. . . ."

The darkness in the room seemed fluid. The air tasted like burning tires. My skin was screaming again. If only she hadn't stopped me. If she'd let me go, just fucking bled, I could have got there. I could have licked the pain away. Mine, hers, the world's. I had Chernobyl bubbling over in my pores, I was no more than toxic froth, and all I wanted to do was hiss. . . .

"It's okay," she said, speaking in a normal voice now. "Hey."

Finally I was hard. The old heroin hard-on. It takes a while to show up, but when it does, it's the last to leave the party. . . .

"You're all I think about," I babbled, maneuvering, trying with both hands to slide myself into her. She wasn't helping. She was lying back, the way she sometimes did. Playing victim. Playing the little girl Uncle used to visit when she was sleeping. When she was pretending to sleep.

I knew everything, except how to make it through the next two seconds. I held her, finally, when I eased in an inch, and tried to give in to the relief. I just wanted to die of relief. It felt like I might come in half a second or sometime next year. But just the movement, just the in and out, might be enough. *Please God!* Might provide some major or minor escape, an off-and-on dance with agony that wasn't going anywhere. *Why was it so hard to die?*

"You really wanted me?" Kitty breathed her query onto my skin. A series of tiny breezes. Each word felt like it raised welts.

"Yes. . . ." I spoke into her shoulder. Her beautiful, swimmer's shoulder. "I came all this way."

"Just to fuck me?"

"Not just that."

"Just to fuck me." She sighed again.

"Okay, just to fuck you. I'm not going to lie. There's nobody else. There's nobody in the world. There's nobody. There's nothing." At that moment I just wanted to fuck the pain away. In taking hers, I could take away mine. That's how it could work. That's how it had to work.

I don't know how long we tore at each other. When I finally came, it felt like the blood flew out of my veins. All the pain squeezed out. And for a minute, for a blessed minute, I was whole again. The spasms stopped.

Until, like some hellish tide, the waves rolled slowly in again. The pain came back. First the knees, the neck, then the burning tongue and the twisting pangs in my stomach. There was, at last, this banging in my skull, a rusty spoon scraped in the hollows behind my eyes, some vicious dirty music that made me want to flush my brain down the toilet, drop this useless, throbbing head in a bucket of acid, a hydrochloric broth. Until the pain was scalded out of me, all flesh and sensation burned away. I could see a skeleton grin in a hissing toxic puddle. . . .

I blacked out for a while and came back gasping.

Kitty slept beneath me. Out like a car wreck. Nothing left but spinning tires and smoke. I paced for an hour. Tried to watch television on her battered black and white. But the people looked like fish. Nothing helped. Nothing at all.

Until, at three o'clock in the morning—I remember because I called up time, asked the tape-recorded lady to save my life—at three o'clock I woke her again. And though she wondered, asked me why, I was on a mission. In another five minutes she was asking me not to stop, and it was all right again.

It went like that all night. I don't know how many times. Maybe five. Maybe six. After two fucks I was coming in a couple of minutes. I don't think I held out more than three. It wasn't like being on heroin. Sex when you're kicking exists as a kind of mutant strain of sex when you're high. It still required Werner von Braun to get yourself hard, but once you were, instead of staying that way until the end of hockey season, you shoot almost as soon as it's in. . . . I'd start to pump, feel that sucking kiss of friction, that juicy nether-clench, and instantly eject my sorry dollop of sperm—no more now than a tired dribble—then roll off her, back onto the soaking pile of blankets.

I was selfish. I was half-dead. But it didn't matter. I'd fuck until I couldn't move. Until she was asleep again. Until the cock that had gone soft inside her got hard again and began to hurt. It didn't matter. It was a better pain, a different pain, than the absent narcotic. Like stubbing your toe to forget the knife in your heart.

By five A.M., for all intents and purposes, Kitty stopped moving altogether. I was fucking a dead woman. Banging a corpse. I didn't care. It was friction. Release. A way out of the pain that wouldn't let me go. . . . I had to work it out. I had to keep going and keep going, to fuck myself to an exhaustion beyond withdrawal, beyond the bony fingers of the opiate monster, the jaws within me that wanted fed.

By six A.M. I was as close to dead as I was going to get. And I wanted to stay that way.

Kitty called in sick that morning. She stayed home and let me use her. Two or three times, I remember, she started to cry. But as she was crying she was holding on to me, pumping up at me with her hips as she pummeled down with her fists. It was the ugliest act I could imagine. And I could not imagine stopping. I had to keep it up. As soon as I stopped, the kick pain came back.

Sun baked the cinder-block walls of Kitty's apartment. Phoenix death rays. She had no air-conditioning. All day we lay there sopping, two half-dead things washed ashore and left to rot. The apartment stank of sweat and sex. Even her dog, an ancient Airedale named Lefty, lolled by the front door, as far away from the two of us as he could possibly get. Kitty showered twice, but I still couldn't make myself.

It was as though my own fumes might keep the pain away, provide a buffer between myself and the demons of withdrawal who wanted to reinvade my skin.

Somewhere in the afternoon I lurched to the bathroom, shut the door and ran the shower, but I didn't get in. I couldn't. I made the effort to keep her from guessing my true condition: if she sensed I was avoiding water, she'd know the truth. Junkies can't stand the feel of water. So I pretended. Dragged my living corpse up off the wet sheets. It was the first time I'd stood up, and the action gave me a lengthy rush. I hung on to the towel rack, hoping it would never end. Gritting my teeth, I held my breath, tried to boost the freebie into full-bore oblivion, but I couldn't get there. I could never fucking get there.

After my faux shower I ran a cold washrag over the foulest parts of my anatomy—i.e., everything—and ducked back out, feeling slightly less disgusting. When I lay back down, Kitty shot me a strange look. I tried to smile back at her.

"What is it?"

"You forgot to turn off the fucking shower. . . ." She got up to do it herself, listing slightly to the left.

Kitty staggered back out, running a hand down her smooth stomach, the natural athlete's body that working with stripped-down sports cars, hauling parts and lifting batteries all day long served to keep firm as an Olympiad's. Even when she was sleeping you could bounce quarters off her belly.

She gave me a strange half smile. "I guess you missed me, huh? I can't even walk. . . ."

"Well, yeah. . . ." I was suddenly too nauseated to talk but didn't want to say so. Postcoital vomit is so hard to explain. Not to mention romantic. . . . But one move right or left and I would have blown polka. And puking was the last thing I wanted to do. I'd done every other disgusting thing since arriving. Each time I went to the bathroom I had to blast the faucets, to keep her from hearing my churning guts.

Kitty had to go to work the next day. I took advantage of her absence to hunker in the dark bedroom, shaking under the blankets and jacking off. My cock was already the consistency of beef jerky, but it was all I had. When she came back I jumped her again.

I don't know how I got through it, but I did. For days and weeks I hung on, I just hung on, distracting myself with food and television and all the baser diversions. Finally I couldn't stand it. Except for Nina, I had no reason to be in Hollywood. Except for Kitty, no reason to be in Phoenix. I had no reason, really, to be anywhere. To do anything. The very air I breathed went in pure and blew out tainted.

Kitty dragged me to the recovery groups she herself attended. I went along, desperate and ashamed of my desperation. Wondering what I would do when the meeting was over. Everybody else had work, had families, had lives. I was somewhere between a has-been and never-was, washed up and unwashed.

"How the fuck can you stand me?" I asked one day, weeks after my quaking arrival. We were riding down the highway after our seven o'clock gathering.

"When I met you, you were so full of life, I wanted what you had." She sighed, sounding older than I remembered. I'd been so busy of late, obsessing on my own problems, I'd given *her* angst scant attention. "You were hurting, but you were, like, *funny.* You were going to make it, go back to L.A. and get the motherfuckers. . . . I thought we'd do it together, you know? We'd live this great life in Los Angeles."

Her soliloquy made me want to rip my heart out and plant it on her dashboard. I felt so guilty, I fell in love with her all over again.

It may have been that morning that I made the fatal call to L.A. Tracked down Towner, got him to overnight me as much heroin as $150 would get me. . . .

I just couldn't handle the residual kick aches. Simply did not think I could make it through another empty day. Could not conceive of looking up from the kitchen table when Kitty staggered in dead tired and feeling the guilt wash over me, as the daily lies about all the writing I'd done, all the calls I'd made, came tumbling out of my mouth like so many worthless coins. . . .

I had no plans. I was living off the last few hundred I'd borrowed. For two days I kept hopping in and out of the apartment to see if the mail had come. It's amazing how, even if you're not physically hooked, just thinking you're going to score, just waiting for it, can trigger an adrenal need so profound, you can barely breathe until you get your hands on the shit. By the third day I knew exactly what the mail truck brakes sounded like. I could pick the squeak out from all the other cars that banged in and out of the asphalt parking lot. . . .

When I finally spotted the overnight envelope—it's red, white, and blue—I all but bowled over the little mail lady, a pudgy Asian woman in striped blue postal shorts that fit like hot pants. I wanted to marry her! I just knew that stiff white package in her hand contained my salvation.

Over a couple of weeks, after half a dozen deliveries, I panicked. I didn't want to get strung again. I used the last shipment I got as sparingly as possible, trying the taper-off method. When I'd made it two weeks without puffing any tar, I celebrated. Sent off my last chunk of dough to get my man in Silverlake to ship me some marijuana.

By now Kitty caught on.

"I have to say something," she said, wearing the smile that played on her face only when she was really mad. "You're completely full of shit. If you think you're fooling me, you're more fucked-up than I think you are. . . ."

I was glad I'd woken up at four and smoked a couple of happy-sticks.

Instantly I was Mister Contrition.

"You're right, Kitty. Jesus, you're right. I'm sorry. . . . Really. Give me another chance, okay? . . . Just . . . just like . . . just hang on."

With this I hopped out of my chair, darted into the bedroom, tugged my suitcase out from under a pile of laundry.

"Look," I said, "look, this is my stash, okay? This is it. I swear to God."

Kitty stood by, impassive.

"I'll flush it down the toilet. . . . No, I'll throw it away, okay? Come on, let's go out to the Dumpster. Right now. I'll just . . . I'll just dump it in the fucking Dumpster, with all the diapers and coffee grinds, whatever the fuck else is out there that stinks so much."

"Jerry . . ."

But there was no stopping me.

"Jerry," she tried again. But I was off. I grabbed her by the hand, dragged her behind me to the stinking garbage heap, where I made a grand display of tossing in my bud-stuffed baggie.

We didn't make it to the meeting that morning. In my full-bore remorse mode, I insisted on keeping her home so I could make her breakfast. "More toast, honey? How about another drop of coffee? No, let me!"

After picking at my culinary offering, a chewy Swiss cheese omelet, she was in her Triumph and off to work by eight-fifteen.

By eight forty-five I was out of the apartment, wearing a pair of work gloves I'd dug out of a kitchen drawer, rooting through the Dumpster until I spotted the gator-bag I'd tossed out little more than an hour earlier. As I'd done a hundred times before, when I'd thrown out needles and pipes—determined to *will* myself to change my ways—I ended up diving right back into the dump, retrieving my stuff so I could resume the business of throwing my own life away. It's one of the awful laws of nature: drugs and cigarettes never taste better than when you use them after you've just quit.

I smoked until my pupils bled. Wasn't that the idea? To get off the hard shit. I was done with hard narcotics. I was *convinced.* Indeed, in my newfound state of determination, helped along by my newly rescued baggie, I was pretty sure I was going to go all the way this time. That's right. I'd even give up pot. What the hell? Why go halfway? It was all clear to me. Clean and sober—completely clean and sober!—that was the only way to go. And, by God, I was going to go that way. I was! As soon as I finished off this batch.

Amazingly, I stayed straight. No more secret smack shipments. No more stashed-away Sensimilla. Come Thanksgiving 1991, I was celebrating ninety days clean. For real. All the bad times, I believed, were behind me. Of course, there were problems. Money, as usual, was tight. I still hadn't found a way to work again. My big fear, as ever, was that I couldn't write without getting high. A problem I resolved simply by not writing. Nor had I faced the ultimate challenge: returning to L.A. and starting my life again.

There was no question, though we never spoke about it, of remaining in Phoenix the rest of my life. For one thing, Progress Valley was still after me for room and board. And it was too painful being away from Nina. The only guilt worse than being loaded in Hollywood was being clean in Arizona. But before I went back, I wanted to make sure my current sober state was not some fluke, arranged by my demon self to send me careening even farther southward.

Never again did I want to leave my baby sitting by herself, in the middle of the living room, while I skulked in the bathroom, shooting up or sucking smoke off a strip of Reynolds Wrap. On the other hand, when I was in there smoking, I'd tell myself, At least I'm not shooting up in front of her. . . .

Never again. That was my sentiment. Surely the worst was over. Thanksgiving, Kitty actually took me to her parents' house. Her mother and father lived in Scottsdale.

They'd both come west from Indiana, both grown up in the same tiny town, a quintessential hub of midwestern Republicanism by the name of Noblesville. It was too perfect. She had two little sisters, both straight-haired college girls.

To my infinite surprise, I found myself enjoying the wholesome exercise. They made me welcome. The father, a slight, bespectacled retired adman with a marked resemblance to Truman Capote, actually took me aside, shook my hand, and told me how grateful he was at the way I treated his daughter. "It hasn't been easy for Kitty," he said, betraying as much emotion as a man from Noblesville, Indiana, probably ever could, "we've made some mistakes. . . ."

"We've all made mistakes," I said, and we shook hands. We understood each other. Two men being men. I wanted to be cynical. But it wouldn't come. These were decent people. It was like being on Mars.

This was a far cry from my standard Thanksgiving activity. For as long as I could remember, this festive day was spent prowling the domestic streets, completely smashed, staring through the picture windows, the open front doors, at all those poor, pathetic families gathered over their miserable hormone-packed turkeys. I was the lucky one! *I was alone!* I had drugs! I'd drive for hours, smoking joints to keep my smack high alive, thanking God and shaking my head at the pathetic lives all those bo-bos had to endure. Family, for me, was something from which you escaped. Not something you aspired to.

Now here I was, clean and serene, in the arrhythmic heart of suburbia, sipping Maxwell House while my girlfriend's mom showed me pictures of her daughter in a cheerleading outfit. Stranger still, I enjoyed it. Some deep and long unacknowledged impulse was finally getting its due.

"I can't believe you," Kitty said as we rode back to her tenement after an afternoon at her folks', "you were really nice."

"I know. It's scary."

In my newfound serenity, I'd even made a stab at work. By sheer chance I'd stumbled on a snippet in the *Arizona Republic* about this new phenom, something called "Smart Drugs," a simmering trend on the unholy cusp of New Age Nutrition, All-Night Rave Society and Corporate Nerd-dom. Embarrassingly, I spent so much time reading local newspapers, it was just a matter of time before something productive came of it. With a whole damn day to fill off the hard stuff, I'd become an inveterate newshound. In my perverse thoroughness I even sucked up the obituaries. People lived a long time in Arizona, which made you wonder. . . . I would, in my newfound clarity, find myself poring over Masie Dobson, eighty-eight-year-old Mormon mother of ten who passed on in Sun City. . . . Or speculating on the final moments of Edwin Skeetop, founder and CEO of Skeetop Sewer and Siphon. "Born in Snerm, Idaho, Edwin Skeetop got his start in the U.S. Army Corps of Engineers, and moved to Bullhead City after World War II." But why? I'd ask. *Edwin, why?*

Try as I might, doing my best to see the good in everything, I just didn't see how people did it. Don't get me wrong, I was down for sobriety. I wasn't about to let what felt like the essential pointlessness of my drug-free existence drive me to a drugged one. I knew, on some level, having to get high every day was what made the old way of life so incredibly focused. Living on the survival level, it was easy to function with what the Buddhists call the One-Pointed Mind.

Life on the natch was a far more amorphous undertaking.

There are no accidents. I suppose, in seeking out my first post-dope employment: assignment by *Playboy* to investigate this new breed of cerebral mind-enhancers, I was unconsciously seeking out a way to stay loaded—but not do the drugs I was used to doing. Smart drugs sounded so . . . smart. Not to mention legal, cheap, mind altering, and—I hope I hope I hope—nonaddictive.

But who knows? It had been years since I'd worked for *Playboy.* Not since before *Moonlighting,* when I'd done a piece on something called "The New Weirdness." Journalism seemed such a safe way to wade back into the world of words-for-hire. It wasn't like I had to be *creative* or anything. All I had to do was fly to San Francisco, track down these New Age eggheads, the slicksters promoting Alzheimer's medicine as a way of boosting executive brainpower, then come home, sit down at the typewriter, and make fun of them.

Ducks in a barrel, right? Nothing to it. Nothing that is, had I actually had a home. Not to mention a typewriter. This was the problem of starting your life again in recovery. The old when-you're-at-your-weakest-you-must-be-strongest dilemma. As ever, I didn't just have to remember how to write, I had to remember how to live. . . .

My friend and editor, *Playboy*'s West Coast editorial mensch Steve Randall, was more than supportive about my return to the Hutch. But coming back to writing after my little holocaust, I was plenty neurotic.

"I have a confession," I whined, after we'd settled on a fee for my foray into the world of megaintelligence medication, "I have a confession. I don't even know if I can still type. What's the middle row again: a,s,d,f? Q's over there on the left, right? On top of A? I mean, I know you don't use Q a lot, but still, a guy has to know. I mean, I can't start an article on brains, for Christ's sake, and not even be able to type I.Q. . . . ."

Randall, a dead ringer for the actor who plays Murphy Brown's boss, listened to my lamentations with his usual saintly tolerance, then interrupted. I had the feeling he'd rested the receiver on his desk, gone to see if the mail had arrived, maybe checked the fax and grabbed a glass of water, then toodled back, knowing I'd still be whimpering in the receiver.

"Just write," he said, neither mocking nor encouraging my long-distance winge. "And make sure you get everything on tape." An attractively normal fellow, whose plain brown wrapper masked a neurosis big as all outdoors, Steve was one of those extraordinary humans who cry out for the title "Honorary Jew." He had that kind of heart. That kind of quirky nervousness. Which he masked by an unwavering calmness of speech and demeanor.

"I'm fucking petrified," I told him after the gig came through, I'd signed the contract, and it was time to fly to San Francisco—the place, not too surprisingly, that the Smart Druggies liked to call home.

"What can happen?" Steve asked, indulging my flair for panic. I could picture him, leaning back on his chair, feet up on the desk as he fiddled with his glasses and stared out from the Playboy building over Sunset Boulevard. "You're talented, remember? You've done this before. If you forget, call me up. I'll send you some of your clips. Besides, you have three months to finish. Relax for a change."

He had my number, of course. I was the guy who'd spend ten minutes trying to get a job, then take two and a half hours trying to talk you out of hiring me.

The long and short of it, with a few months' clean time, a contract in my pocket, and the promise of a generous per diem and hotel waiting in San Francisco, I bade loving farewell to Kitty. The plan was to stop in L.A. and reacquaint myself with Nina, squat in Eric's garage while I did some research, and then, in the middle of December, hop a shuttle to San Franscisco to go back to work.

At least it *sounded* good. . . .

• • •

If I believed in omens, I'd have doubtless read something into the first sight that greeted me when I hopped out of the taxi into the Phoenix Hotel, the San Fran hot spot I'd selected to ride out my time in pursuit of smart-dom. For who should I see hanging about the tiny lobby than the absolute ne plus ultra of grunge-dom, the Nineties' number one name in creative opiating, the junkie's junkie, the late Kurt Cobain.

Call it prophetic. Call it pathetic. All I know is, after going all this time with nary a Reynolds Wrap–ped speck of smack, it was disconcerting to bump into a swell who'd more or less made a career of, for lack of a better term, what might be called the anti-AA: Alienation and Addiction. The very stuff that put Seattle grunge on the map.

Not, mind you, that the modest fellows checking into my hotel at the same time were broadcasting their chemical proclivities. Not at all. They looked like any other gaggle of goatee-and-flannel guys. One was low-key. One was tall and goofy. The other I don't even remember. When you're trying so hard to avoid something, it's vaguely disheartening to find evidence of it everywhere you turn. So there I am, planning to have this clean and sober getaway, to prove to myself IT CAN BE DONE, when who do I bump into but living proof of exactly what I did not need proved. To wit: You can do drugs and still be successful. You don't even have to hide. You can be flagrant. You can be loose. You can be . . . *Nirvana.*

I wouldn't call myself a fan of the band. (I'd been sitting by myself in bathrooms so long, I just found out that Disco died.) How could an AIDS-era smackster *not* love an album called *Bleach*? If you knew what they were referring to, well, then you *knew*. . . . You were part of it. No different from the sixties acidheads who smirked when Grace Slick sang *"feed your head."*

Different generation, different drugs. Just being conscious at the dawn of the American Nineties, it was hard not to be aware of the statement being made by Perry Farrell, Layne Stanley, Nick Cave, or any of that breed of happening young junkies who were, by their very existence, with every note they played, saying "Life's so fucked, why not stay fucked-up? . . . *We are!*" to those inclined to hear the message. For every River Phoenix, how many lesser unluckies do you think you're not hearing about?

Whichever way I turn my head, down there on Eddy, down on Ellis or O'Farrell, in front of the SRO hotels, next to the liquor store, every-fucking-where, I'm sensing these deals going down. It's one thing to fight the itch when there's nothing around to scratch it. Call me a jelly-spine, this is harder. Here I am, in this strange city. Money in my pocket. A swell hotel room. Gee whiz! Nothing but tombstone eyes under every set of eyebrows. And in no time what starts as mild "professional" interest turns terribly urgent.

Right off, I can spot the crack maggots. It's the more mature, chronic face-rubbing crowd holding down a stoop to my left that interests me. Crackheads don't get old. These guys rubbing their noses, scratchin' and chattin', they've got those hard, steady moves. This real slow, nothin'-gonna-bother-me kind of walk. Not the herky-jerky dance that the pipe gives you.

Wherever crack's on sale, you see these hunched-up skeeks spazzing up and down with their eyes on the sidewalk, scoping for dropped rocks. That's one of the mysteries of the drug. No sooner do you smoke it than you're on your hands and knees, scarfing crumbs up off the carpet, the cruddy linoleum, the gutter, wherever.

Half the 'basers in the goddamn Emergency Room aren't even in there for coke. They're in for smoking plaster or paint chips, anything that even looks close. I've done it myself. You haven't lived till you've sucked in a lungful of flaming paint chips.

No, the upright citizens I had my eyes on were not in the 'base business. They were the old school. Closer to Ray Charles than Ice T. Pre–gangsta rap African American fellows in overcoats. Tattooed Latino dudes. Bus station white guys. Ladies whose best days on the streets are behind them. My kind of crowd. In spite of my best intentions—I'd only left the hotel room minutes ago, only gotten off the damn airplane an hour or so before that—I found myself . . . *hovering.*

In a perverse bit of behavior I couldn't shake, I still dressed for the part. No matter how clean I got. Even if my arms had healed, you'd never have known it from the black leather trench coat. The three-day growth. The slouch I just seemed to cultivate in the vicinity of the thing itself. . . .

"Y'all in town doin' a gig?"

For a second I froze. The man had a voice like Lou Rawls. But my first thought was, "heat," expecting one of those plainclothes types who come on like one of the fellas.

He looked like anything but a cop. Unless the cops were hiring used-up, sixty-plus black men with bad teeth and ratty suit pants. He saw me giving him the once-over and chuckled. Again his voice resonated with its own powerful music.

"You lookin' at my kicks, right?"

He laughed again and raised his right foot off the ground, delicately lifting the pant leg to give the full effect. He did, indeed, sport a classy pair of shoes. Pointy alligator numbers, tasseled and faux-grainy, on the green end of greenish black. "Got these at Florsheim. Ain't gonna catch me wearing none of that Thom McAn. I'm a Florsheim man. Always have been, always will be."

He gave a quick look at my own mega-scuffed Italian fence climbers. Shook his head with a dismissive little sniff.

"See you in the market for some footwear yourself."

"Yeah, well . . ."

A tad defensive, I started to answer, then caught myself. What the fuck was I doing talking shoes, in the middle of the Tenderloin, with a guy who was clearly either crazy or working me for a tap?

"You know, Duke used to say, 'I don't care how down-and-dirty a man let himself go, you put a new pair of shoes on him, he's gonna feel fine.' "

In spite of myself, I stopped. "The Duke?" I said. "John Wayne and you had a conversation about loafers?"

"John Wayne! Shit, that's good. Man, I had you pegged for a musician. Now I'm gonna have to revise myself. You must be a fucking comedian. John Wayne. Hah!" He paused, made an elaborate show of spitting two inches left of his Florsheim. "When I say 'Duke,' son, I'm talkin' about Ellington. Duke Ellington, you ever heard of him?"

"'Course I heard of him."

"Indeed you have," he said, "indeed you have. Step over here, son."

He stood no taller than me, six feet or so, only he held his head higher. Imposing in a way that kept you from noticing how incredibly thin he was. He looked like the unshaved skeleton of a born aristocrat. In spite of the ratty clothes, stained gray overcoat, and gold front tooth that glowed among the gaps and chips in his mouth, there was something formidable about him.

"Y'all a player?" He phrased it as a question, smiling now and offering his hand. "I'm gonna guess drummer. Lots of times a drummer has class, but he gotta be an animal, too. Now Philly Joe was like that. Class right down to his toes. He had that touch, but he had power, too. Used to play a little ahead of the beat. Drive the guys crazy."

"Philly Joe Jones?" I said. For some reason I wanted him to know I got it.

"My man," he said.

He gave my hand an extra squeeze, pulled me a little closer. "You tryin' to cop in TL, you gotta be careful. They don't know your ass, they ain't gonna sell to you. This ain't like New York, you know what I'm sayin'? More of a neighborhood thing. Same folks day in day out."

"I'll take my chances."

He backed off and looked genuinely offended.

"What's your name, son?"

"Nicky," I said without thinking.

"Well, look, Nick, I been stuck in this fucked-up street, in my fucked-up hotel room, for five motherfuckin' years, and you think I go round hustlin' motherfuckers to get me my medicine every day, you fucking wrong. You ask anybody down here about Tommy Johnson, they'll tell you that I'm what they call the old school. All I wanna do is get my motherfuckin' her'on, so I can play my music and get the fuck on with it. You hear what I'm sayin'? That's the way I come up. I seen you, the way you move, I figure this guy's in town, he got a gig, and he got to cop—and he gonna get himself burned. In the old days, man, cats looked out for each other."

By now we'd stepped back off the sidewalk, into a niche between two tenements, a little door to nowhere. I didn't know what to say. It was like he'd looked into my mind, picked out the fantasies I'd held on to since I was nine, and laid them back out for me. Ever since I was old enough to know what cool was—and to know I wasn't—I wanted to be a musician. And I wanted to be black. This Kreskin of the Tenderloin picked them both right off, and laid them back out for me.

"I ain't lying to you, Nick."

I kept my expression blank. Tried to catch his eyes.

The whole thing was so off the wall. So anti everything you learn on the street: don't talk to people, don't tell 'em your fucking business, most of all, don't give money to anybody who says they're gonna cop for you because they're gonna go in one door of a building and out the other.

I knew all that, but I had a feeling. I liked the guy. "All right," I said, "so what's the deal?"

"No big thang," he said, spitting his contempt. "I introduce you to Paco here—no, don't turn around—and tell him you're good people."

"That's it?"

"Well, I wouldn't say no if you wanted to make like Baskin-Robbins and give me a little taste. . . ."

This was, as things turned out, the start of a beautiful, completely, terminally, unalterably self-destructive friendship. Tommy lived on Larkin, in a seedy, bathroom-down-the-hall, "NO GUESTS AFTER TEN" SRO.

He introduced me to the man with the stuff. It was the cat in the bandanna, the one who'd fired a grin when the old man first let out his laugh. It was very chummy-chummy. We shook hands, I dropped a quick hundred, got what seemed like an enormous amount (turns out dope's half price in S.F., another cause for tourist exultation), then my guide steered me back down Larkin just below O'Farrel, where we met a mountainous woman, somewhere between fifty-five and ninety, hunkered on a milk crate beside a Chinese restaurant.

"You're lucky it's Sunday," he said, "everybody out sellin' on Sunday. You want rigs, Sunday's your day to buy."

"Yo, Sister Betty, this here's my man Nick, he's all right," he said when we steered aft of the lady.

He leaned close, until his lips almost pressed into her gleaming hair, a wig full of lustrous black curls that didn't quite cover the white frizz underneath.

The lady aimed her head a bit left of me when he spoke, saying nothing. Tommy reached down and tapped her hearing aid. Then he stuck an elbow in my ribs and cocked his head toward her face. "How's the cataracts, Sister? Did we get our operation yet?" He gave me a wink.

"Tommy," she sang, and held up one blistered hand. "That has to be Tommy!"

"Twenty," he mouthed, and I slipped it to him. He pressed the cash in her palm as he raised it to his lips to kiss. Smiling, Sister Betty groped beneath her enormous haunches and produced a battered old leather purse wrapped in twine. Still beaming up in our general direction, she plucked out what looked like a clump of Kleenex and handed it over.

"Bless you, Sister. Say somethin', Nick, so Sister Betty get to know your voice. This lady ain't jus' beautiful. She remembers voices like the FBI remember fingerprints."

The old lady flushed. It was a Kodak moment.

"Well, go 'head!" he laughed.

I opened my mouth. I closed it again, swallowed, looked helplessly at my beaming benefactor. That morning I'd woken up in Los Angeles and sipped chamomile with Eric and Tina in their genteel kitchen. Now I was handing cash to a blind fat woman with doll hair for something I wanted in her purse. I couldn't talk.

As we move back toward his hotel, the King George, I feel the package in my pocket. Count out five syringes.

In a few minutes we're humping up the seven steps to Tommy's building. From what I can see, it's full of ravaged old guys given some place by the city to live. They are all Tommy's age or a little younger. All burned out. All eyeing me with fuck-you eyes even after Tommy makes his "This is my man, Big Nick. . . . You probably know him. He's a musician. Doin' some gigs in town. . . . Goin' incognito. If you see him, he's comin' around to see me."

When Tommy nudged open his door, when I looked in and saw the shabby, solitary room, it was like I'd been traveling all my life and had just come home. We're talking about four cracked-plaster walls, a shitty sink, and a bed. Just big enough for a man and his needle. . . . Everything I ever wanted. What does a room matter, as long as the blinds are drawn? Except here in Tommy's lair, I couldn't help but spot the tattered black-and-white photos taped here and there on the wall. Despite the mangy state of the room and its fixtures, there was magic to it. In one picture this rail-thin, fully conked young cat stands next to a white guy with fucked-up teeth. They both wore workshirts buttoned to the neck. Side by side, they look like IV poster boys. In spite of the work at hand, I stared and stared at the old photo. Found myself squinting until, abandoning my needle check, I got up, stepped around the made-up single bed with its army corners, and leaned closer.

"Is that . . . ? No, it couldn't be. . . . Is it—" I started to ask, then caught myself, leaned closer again. "Fuck, it is, that's Art Pepper!"

"San Quentin, class of 19-fuck-if-I-know." He laughed.

He came over, aimed his bony finger at another snap, this one curling around the edges. Tommy alongside a guy who looked like a god. A head taller than he was, with the dreamiest smile I've ever seen. "Dexter Gordon. He was a Folsom man." Down across the wall, to a photo with a group of guys, one of whom, too smudged to make out, he tapped with his fingers. "Frank Butler, a terrific drummer. . . . And, over here"—we jumped to another ancient shot—"Frank Morgan." He shook his head, nodded somberly, I sensed, to convey a sense of the man's greatness. "This guy spent damn near his whole life inside. But he's out now. Doin' great, too, God bless 'im. . . . Oh, and this cat? This cat here was Ray Draper, played this crazy-ass bass trumpet. You never heard nuthin' like it . . . Ol' Ray Draper, he's gone now. . . ."

He sighed, turned back to the sink, and picked up the water.

We sat back down, me on the folding chair, Tommy on the edge of his cot, and for a second we both just stared at the feast before us: a few knuckles of smack, a fistful of clean rigs, and—though I hadn't seen him produce it—an open bundle that must have contained a gram or so of fluffy white powder. It wouldn't have surprised me if he'd stopped and said grace.

Instead he waited till I caught sight of the coke and cackled. "Don't want you to think I ain't bringing nothin' to the table, son. Man always got to bring something to the table."

"Hey, man, you brought the fucking table. . . ."

"Shee-it!" He held out those scythelike fingers, palm up, for me to slap him five. "Nick, man, you are what the guys on the yard used to call a real gazoonie."

Still chuckling, he cracked open a plastic bottle of rubbing alcohol he slid out from under the bed. Reached back under and fished out a crumpled paper bag. The bag, when he dumped it out, turned out to be full of cotton balls. Pressing one to the top of the alcohol, he turned it over, then soaked the cotton and ran it carefully over and between his fingers. Then he pushed the cotton and alcohol toward me, with the clear directive that I do the same.

"Old habit. The boys used to call it 'cleanin' for Aunt Hazel. Don't wanna shoot Aunt Hazel with dirty hands."

"Aunt Hazel, Christ, I love that."

"You never heard 'bout Aunt Hazel? That's what all the cats used to call it. 'Well, boys, time to visit Aunt Hazel. . . .' Like that, you know. Man, that was a time. . . ."

"Fucking great," I said. "This is so fucking great. . . ."

And it was, it was. We were goofing, but there was a real gravity to the process. We were like two surgeons, prepping and fretting for the operation of a lifetime.

I fixed first, a speedball that sent my back brain skidding across the linoleum. When I finally exhaled—the cocaine blew your brains out and the smack glued them back together—I reopened my eyes to see the old man twisted on the bed, his back to me with his pants half dropped, taking his fix somewhere between his legs that I didn't want to think about.

He tugged his trousers up, turned back around, and in a voice that betrayed nothing of the enormous quantity he'd just jammed into himself, announced: "You really should think about finding another spot to shoot, son. Look at this."

He rolled up his sleeves and showed his arms for inspection. Nothing but a few ancient, faded scars on the ropy veins that seemed to run from his shoulder right down to his hands. Otherwise Ivory soft.

It must have been three, four in the morning by now. We'd been hanging out, getting high for so long, and so hard, it was tough to remember I'd ever been anywhere else, done anything but sit there getting high and shooting the shit.

It was getting on that time of night when, no matter how high you were, how high you'd been, reality was impinging again. The world was out there. You couldn't keep it at bay forever. I was already thinking about laying something aside to be able to function the next day. Veering between trying to prolong the pleasure I'd induced and giving in to the regret that was, sure as the sun follows the moon, already starting to rear its devastating little head. Regret that I'd gotten high at all.

"Hey, Tommy," I said, breaking the mutual silence that had enveloped us both for an hour or so. "What about you? What did you play?"

"You seen the pictures, right?"

I wouldn't say he sounded angry. Just more brittle than I'd noticed before.

"I seen them," I said.

"Well, then you know I didn't carry no instrument. Whassat tell you?"

"I don't know. Either you hocked your horn or you're a fuckin' singer."

"Ha!" Tommy let out a snort. Shook his head like he had to laugh in spite of himself. "My son! My son!" he cried with a look in his eye I hadn't seen before. His voice took on a peculiar resonance. "You do not know the truth you speak."

"What?"

"What?" His grin turned almost feral. "The white boy says 'What?' "

He pounded the tray, all but spilled the contents onto the carpet, then steadied and caught his temper with a long, slow breath that seemed to take every ounce of control he had.

"Do you think," he began in this low, chilling delivery—James Earl Jones on the nod—"do you think a horn is the only thing a man has to hock? You really think that? Well, let me tell you something, my young friend. And when I tell you, I want you to listen."

He shook his head again, plucked a rig off the table, and held it in front of him. He waved it in my face, his eyes burning. "A horn is the very least thing a man can hock, do you understand me? A horn is shit. When a man tangles with this skag, he will walk into that pawn shop, he will get down on his knees, and he will beg that motherfucker, he will plead with that little man behind the counter."

Here his voice went a little screechy. High-pitched and hysterical. I couldn't tell, for a moment, if he was being funny or truly insane.

" 'Oh, Mister Pawnbroker, here is my talent! How much will you give me for that? Huh? Here are my dreams! Here is my blood. . . . Here is my future. . . . Here is my fucking life. . . . Oh, please, please, Mister Pawn-Shop Man, take it all away from me! Please, take it all so I can get me another shot. . . .' "

He paused. Stopped dead for dramatic effect. Let his voice drop down to bass again. It was almost frightening.

"And when he walks out," he hissed, "when he's got that fifteen dollars in his sweaty hand, when he's copping that bag, he don't know he ain't gonna be getting it all back. Ho-no! He thinks, This is just now, this is just for a little while. But we know. We know, don't we, Nick?"

He craned his neck, planted that elegant, war-torn hatchet face close to mine.

"Well, yeah. . . . Yeah. Tommy—"

"Yeah, you see them cats on the wall? I knew them all right. Maybe I jammed with them, too. I could sit here and tell you I sat in with fucking Thelonius Monk, and you know what, maybe it's true, maybe it's true, but so fucking what, huh? So what? *I sold it,* man. I traded it all in . . . for THIS."

I thought he was going to throw the rig back down, maybe throw it at me. Instead he just got quieter. Aged twenty years and sat down on the edge of the bed.

He reached for the spoon, checked to see there was still a chunk of dope left for the cradle, and raised his face my way. His eyes glittered under the single bare bulb. Something shimmered there. Then he smiled. But the smile on his lips was a thousand miles from the look in those eyes.

He threw back his head, and that laugh, that scary, bitter, amazing, who-knows-what fucking laugh, just tore out of him.

"I'm a jazz man, motherfucker. I shoot dope. *I'm a fuckin' jazz man. . . .*"

As I fumbled with the key back at my own hotel, I was struck by a kind of blind pang, some indefinable sadness that, despite my own sorry condition, was not even about me. It was about Tommy. Or so I thought.

"Jesus Christ," I heard myself mutter, "Jesus Christ. . . ."

I suddenly remembered the guys on the King George stoop, the way they'd looked at him when we walked by. Like he was a fool.

He had that great voice, sure. And he knew his jazz. He'd probably even sung some. Done a couple of gigs. Even knew, or at least met, some of the guys in the photographs. That was him and Art Pepper, no doubt about it. It's just . . . only a couple of the snaps actually showed him with anybody. The rest were no more than clippings he'd cut out and taped on his wall.

He was a guy who'd just never made it. A guy who probably even had the talent. Who had all the chances. Until time ran out. And he went for the needle instead. A guy like me. . . .

You old motherfucker, I thought. I think I was even laughing when I passed out.

The next day I entered the world of John Morganthaler, the neat little man at the helm of drug's squeaky-clean side, the Boost Your Intelligence Movement.

Along with an ex-navy gerontologist named Ward Dean, Morganthaler wrote the movement bible, *SMART DRUGS AND NUTRIENTS: How to Improve Your Memory and In-*

crease Your Intelligence Using the Latest Discoveries in Neuroscience. As the visionary who personally dreamed up the term *smart drug*, Morganthaler bore about as much resemblance to your basic "drug-guru" as Dan Quayle to Charlie Manson.

Morganthaler came across like a young Republican. His hair was parted Beaver Cleaver–style, his buttoned-down shirt pressed just so. Sitting behind his computer in his San Francisco condo, he even kept his socks neatly balled up and stuffed, side by side, in his Reeboks.

It was impossible, fixing my gaze on his as I let my Sony microrecorder do all the work, not to drift back to the previous night, back in the Tenderloin, when I sat communing with another narco-ecstatic. What was Tommy J.'s allegiance to heroin, really, but the negative image of this clean liver's full-time devotion—and promotion—of *his* chemicals of choice? All that differed, really, was the narcotic.

Morganthaler was the Ralph Nader of mental technology. His life has been devoted to the singular proposition that stupidity, like polio or shingles, was a disease, and he'd been put on earth to help obliterate it. Even as he spoke, and I sat there knitting my brows, nodding somberly to let him know I shared his every value, the parallel between forties bebop junkies and nineties executive pill-poppers was so profound, I had to bite my lip to keep from telling John about it. I imagined, in my monstrous hung-over state, Tommy sharing a room with John. Tommy talking about how slamming that heroin helped Coltrane practice twenty hours a day, Morganthaler prattling on about Hydergine giving Silicon Valley lugs a leg up on the competition.

"Our athletes," he declared, "have been into this for a while." His voice rang with conviction, the earnest certainty of the true believer. "I'm not just talking about steroids. There are lots of drugs that increase red-blood-cell production. It's common for athletes to use megavitamin therapy. Anything they can use to enhance their performance, to get just a little bit of edge, is critical. What we are talking about is making ourselves better than what is considered normal. Today's executives on the go need the extra intellectual boost these products can give!"

Whatever the *real* truth, my trim and gym-fit subject looked me right in the left eye, est-style, and declared proudly: "When I think of taking smart drugs, I feel like I'm upgrading a computer. Like going from a 286 chip to a 386."

I interviewed any number of these guys, and the whole time, all I could think was, *No wonder I'm ashamed to be white. . . .*

Worse than this Square-And-Proud-Of-It flank of Smartdom, though, was the self-proclaimed cool group: the Raver Wing. This branch, see, looked right down their pierced little noses at the pharmaceutical wing. They preferred amino acids and herbs to actual drugs. Instead of Vasopressin, or Piracetam, their brain fodder boasted names like album titles: "Fast Blast" and "Psuper Psonic Psyber Tonic."

Somehow the youngish trendoids at the organo-end of Smartness depressed me more than the buttoned-down boys. Earth Girl, the terminally perky young redhead pushing her own brand of amino drink, dubbed "Energy Elicksures," took one look at my head-to-toe blackwear when I showed up to interview her and laughed in my face. "Oooh, Gawd, look at you! You're so . . . late-Eighties."

And it just got worse. By way of research, I signed on to attend to the Smarty-pants event of the season, a full-on Rave, to be held New Year's Eve at San Francisco's humongous Fashion Center. I didn't think much of it when I agreed to hit the party. But once I was actually there, surrounded by legions of twenty-plus Ecstasy-ingesters in *Cat in the Hat* stocking-caps and Day-Glo stripes, scarfing amino drinks and stomping their little hearts out to that Tribal-Techno beat, I had an epiphany that doomed me to extremes of existential wallflowerdom.

These Rave-a-holics were like microscope polyps that,

clumped together, formed a giant coral. What they celebrated was the reef, not their isolation within it. . . . And this was how I celebrated my New Year: in this giant room with a thousand dancing strangers, all of whom were best friends with each other. My tortured loner routine was as out of place as an atheist at a snake-handling convention. I was less likely to get laid than I was to be shoved in a circle and laughed at by a hundred neo-hippie adolescents.

Invoking some cosmic law of checks and balances, I figured it this way: Since I was so far gone on "dumb" drugs, after ingesting an equal and opposite amount of "smart" ones, shouldn't I be able to walk away more or less neutral? God knows, for some of the mornings after I was having on this road trip, stupid didn't do justice to the state of my brain. So, waking up and popping a fistful of the Piracetam and Hydergine Messrs. Rennie and Morganthaler passed my way, I sat around waiting for my IQ to climb out of the sixties so I could find my shoes—or remember how to tie them.

No luck. When the pharmaceuticals failed, I went for the drinks. I'd met a gorgeous Oriental woman with a shaved head who called herself Go-Girl, so I started off with her stuff. It was called "Brain-Goose" or "Cortex-Tickler" . . . I forget. Whatever, it must have worn off.

In all honesty, though, the potion helped at the time. Really. Of course, when I read the ingredients—along with those posted on my jugs of RENEW-U and PSUPER-PSYBER—I realized that along with all the New Age Wonderstuff: your phenylalanine, choline, *Ginkgo biloba,* ephedra, and so on, there was plenty of that old standby, Mister Caffeine. RENEW-U's label actually boasted "a renewing and alerting brain neurotransmitter mix created to revitalize an overstimulated body and mind."

There was one nootropic treat, peculiarly enough, that did the trick for both Tommy and me. It was called Vasopressin. And it wasn't even a pill. It wasn't a drink, either. It was, and this is really strange, a nasal spray. Chock full, according to the pro-Smart Bund, of nothing less than a pituitary hormone. An excess of which packs enough of a swirly wallop to make a cadaver stand up and recite the Gettysburg Address. It was pituitary deficiency, see, that caused what civilians like to call "hangovers." So a few whiffs of Vaso was served up as the first genuine hangover helper.

In that condition, which the two of us reached two or three times a night—till we got it together to head down the steps and back out to the street to cop some crack—the Vasopressin worked like that gunk you pump in flat tires to keep you rolling to the next station. You couldn't go far, but you didn't have to lie down by the side of the road and die, either.

By the end of my San Francisco jaunt, my work all but done, I hung on, shifting south from the legendary rock 'n' roll fixture, Hotel Phoenix, down the street to the Hotel Adeline, off of McCallister. There was no reason, really, for me to still be in the city. Soon enough the initial rush of my plunge back to Big League IV-dom lost its luster, and my daily jaunt down to the Tenderloin, to Tommy's SRO to scarf up the next batch of dope, had degenerated to just another day's work.

In the way of such streety alliances, Tommy and I had it down to a routine after a day or two. We'd hook up around ten or eleven, lay in enough stuff for some serious using, and be back up in his tiny room by noon, cooking up the first hit. I never pursued my hunch about his career as jazz man—any more than he pressed me about the supposed "gigs" I was up in Frisco to do.

I couldn't say exactly when the really bad depression kicked in. The initial allure of shooting dope with an old bebop dude simply faded away. Another white boy fantasy. I'd actually managed to kick the shit, and I'd used my new friend to justify walking back into the narcotic maw.

• • •

Where did I go after San Fransicso? Back to Phoenix, then back to L.A. For a month or so, maybe longer, I slimed back and forth between the two cities. Barely noticing, let alone caring, where I happened to be. It didn't matter. Wherever I went I always met myself there.

The evening I flew in, I was too torn up even to absorb the daggers Kitty was shooting me. She'd dressed up in her best capris, slapped on the six-inch fuck-me heels I loved more than life itself. And couldn't get a rise out of me.

I stayed in Phoenix, putting up with Kitty's daily disparagement, until I knew for sure the Blakeneys were headed for their Napa vacation home, then bounced back to L.A. Here, of course, I must be careful not to sound like an ungrateful boor.

I was like a zombie who was just alive enough to know he was one of the Living Dead—and just dead enough not to be able to do a thing about it. Of all the fates I'd imagined for myself in my worst back-to-the-wall, smack-and-crack-induced nights of terror, this was one I'd never anticipated. I felt, in the end, blander, more completely square, than any TV writer, any certified public accountant, any bought-and-sold flank of philistine humanity I'd ever condescended to.

In desperation I'd phoned up an old editor, from *Los Angeles* magazine—the very first place I'd freelanced in L.A. some twelve years earlier. At one time I'd been their rising star. They had, after a few features, given me my own column, "Outer Limits." In my arrogance I'd decided they were too lame for me and moved on. Snubbed them for better magazines, better gigs, better money. . . . All the better things that brought me to the better spot I was in now.

The editor was friendly enough. He did not, though I heard him start, ask me where I'd been. Did not ask because he heard the tremor in my voice. The cringed-out, desperate plea behind my attempts to be casual. In my glory days on the mag, we'd endured a major conflict over my refusal to take on assignments of a type I simply deemed unworthy of me: celebrity journalism. Star profiles. Fawning, nipping-at-the-heels-of-the-famous "Lifestyle" pieces. Which, of course, is exactly what I proposed now. *"I've got this friend, see . . ."*

So I ended up on the business end of a celebrity profile of my old pal Mark Mothersbaugh, onetime lead singer of DEVO turned TV and film score composer. I'd met Mark when his girlfriend Nancye starred in *Jackie Charge,* a bit of bizarro theater I'd written with Rinse Dream, my old *Cafe Flesh* collaborator.

Seeing Mark invited all the usual well-meaning queries. The ones that stung like salt in open psychic wounds. I didn't look bad enough to send for an ambulance. Just kind of diminished. I was the guy who was always about to DO something but somehow never had.

I hooked up with Mark at Le Gustia-Bustia, or Bustia-Gustia—something like that. Some mega-trendy breakfast joint on Sunset Plaza. The kind of place where people who routinely started off their day with a trio of power breakfasts might be sitting down to their second round of deal-making croissants.

It had been so long since I'd tarried in that Glitzville atmosphere. I remember stepping off the bus half a block up Sunset from the cafe. A waitress who'd happened to catch me alight from the RTD backed away, touched her hand to her collagen-packed lips, actually called the manager when she saw me—a bus rider—step over and sit down at one of her outdoor tables.

"Jerry, *Jesus Christ!"* Mark gasped when he saw me. "Did you just find out you had cancer?"

Much as I wanted to, I didn't answer yes. It would have made the whole deal easier. Instead I gave him the abridged Jerry Stahl Saga.

"But why?" Mark kept interjecting in my tale of woe. "But why?"

I didn't have an answer. After breakfast he invited me back up to his house in the Hills. He was riding a red scooter the Honda people had given everyone in the band for a commercial they did five years ago. Since he didn't have an extra helmet, I just hopped on the back, headgear free, thereby violating L.A.'s new-that-year-helmet law and invoking their wrath.

An officer who hadn't started shaving yet burst out of a concealed driveway and pulled us over. I gave the boy-policeman what used to be called guff. "There's not enough fucking crime to go around, you've got to nail people on scooters?" Reward for which, he arrested me. Mark turned to the officer and informed him just who he was.

"DEVO," the young officer repeated. "DEVO? Never heard of it. . . . I don't go much for country-western."

At which point Mothersbaugh sighed heavily, covered his face in his hands, and started bawling. "He hasn't heard of us . . . Nobody's heard of us . . . We're washed up . . . We're fucking washed up. . . ."

To which the officer, melting from his former fury at my obnoxious behavior, now responded with genuine alarm.

"Is he . . . is he okay? Jeez! I didn't mean to insult you fellas. . . . Were you really big or something?"

From there it was easy-picking. Officer Aqua Velva relented on the spot. Settled on writing me a ticket—apologizing even for that—and making me promise my friend would seek professional help.

By the time I concluded my humbling Mothersbaugh business and headed over to Towner's, it was as if everybody on the street had ingested bad speed. People on the bus fought over seats. The driver was openly hostile. The crowd of Gen X'ers planted on Towner's couch carped excitedly about anarchy. I was so out of it, I was hardly aware of the source of their strange excitement. I didn't read the paper. Never watched TV. All I knew is that, in his distraction, Towner left his dope drawer open, the top left one in his bedroom desk. And when he dashed out to catch a news flash on the tube, I wasted no time popping the top off the film can he kept the tar in. Stashed a pair of weighed-out grams in my mouth before jamming the lid back on.

Then I followed him out to the living room. Figuring, as I always did when I stole brazenly, maybe he'll find out it was me, stop selling to me, make me go back to copping on the street so I can just get fucking popped, fucking killed, *something* . . . to get me to stop doing this shit.

You see, I already knew I'd never stop on my own. It would take an Act of Nature. An Act of God. Some *Dope-us Ex Machina* to blast out of Nowhere and pluck my ass from this dope-laden quotidian into some new way of life.

Which, thank you, Darryl Gates, turned out to be just what happened.

Maybe I *was* primed. Maybe it would have happened without the riots. I didn't like what I saw about myself that day. It wasn't so much that I'd given up hope as that I'd forgotten it was even an option. It was easier that way. And seeing an old friend; being confronted by the long forgotten notion that somebody cared—awful thing—forced me to wonder if maybe there was a way back. . . . Forced me, conversely, to work that much harder to forget there was.

Fuck it! I heard myself say out loud back inside my garage-cave. *Fuck it!* behind the locked and vacant house I was not allowed to enter. In the city I lived in but had nothing to do with. I stepped outside, intent on sucking up the biggest chunk of smack I could in as short a time as possible. On getting myself back to where I was. Back to no-place. No-thought. To the dry, empty center of pointless existence.

I didn't know, when I stole the dope, that it would have to last me. I'd been so broke, it had come down to my smoking as much as I could on the house at Towner's, making off with no more than a pinch to get through the night, then scurrying back the next day to do it all over again.

Had I known, maybe I would have made it last. Next morning, after passing out with my eyes open until the dawn, I decided I had enough to stay put. There was no food in the garage. Nothing to drink. But what did it matter. Upon arising, I checked my shoe for the knuckle of tar I'd stashed the night before. And reveling in the perfection of the day to come—perfection, for me, meaning no more than Zero: a day when I had to go nowhere, say nothing, think no thoughts, see no one—I promptly got off.

This was it, for me. Beautiful Zero. I smoked and I smoked, and gradually, as the sirens began to wail, as the acrid taste of burning rubber began to sting my eyes, the day passed into night and I passed out of consciousness. Perfect.

All I wanted was this timelessness. I was like a man doing acid when they dropped the atomic bomb. I already saw the clouds and colors. What difference did it make if they suddenly became real?

Maybe it was the same day. Maybe it was the next. I hadn't even made it to the cot. I'd fallen out in a chair, woken up staring. When you are nothing, when you have nowhere you really have to go, you can live like that. Can go to sleep and wake up not knowing if it's been ten minutes or ten days. The chunk of tar was almost gone, but that was not a problem. I'd take my time. Saunter down to the 7-Eleven by Pico, pick up a Tiger's Milk bar. Pick up water. You could live on that. You didn't need food, really, if you had the dope.

Early evening. Police cars raced by, going north. Then they raced right back, going south again. Strange, too, it looked like the police cars were packed. Not the usual driver and shotgun. But three in front, three in back. The way they looked at me, too, I thought: Can they tell I'm high?

And then, So what? I'm not carrying. I don't have tracks.

What are they going to bust me for, slobbering? Still, the strange quiet. The edgy silence on the ground and the roaring overhead. Chopper after chopper.

What was in that shit? Maybe it wasn't even tar: maybe I'd stolen some weird sticky opium. Maybe I'd smoked fucking opium instead of junk . . . The unreality is palpable. I weave toward the 7-Eleven.

A BMW, also packed—why is it there are almost no cars on the road, but the ones that are, are full?—tears by, black faces howling, mouths forming big pink O's.

Jesus! And then, in front of the store—what? What, as they say, is wrong with this picture?

"Do it! Do it! Do it!" The cry rolls out of the store as I move toward it. Thinking about walking in. Thinking, because I've had to stop, right in the parking lot, facing a primer gray Chevy, motor still running, purring like an amphetamine-fed puma . . . Thinking: Where is the door? I don't remember not knowing where the door is. AM I THAT HIGH?

Shit! That's when I see, there is no door, the glass front of the convenience store has been shattered, one whole pane of it lies across the hood of the Chevy. I think: accident. The car plowed farther into the front of the fucking store and backed out again. Glass is everywhere. It crunches underfoot. And everyone inside the store is moving fast. A man who looks like a Mayan sun god reels out with a stack of Budweiser twelve-packs, throws them onto the front seat of the Chevy, turns fast, and bumps into a woman who looks just like him, carrying Huggies, stacked just as high as the Buds.

I go inside, see the Indian owner, weirdly dignified in turban and 7-Eleven jacket. *"Policeman!"* he cries into the phone. *"Policeman!"*

Three black girls, no older than fourteen, all breathing hard, tear out with arms full of frozen food. It looks like they've hit the TV Dinner lottery. In and out. More people of color. All silent. All moving fast. A Latino family, five or six kids, apparently related to the divine Mayan, come out and throw six-packs of Coke in the backseat of the Chevy. They've all got the same thing: Coke in cans. Coke in glass bottles. Coke in jumbo plastic.

I forget what I came for. Stand stupidly in front of the cooler. Finally reach in and select a bottle of Perrier. I remember now. I'm thirsty. I hold it, for some reason, with two hands. Turn around. See the place is full now. Mobbed. Half black, half brown, and me. El Anglo Estupido. I start for the counter. Reach in my pocket. I haven't got the hang of looting. I've just realized it *is* looting. It's like gravity has stopped working. Some fundamental law has not been violated so much as reversed. Things float off the shelves, out of coolers. They jump into your hand.

I stand at the counter. Am I demented? Do I expect Gunga Din here to drop everything and collect my dollar thirty-nine? What is *wrong* with me?

I can't tell if I'm high or this is how it feels when the world goes insane. I'm scared. Confused. I step slowly out of the store—I see this clerk every day; will he remember? Will he feel bad if a regular customer steals in front of his face?

Outside, the Perrier in my hand, I see the police car careen over the curb and screech to a halt behind the primer Chevy. Tires crunching glass. The police radio crackling static.

A black policeman, tall and muscular, leaps out of the passenger side, shotgun in one hand. "Freeze!" His uniform is so tight, I think idiotically. How the fuck can he move? The white cop behind the wheel jumps out after. He's fat. Red-faced. Both hands on his baton. "Everybody out," he shouts into the store. He does not go in. "Everybody against the wall."

I see them all. The Chevy people: Grandma, Grandpa, two boys, and three girls. The youngest can't be more than four. The oldest girl thirteen. I don't know what happened to the three black girls. Maybe they ducked in the back.

Just me and this poor fucking Latino family. I stand there. Is this it? I'm going to be arrested for looting a fucking Perrier?

I can picture it now. "What are you in for, man?" "Oh, I looted a Perrier. . . ."

Jesus!

"You, get the fuck out of here!"

It's the tight black cop. Pointing with his muzzle. Fat white cop marches out with the trio of black girls and a light-skinned black fellow about my own age I hadn't even seen. The brother's got a Raider's jacket zipped half up. Lunch meat spills out of the top. He's got his hands full of sliced bologna. The white cop pushes him with the baton.

We're all lined up in front of the store. Another cop car tears in. Doors open at once. Five cops pile out. The fat one had already tugged these plastic cuffs out of his pocket. The Latino family is kneeling. Like they're at mass. Like they're about to be shot. The old man is already cuffed. The white cop is leaning down to cuff the woman.

"You, go," the black cop barks again.

I start to protest. Lunch Meat looks at me. Our eyes meet. I want to say, "No . . . you don't understand . . . *I'm just like you . . .*"

But of course I'm not. I never will be. For some reason I think of Sammy. Of Ruleena. Wonder if they're still downtown. Still on the Crack Wagon.

"Get the fuck out of here," one of the new cops says, but quiet. Man to man. *We're all white guys here.*

I start walking.

I don't look back. Smoke fills the sky somewhere south.

More cars tear past, but I don't see them. I don't look up.

Back in the garage, I put down the Perrier. Find the dope. Put the rest of it, an enormous chunk, on the foil. I want to smoke it all NOW. I want to get high NOW. I don't care about later. There is no later.

I gulp the first puff hungrily. Squeeze my lids shut. But it doesn't help. The light-skinned black man, the Lunchmeat King, is still staring. Saying nothing. Staring. His eyes doing all the talking.

I hold the smoke in my lungs. Do not exhale. Walk slowly, deliberately, to the TV. I have not turned it on since I moved in here. I don't know if it works. It does. I get Channel Seven. Paul Moyer, of all people. He can't wipe the expression he always wears off his face. Smug, cute. He might as well be reporting from a beauty pageant. I turn off the sound. Burning buildings. Black smoke pouring out of windows. A happy guy with bad teeth holding a portable TV. I turn the sound on. "Hey, Grandma," Happy says, laughing. "Don't worry, I got one for you."

Why am I even doing drugs? I wonder. Though I don't know where the thought comes from. What it means.

Even though I know I'm going to want it later, I light up again. Hold the flame just under the tinfoil, follow the melting trail of tar from one corner of the perfectly flat foil all the way down to the other end. Stare at the TV. Almost dark. I recognize the Sears on Santa Monica Boulevard. Ten minutes east. Sound still off, I see my reflection in the TV. My bones and eyes. A ghost image imposed on the picture. So the people on TV are looting my face. Stealing appliances right out of my forehead.

"You can have it," I hear myself say. "Take my brain. I don't need it. I already gave it away . . ."

I leave the TV on, sound off. Lean back on the cot while night roars on all around me. I hear a scream from the street. Maybe it was just a laugh. I don't know. I wonder, are they going to get houses, too? Are they, I wonder mildly, going to kill people?

As long as I'm high, they can shoot me. As long as I'm high, I hope they shoot me. Because tomorrow . . .

I feel for the nub of dope left unsmoked on the foil. That's it.

All night I listen to the distant war. Watch the silent footage on TV. Then, just after dawn, something happens. A muffled groan. Like some large animal dying. And the pictures flicker off the tube. I try the light. That's gone, too. No power.

I check the foil again. I still have that nub. Maybe two puffs. Three if I go easy. Shit. I pick up the phone. Who am I going to call? That's dead, too.

I have no watch. Eric left an alarm clock before taking the family to Napa, but I don't know where it is. I don't particularly want to move. But I have to. If I smoke the rest of what I have, I can handle the bus ride to Towner's.

Shit. I don't even want to get high. I'm not hurting. But I don't want to start jonesing, either, in the middle of a bus ride. Standing there inhaling the chemicals from the blue-haired ladies who get on and off at Fairfax. Why do they do that? I find myself thinking. Why blue? When you sit next to them, it smells like an Earl Scheib outlet: *$99.99! We paint any hair, any time. $99.99 . . .*

I'm at the bus stop on Fairfax and Olympic for what feels like forever. There's another guy with me. An old guy. But we don't talk. He looks worried. He's got one piece of newspaper. He keeps his nose glued there. I can see it's classifieds of some kind. He probably found it in the trash.

I must look scary. I can't remember when I last washed. Or changed my clothes. Sometimes Towner let me shower there. He knows I live in a garage. . . . Maybe I'll shower today. Borrow some socks or something.

Finally a car pulls over. An old blue Oldsmobile. An older couple in the front seat. They look nice. "Herman," the lady calls. "Herman. . . ."

The man is still staring at the paper.

"Herman!"

I tap him, and he looks up, startled. Then sees the lady and breaks into a smile.

"Herman, we are so lucky to find you. They stopped the buses. On account of the riots. It's terrible."

The man named Herman looks dazed for a second, then the lady reaches behind her, opens the rear door, and Herman steps forward, folding his paper, and gets right in.

The lady looks at me for a second. How long since I checked myself in a mirror? What I must look like. I can sense her dilemma: do they offer me a ride? I'm embarrassed for her. I don't want her to feel bad.

When they pull away—me pretending not to even want a ride—I stand there for another minute. The full import of this has not hit me, but I know it will. I know it's going to. I start walking back to the garage. Down Fairfax, across Olympic . . .

The thought I do not want to think grabs me halfway across the street. I could not put it off, it seems, for more than twenty seconds. "I AM OUT . . ."

Shit. . . . I am out of stuff. No more . . . I walk slow. Try to make myself believe that if I walk slow, that if I conserve my energy, if I do not think about the situation, the situation will not exist.

I will be cool, I tell myself. *I will be fine.*

And yet, the second I'm inside, I tear through the garbage, I root through the crumpled tinfoil, for a crumb I missed. I instantly unroll the rolled-up tube I've been smoking through. There's enough residue, maybe, for a hit and a half. That will hold me for ten minutes, maybe, when things get bad.

But they will not get bad, I remember to tell myself. They will be fine.

I pick up the phone—though I know it's dead. Then I try the TV. Still no power. Shit. I've even drunk most of the Perrier. Why did I do that? . . .

There is nothing to do but wait. Sit. Breathe in—but the air tastes like battery acid. Breathe out—but the smoke makes my eyes water.

I am not crying. It's the air.

"It's okay," I say to myself. "It's okay. . . ."

I hear people shouting. I hear groans, hyena laughs, tearing metal, shattered glass. I hear shrieking, but it's far away. Or so I tell myself.

The first shivers do not start till dawn. I've gotten through a day, somehow, a night without moving. If I stay still, I've decided, I will be okay. If I expend no energy. Since coming back from the bus stop, the morning of the day before—was it yesterday? Is it still today?—I have not moved.

Finally the cramps hit. And, cowering like a sick cat, I find a corner of the garden, behind a cluster of mint, where I squat down and relieve myself of what feels like a half a ton of poison bile. I have no toilet paper. No newspapers. Nothing but old copies of *Travel & Leisure.* Whose upscale pages I use to get myself as clean as I'm going to get. Somehow these genteel images of Royal Homes of the Netherlands feel easier on my chafed and aching sphincter than any other printed matter. I wouldn't want to test this scientifically, but in the state I'm in, you take your perks, such as they are, where you can find them. . . .

There is no water, which is the worst. I'm sure there's a hose attachment somewhere on the house, some exterior spigot, but I'm too sick to crawl out and look for it. In my paranoia, which has clocked in along with the kick-sick, I imagine the neighbors seeing me skulk along the side of the house, like I'm looking for the right windows to break. I don't know, if I could be sure they'd shoot me, just open up with a fucking .38 and catch me between the eyes, I wouldn't mind so much. My big fear is that they call the police. I didn't realize, at the time, that the police had taken a powder of their own. The folks at Florence and

Normandie got that news first, but in my neck of the reality I was a little cut off.

The power came on for a while that morning—I think it was DAY TWO—so I could lie there, clutching a pillow to my chest, sweating in my airless box, watching those images of taxi-riding looters, wild-eyed rock-throwers, the soon-to-be-legendary Reginald Denny getting his skull redesigned by the soon-to-be-legendary Damian Williams.

I would laugh if I weren't so close to crying all the time, if my mouth weren't full of this green slime I don't even want to know about . . . The puking started after the shits but before the weeping. These things all have their own cycle. Why the shits couldn't kick in after dark, when I wouldn't feel like I was squatting there with someone's high-powered lens fixed on my every twitch . . . It's one of those cosmic queries I just don't have the energy to pursue.

No, it's easier to just curl up on my stomach, flipping the pillow over every time it soaks through, which happens every half hour or so. Though this is a guess, too. I have no clock. No real sense of time. I break the day into the space between trips out to the bushes. I made the mistake, in a weak moment, of letting my bowels rip in a patch of vegetable hell that turned out to be just outside my window. And when the sun flames down, which it seems to be doing with a vengeance, as if the neighborhood fires weren't enough, it wants to add its two cents, well, I don't have to tell you.

I don't know what the rest of the city's feeling. I watch it on TV, but I keep forgetting it's happening two miles away. I might as well be watching Vietnam footage. Thanks to my twisting guts, the wrenching spasms in the back of my neck, I forget I'm sitting here in the middle of Saigon . . . That's the one blessing of my condition. I am so far away from everything. . . . I have torn the sheets off the mattress now. I soaked it through, and it won't seem to dry. So I've just ripped the sheets off, pulled them onto the floor, where it's cooler. If I press my forehead into the linoleum, it's almost soothing. Almost like . . . relief.

I go to sleep, or something like it, with the TV on, and when I come to I cannot tell if the words that echo in my brain are coming from the television or out of my mouth. Or maybe both. The images on screen have invaded my dreams.

I AM A CITY IN RUIN, I hear myself declaiming at one point. I AM BURNING BUT I CANNOT BE CONSUMED . . .

The phrases come out of me, scare me, wake me out of this half stupor I struggle to maintain. If I knew how to hang myself I would. But I have never been very good with knots. Never been good with my hands. I have never, I think, been good with anything.

The scariest is when I come to outside, facedown in the dirt, my mouth full of wet mud, tongue clogged with earth soaked through with my own urine, my own liquid puke. I can't tell the mud from my puke. And when I try to stand, at least raise myself up enough to crawl, I feel my fingers sink, squish, into the steaming shit I've left everywhere, trailed behind me like some kind of diseased slug.

Fuck, but I am cold. . . .

And, gathering my strength, I wrap my arms about me, feel this strange wet sheen. . . . Fucking Jesus, I'm naked! I manage to turn my head, see the pale sheet I've dragged behind me. I must have walked out—did I walk? did I start out crawling?—must have, at any rate, left the sanctity of my close quarters wrapped in this stinking percale . . . I don't know. However I started out, I think, this is how I ended. And isn't that the story of my life? Isn't that, ladies and germs, all there is to say?

Somehow I manage to roll over. The mud feels better under my back than against my stomach. And as I lie there, I imagine I can see flames. The orange tips of fire licking at the sky. Staining the green tops of the trees that sway above me to something like pale gold, pale and shining gold.

Something tickles my skin. I feel it, on my face, think: Feathers? Could it be? Have I entered some García Marquez story, where my life ends with silent feathers wafting from the heavens onto my ravaged flesh? But no, I realize, no, it isn't feathers, it's soot . . . the floating, lighter-than-air remains of God knows what. Because the sky, by now, is black. Well, maybe lighter. . . . A deep and dirty-looking gray. An unnatural but, to me, oddly soothing shade. Soft as a pigeon's belly. Soft as ash. That's all I want now, to rest in a bed of ash, to float away myself, carried by the heavy air, wafted off and forgotten . . .

The underside of the world, I think, gazing through my itching eyes, the bottom has become the top. *Does this,* I think, smiling in spite of myself, feeling my lips break the shell of tainted mud that has coated and dried over them, *does this mean the dead will come drifting down from the sky . . . poured out of the earth they were buried in . . . ?* I would like that, I think. I'm ready for that. I'm prepared.

Maybe that's all this was. . . . All everything that led up to this moment in the dirt ever was, preparing for a meeting with the dead. Preparing to see my father. My father, who I have not let myself miss. Who I have never mourned. Who is, even now, I think, watching my every move, shaking his head, furrowing his brow at the sad dynamic that drives his boy to just get worse, just sink farther and farther down. . . .

Far enough to meet you, Daddy. If I sink far enough I will be in the ground with you. . . .

And what will you say?

I will say I'm sorry.

And what will you say after that?

I will say it's over.

And so, miraculously or not, so it was.

I came to again, on the garage floor, on what I thought was the morning of the third day. It felt as if I'd slept a thousand years. I felt a lightness. Product I knew, not just of the kick, but of fasting for so long, of purging myself, with tremendous fury, from every exit. My father, it suddenly hits me, expired in a garage.

Once on my feet, peeled out of the filthy stiff sheets and blankets, I stepped outside, to the small patio between my garage and the locked-up house. As if in a bad B movie, the sky now shone deep-blue. It might have been the moment, in *The Wizard of Oz,* when Dorothy steps out of her spinning farmhouse and the world bursts from black and white to color.

In front of me, as if it had been there all along—which of course it had been—I spotted the coiled hose. I don't know how I could not have seen it. Perhaps I did not want to.

I no longer worried about the neighbors. By now, I assumed, they had more to worry about than a mud-caked white man hosing off his own puke in the backyard next to them. It wouldn't thrill them, I am sure, but in the past few days, I reasoned, everyone has had to deal with fears they never before expected to have to deal with.

So many hells that were once potential were now fully realized. For me, in my peculiar lightness, this was incredibly reassuring. There was nothing else to fear. Because what I feared had already happened. I had made it happen. And here I was—relieved as only the dead can be.

I suspected, for one strange moment, that I actually *had* died. And caught myself looking over my shoulder, back through the open door of the rank garage, into the shadows, just to see if my body was still in there. It would not have surprised me, either way.

It didn't matter now. Nothing did. The scum had boiled to the surface and burned off, and what remained was all that had to remain.

I held the nozzle over my head, turned the spigot, and raised my face to the streaming water.